"Beautifully written, relentlessly insightful, and methodologically innovative, *Playing to Win* expertly captures the perspectives of parents and children regarding the importance of after-school activities for socialization and childhood in contemporary American society. Hilary Levey Freidman has produced a sociological gem."

—William A. Corsaro, author of *The Sociology of Childhood*

"Hilary Levey Friedman's *Playing to Win* is an essential social science volume that transcends the boundary between scholarship and popular critique. Levey Friedman successfully explains how upper-middle-class Americans think about their children's engagement in serious leisure: competitive chess, dance competitions, and youth soccer. Listening carefully to both parents and children, she reveals the tensions and contradictions, benefits and drawbacks of intense competitions, and provides a perspective necessary for researchers who examine child development and for parents who wish to raise happy, healthy children."

—Gary Alan Fine, author of *With the Boys:
Little League Baseball and Preadolescent Culture* and
Gifted Tongues: High School Debate and Adolescent Culture

"The world of twenty-first-century childhood has found its superb interpreter. With sparkling arguments and fascinating evidence, Hilary Levey Friedman's *Playing To Win* introduces us to one of America's most remarkable contemporary innovations: the proliferation of organized, competitive after-school activities. An important contribution to the sociology of culture and inequality."

—Viviana A. Zelizer, author of *Pricing the Priceless Child:
The Changing Social Value of Children*

"Hilary Levey Friedman has managed to convince numerous upper-middle-class parents and their children to pause in their mad dash between extracurricular activities to explain why they have chosen this lifestyle. Using information from detailed interviews across a variety of activities, she provides a revealing account of the motivations that lie behind the dramatic rise in competitive children's activities. This fascinating book forms a key part of an emerging body of research that links the increase in time devoted to childcare to parents' worries about their children's economic futures."

—Valerie Ramey, Professor and Chair of Economics,
University of California, San Diego

Playing to Win

RAISING CHILDREN IN A
COMPETITIVE CULTURE

HILARY LEVEY FRIEDMAN

UNIVERSITY OF CALIFORNIA PRESS
Berkeley Los Angeles London

University of California Press, one of the most distinguished
university presses in the United States, enriches lives around the world
by advancing scholarship in the humanities, social sciences, and
natural sciences. Its activities are supported by the UC Press Foundation and by philanthropic contributions from individuals and
institutions. For more information, visit www.ucpress.edu.

University of California Press
Berkeley and Los Angeles, California

University of California Press, Ltd.
London, England

Library of Congress Cataloging-in-Publication Data

Friedman, Hilary Levey, 1980–
 Playing to win : raising children in a competitive culture /
Hilary Levey Friedman.
  pages cm
 Includes bibliographical references and index.
 ISBN 978-0-520-27675-8 (hardback) — ISBN 978-0-520-27676-5
(paperback)
  1. Competition (Psychology) in children.   2. Student activities.
3. After-school programs.   4. Sports for children.   5. Parenting.
6. Child development.   I. Title.
 BF723.C6F75 2013
 306.874—dc23   2013021947

Manufactured in the United States of America

22 21 20 19 18 17 16 15 14 13
10 9 8 7 6 5 4 3 2 1

In keeping with a commitment to support environmentally responsible and sustainable printing practices, UC Press has printed this
book on Rolland Enviro100, a 100% post-consumer fiber paper that is
FSC certified, deinked, processed chlorine-free, and manufactured
with renewable biogas energy. It is acid-free and EcoLogo certified.

For my Family—
Past, Present, and Future

Contents

Preface: Enter to Grow in Wisdom   ix

Introduction: Play to Win   1

1. Outside Class: A History of American Children's
    Competitive Activities   24

2. More than Playing Around: Studying Competitive
    Childhoods   50

3. Cultivating Competitive Kid Capital: Generalist
    and Specialist Parents Speak   81

4. Pink Girls and Ball Guys? Gender and Competitive
    Children's Activities   121

5. Carving Up Honor: Organizing and Profiting
    from the Creation of Competitive Kid Capital   153

6. Trophies, Triumphs, and Tears: Competitive Kids
    in Action   180

    Conclusion: The Road Ahead
    for My Competitive Kids   214

*Appendix: Questioning Kids: Experiences
from Fieldwork and Interviews*   229

Notes   245

Works Cited   265

Index   283

Preface

I have a favorite gate.

Dexter Gate is one of the walking entrances into Harvard Yard off Massachusetts Avenue. Across the street from Harvard Book Store it proclaims, "Enter to Grow in Wisdom."

I first walked through the quiet, darkened archway of Dexter Gate as a gawky seventeen-year-old, a recently admitted student visiting campus for the first time from a world away, my hometown in the suburbs of Detroit. At that time I thought anything was possible in the world. I thought that being a college student meant endless opportunity, kindred spirits, and a level playing field. On most counts, I was right.

However, during the first weeks of my freshman year I quickly learned that there was much I did not know. People living in my dorm had gone to historic high schools that I had never heard of. On campus many of them seemed to know each other through some magical network that I was lucky to realize even existed, given how removed I was from it. I did not attend a nationally known high school; I did not know what "crew" was;

and I did not have any family connections to the university, or to any Ivy League school, for that matter. In fact, when I called my father to tell him I had been admitted to Harvard, he said, "But only rich people and the Kennedys go there!"

My first semester I stumbled upon a sociology class. Having never considered studying anything besides history or government before, I was quite taken by this new-to-me social science. That course on social stratification helped me make sense of the new community I was suddenly part of by exposing me to research on class, status, and prestige.

Fourteen years later, I am still trying to make sense of the world using the sociological tools I learned about in that class. After graduation I left Harvard for other Ivy-covered campuses, where I studied parental aspirations for their children. During that time I wrote a dissertation—the basis for this book—on competitive after-school activities (specifically chess, dance, and soccer) in which I link parental anxieties about their elementary school–age children's futures, especially anxiety about the increased importance of educational credentials, to their parenting behavior and strategies in the present.

At heart *Playing to Win* is a story about social reproduction. I am interested in how everyday parental decisions impact the social structure across generations. My research shows one way that these practices have been institutionalized: through the professionalization of children's competitive after-school activities.

In contemporary sociology the question of how social reproduction occurs is often approached from the "bottom up,"[1] looking at those toward the lower rungs of the social class ladder. But it is equally important to know how those in the middle and upper-middle class get there and how they prepare their children to stay there (or move up in the class structure). This is especially important given the increasing inequality in the United States over the past quarter-century, particularly when it comes to childhood and parenting.[2]

My findings on children's participation in competitive after-school activities provide a small but revealing window into how social reproduction happens as parents actively strategize about child-rearing practices. Training a lens primarily on the affluent middle class helps us understand how and why decisions made during childhood might have long-term consequences for future credentials acquisition and careers—which in turn deepens our understanding of how less advantaged parents can leverage cultural activities to help their children.

I should know because I didn't grow up like most of the children I studied. I never played travel soccer, nor did I play on any athletic team. I took dance but never participated in a competition. And I never even learned how to play chess, so forget about playing in a tournament. In fact, I never competed in any activity in an organized way before middle school, and even then I competed only in the school-sponsored activities of reading and public speaking competitions. I was definitely a competitive child and thrived in any high-stakes environment, especially in educational settings, but not in the way the kids I study do today.

And yet I ended up walking through Dexter Gate. My own interest in how people from different backgrounds can end up in the same place has shaped my sociological imagination, and it is one of this book's motivating factors.

I am married to a man who had a much different childhood, one that more closely resembles that of many of the kids in *Playing to Win*. He was born and bred in Harvard's 02138 zip code and attended Philips Andover Academy (one of those historic boarding schools I had never heard of before college), where he was captain of the cross-country team. He also played select soccer while still in primary school and learned chess at his elementary school. His father graduated from Harvard, where he is a professor, and his mom graduated from Smith, one of the Seven Sisters.

Despite our varied upbringings we were in the same college class. Some believe that once we passed through Dexter Gate as freshmen, we were equal. But the sociologist in me knows this is not the whole truth. We brought with us very different views of the world and bundles of resources when we entered Harvard Yard, ushered in by the gatekeepers who read our admission files. For instance, my husband brought with him all the cultural capital that comes with attending an elite boarding school; I brought with me all the wisdom that comes from growing up with a hardworking single mom determined to provide her daughter with the best educational opportunities she could.

So how did I get so lucky on a day back in November 1997, when a Harvard admissions officer decided I was worthy, despite my lack of an elite high school education and participation in myriad organized, out-of-school, competitive activities? I have asked myself that many times, and as part of my work I have spoken with admissions officers at Ivy League schools. One of them explained to me why participation in extra-curricular activities is so important and in the process helped me understand why my application ended up in the admit pile.

Ivies are looking for smart students with a great deal of ambition. But it is hard to measure ambition. Participation in activities—and awards and leadership earned through participation—are a proxy for that ambition. The specific activities are less important; what matters is that you play a sport or seriously participate in an activity such as debate or drama. But you should also do something else—perhaps play an instrument or be part of a Model United Nations team or volunteer or compete in dance competitions. While in high school I participated in Model United Nations, drama club, literary society, French Honor Society, National Honor Society, and more.

What Harvard, and schools like it, is looking for are ambitious individuals who are not afraid to take risks. When freshmen get to campus they will be exposed to new activities and academic disciplines, as I was. Admissions officers want to create a campus full of ambitious kids who are willing to try swimming or journalism or glee club or anthropology for the first time. So to be admitted you can't do just one thing; you need to show you are flexible and versatile. Of course, you are still expected to excel in whatever you try, especially in academics first and foremost, but you must first be willing to try.

Being ambitious and versatile and taking risks are traits that many also think of as being American, part of our nation's DNA. A former president of the American Psychological Association said that America is "a success-oriented society whose attitudes toward achievement can be traced to our Protestant heritage with its emphasis on individualism and the work ethic."[3] When Alexis de Tocqueville toured the United States in the mid-nineteenth century he famously wrote about the participatory nature of Americans, declaring that we are a nation of joiners.[4] When another European, the developmental psychologist Jean Piaget, toured the United States, he was also struck by the degree of social involvement of Americans—specifically American parents. Piaget was shocked by how many parents asked him whether it was possible to speed up children's development.[5] He named this concern "the American Question" because he said Americans are always trying to hurry things along.

"The American Question" symbolizes not just ambition and involvement; it also symbolizes competition. In his book on competition in the United States sociologist Francesco Duina argues that competition is central to finding our place in the world in both a physical and a symbolic sense.[6] Why? Because competition allows us to prove our worth (to ourselves and to others) and offers a way to determine whether something, or someone, is actually working well and succeeding.

It is no secret that Americans have long loved competitions and rewarded winners. General George Patton often declared in his speeches to troops during World War II, "When you were kids, you all admired the champion marble shooter, the fastest runner, the big league ball players, the toughest boxers. Americans love a winner and will not tolerate a loser. Americans *play to win* all the time."[7]

In contemporary American society competition seems to be everywhere. Organized, tournament-like competitions are held for the seemingly mundane, the inane, and the arcane. We have beauty pageants, bodybuilding competitions, spelling bees, and video game tournaments—not to mention organized competitive events for any sport you can imagine, from soccer on inline skates to childhood games such as dodgeball.[8]

On top of the tendency to make everything competitive, Americans also like to do everything *big*. In a book on competitive eating competitions the author explains, "[America is] different because we have more of it, more types of contests in more places. We do it broader and bigger, and unlike the British, the French, and the Germans . . . we make no apologies."[9]

One of the most competitive domains in American life remains the labor market. Individuals are rewarded for being competitive in the workplace, often with higher salaries, which can also bring more status and prestige. In her comparative study of the American and French upper-middle class, Michèle Lamont found that what was highly valued in the U.S. workplace was having a "competitive attitude, fighting to be the best, to be 'number one.'"[10] Today workers not only want more money, they also want more titles and accolades, so it is easy for others to determine if they are indeed number one.[11]

It appears that a huge part of succeeding in the labor market is going to the "right" schools, where you can make the "right" connections.[12] A recent study by Lauren Rivera found that elite employers not only rely on a degree from an elite university to signal employability, but they also pay attention to extracurricular activities, including lacrosse, squash, and crew.[13] Parents who want their children to someday gain employment at management consulting firms, investment banks, and law firms are right that they need to start early.

Not surprisingly the quest to be number one and get into the "right" school begins in childhood, and this process of learning about competition is beginning earlier than ever before for American kids. Not only is there Phi Beta Kappa in college and the National Honor Society in high school, but now there is the National Elementary Honor Society (founded in 2008). Not only is there test preparation available, for a price, for graduate admissions tests (LSAT, MCAT, GMAT, and GRE) and college admissions tests (SAT and ACT), but now there is also test prep for kindergarten and preschool admissions. Some parents will pay up to $450 an hour to ensure their kids are prepared for a preschool admissions test.[14] In 2009 a company called Bright Kids NYC started a weekend "boot camp" to help children prepare for the gifted exams, and they quickly had a waiting list for their sessions.[15]

Many kids today who win a competition, do well on an exam, or gain entry into a select group receive a trophy or some other tangible reward.[16] Yet research shows that it is best for kids to be intrinsically motivated if they are to stick with an activity over the long haul. Intrinsic motivation happens when you are motivated to compete in order to excel and surpass your own goals and previous performance, and not just beat others.[17]

In a seminal study by psychologists Mark Lepper and David Greene, preschool children were observed drawing a picture.[18] Those who expected a reward based on their performance showed less interest in

drawing just a few weeks later. The reward created more extrinsic motivation instead of intrinsic motivation.

What happens when we extrinsically reward kids yet demand intrinsic
motivation from them just a few years later, when they apply to college? It
makes American childhood a confusing and contested time. Tensions
about children's achievement and the "right" way to raise kids were mag-
nified during the furor surrounding the 2011 publication of *Battle Hymn
of the Tiger Mother,* written by Amy Chua, a Yale University law professor. Chua's daughters were expected to play to win at their music competitions; she wrote, "The only activities your children should be permit-
ted to do are those in which they can eventually win a medal . . . that
medal must be gold."[19] Chua claimed her American-born daughters were
at a disadvantage relative to their Chinese counterparts because her husband and his family wanted the girls to have fun. She wrote about her
mother-in-law, "Florence saw childhood as something fleeting to be en-
joyed. I saw childhood as a training period, a time to build character
and invest for the future."[20]

Later that year Chua's eldest daughter, Sophia, was admitted to Harvard (the Holy Grail for many competitive parents) during the most competitive admissions cycle to date, when only 6.2 percent of the roughly
thirty-five thousand applicants were admitted. Meanwhile thousands of
parents whose children would be applying to college sometime in the
next decade worried that they should be parenting like Chua.

All of the parents I met while studying competitive after-school activities expressed ambivalence about their elementary school–age children's
participation in these activities. But no one wanted to deny their child
the opportunity to succeed. No one was willing to take the chance of not
enrolling their kids in competitive activities, especially when all of their
classmates appeared to be playing to win all the time.

And yet, some of the two thousand students admitted to Harvard in
2011 were like me: ambitious students who worked hard without a background in organized, elite competition. At the same time some of the
lucky admitted students were reared to be Ivy-bound from a young age
(like Sophia Chua), fortunate to grow up in affluent families. Many of
them worked hard and deserve their slot. But what happens to the equally

smart and talented kids who don't have access to the same resources, who don't even know to take the chance to try to get past the Ivy gatekeepers?

We tend to hear about the kids who beat the odds, like when the child of the driver for a rich family gets a slot at an Ivy over the boss' child, because it makes a good story.[21] But for every one success story there are thousands who did not make the cut, or who did not even try. In many cases this failure to try goes beyond differential material resources—it is the result of a different way of seeing the world. Sociologist Dalton Conley put it eloquently in a piece on social class: "Just as the social reproduction of the working class involves a constraining of the horizons of the minds of its members, the construction of an upper class involves the expansion of the sense of possibility among its members."[22]

Playing to Win tells the story of how parents work to expand the sense of possibility among their children by developing what I call "Competitive Kid Capital™." This book is not a diatribe against crazy parents. Are some of the parents I met overinvolved? Yes, but instead of simply condemning them I put their choices into perspective by detailing the historical development of competitive after-school activities. I also situate them in the present day, a world filled with businesses advocating for competitive childhoods. I am not uncritical about all the parenting decisions discussed in *Playing to Win*, but I do place them in context, a process that ultimately reveals middle-class insecurity and concerns about children falling behind.

In the rest of this book you will find the story of what many think you need to do at a young age to successfully get to Dexter Gate, or the gates of other institutions of higher education, and beyond. You will also find a story about the ways in which competition is a central focus of American family life, shaping the lives of young kids who tend to view their competitive activities simply as fun.

Introduction

PLAY TO WIN

It's just after lunchtime on a Saturday in June. In the basement cafeteria of a public elementary school the smell of Doritos, doughnuts, pizza, and McDonald's fries hangs in the air. Although there is a chess tournament in progress in the gym, less than fifty feet away, the atmosphere in the cafeteria is boisterous. Some children are entertaining themselves by running between the tables. Others, almost all boys, are engaged in rambunctious games of team chess, known as "bughouse."[1] A few kids sit apart, absorbed in playing their Game Boys. The youngest of the children are huddled at the back of the cafeteria, drawn to a table that has been set up near a wall of industrial-size, silver-colored refrigerators. Mesmerized, the kids stare at, and sometimes tentatively touch, the shiny gold trophies that cover the table's surface. Together they try to count all the trophies—but some are too young to count high enough.

Their parents pass the time in their own ways. Groups of dads sit together, some talking, others gossiping about the event and the other children. Mothers sit by themselves or in pairs. One mom reads *The Kite Runner*, another labors over the Sunday *Times* crossword puzzle, and still another keeps an eye on her son while her knitting needles click rhythmically.

Close to half of the parents are not sitting, however. They are jockeying for position in front of two sets of doors that lead from the cafeteria into the gym, where the tournament is taking place. Those closest to the doors strain to see through the single, one-foot-square window in each door to get a glimpse of their child's game board. Parents are banned from the tournament room because of poor behavior at previous tournaments: helping their children cheat, distracting other children, or even getting into fights with other parents. Some pass messages back to other parents—"He's down a knight," for instance—but most fret silently. Every so often a child exits the gym. As the doors swing open, they slam into the faces of parents who had been peering through the windows.

As soon as a child emerges, the interrogation begins. The first question is rarely "Did you win or lose?" A child's body language usually makes the outcome of the match obvious. Instead parents ask, "What happened?" One girl answers simply, "I blundered my queen." A boy launches into a blow-by-blow description of the game: "I put my knight on e6 and he put his pawn on f4 and . . ." Some parents, especially moms who generally know less about the fine points of chess, just praise their kids for their success or offer them comfort for their loss.

Within the din of this 140-player tournament, many languages can be heard, including English, French, Spanish, Chinese, Japanese, and Arabic. One tournament participant is deaf. Not everyone in the overcrowded, noisy cafeteria is friendly. When a boy, no older than eight, asks a dad standing next to him if his section has been called to play the final round, the man replies tersely, "I don't know. I don't work here. Go ask someone over there," as he gestures toward the trophy table, where tournament organizers are standing.

The youngest players, who are soon to graduate from preschool or kindergarten, finish their four games quickly. The tournament directors hold the awards ceremony for this group early in the afternoc children sit down near the trophy-filled table they had been inspecting so closely earlier, their parents gather around, cameras at the ready. The tournament announcer explains that this section had seventeen competitors. Miraculously they have all tied for first place.

"Quite an achievement," the announcer intones, deadpan, as the parents look at one another and laugh.

The children clap excitedly. This section is the only one in which all the players receive a trophy for participating. A father whose child is too old to compete in this group laments to another dad, "My son is going to explode if he doesn't get a trophy."

Another father, sitting in the back of the cafeteria with his wife (they are one of the few couples present), watches the youngest kids with a smile. His son is a second-grader who is already playing in the tournament's most advanced section. This father and son seem to share a special bond, signified by their matching T-shirts emblazoned with characters from *Toy Story* and a tagline from the movie, "To Infinity and Beyond." As his son prepares to play his last-round game, the man turns to me and declares, "I never would have thought I'd end up spending my weekends in a cafeteria basement, waiting around for my son!"

Why do so many families spend their weekends watching their children compete? To answer this question I present evidence from three case study activities (one academic, chess; one artistic, dance; and one athletic, soccer) drawn from sixteen months of fieldwork with ninety-five families who live around a major metropolitan area in the Northeast—including 172 separate interviews with parents, children, and teachers and coaches. I argue that the extensive time devoted to competition is driven by parents' demand for credentials for their children, which they see as a necessary and often sufficient condition for entry into the upper-middle class and the "good life" that accompanies it. I develop the concept of "Competitive Kid Capital" to explore the ways in which winning has become central to the lives of American children.

TO INFINITY AND BEYOND?

The "To Infinity and Beyond" dad, Josh,[2] and his wife, Marla, are dermatologists in private practice. They work full time while raising eight-year-old Jeremiah in the center of Metro, a large city in the northeastern United States. Marla and Josh also have an older daughter who is a freshman at Duke University.

Jeremiah attends one of the best independent day schools in the country and has already distinguished himself outside of school. He is one of the top fifty chess players for his age in the country, and he plays on one of the most selective travel soccer teams in the city. Jeremiah also takes private piano lessons and a music theory class at the "top" local music instruction school.

Josh, who grew up outside of Pittsburgh, says that Jeremiah's childhood is "totally different" from his own. "I never played in an outside-of-school sports thing," he explained in a soft-spoken voice. "I didn't play soccer, except pick-up games. I guess I played some neighborhood softball games. But I never did chess in an organized way, and I never did soccer in an organized way. My dad was never involved as a coach." In contrast, Josh acts as an "assistant coach" for Jeremiah's team, which like many travel teams, employs a paid non-parent head coach.

Both Marla and Josh are familiar faces at chess tournaments and on the sidelines of Jeremiah's soccer games. Marla often sits perched in a chair, reading a book or socializing with other parents when they approach her. Josh is more gregarious among the chess parents from Jeremiah's school. He thinks of most of these parents as a "pretty compatible and nice group" and told me, "I was imagining [starting] a book club because we sit around during these tournaments."

Josh and Marla get a lot of pleasure out of hugging the sidelines while Jeremiah puts himself through the paces of these tournaments. "It's a tag team thing," Josh explains. "[We] both want to, if not hunger to, participate in his ups and downs." Of course that's often difficult to manage with work and family obligations and community and religious responsibilities. Marla describes how they handle the details of Jeremiah's extracurricular life: "Things that Jeremiah does on Thursdays and Fridays, he does with our nanny. But Monday, Tuesday, and Wednesday, it's Josh and I. Monday, Wednesday it's me; Josh is Tuesday."

Marla thinks that at this stage, Jeremiah should avoid specializing in any one activity. He should pursue chess, music, and soccer at the same time, even if that means hiring additional help for the family to manage the logistics. "I would not want, at this age, unless he were a prodigy of some sort, for the focus to be only on one of those things," Marla says earnestly. "I mean he's my son, I think he's a great kid and he's got a lot of talents, but he's not a prodigy. At this point, he needs to develop all sorts of aspects of his interests."

Josh articulates his parenting philosophy in a slightly different way, explaining that Jeremiah has "got lots of muscles and it's exciting to think of him using them all and making the best of them." Being well-rounded and benefiting from the exposure to many different activities, hence working different "muscles," seems to his parents the right strategy for Jeremiah, especially since he is not the absolute best in any of them. Breadth muscles, and not just depth muscles, are necessary to reach infinity and beyond.

But Josh describes his son as primarily a "ball guy": "Well, Jeremiah gravitates toward any round object. When he was younger he could maneuver a little round object, like dribble it, and to see that little toddling creature, that was amazing. . . . So it was clear that he was a ball guy."

In conversation Josh highlighted Jeremiah's soccer skills, likely because soccer draws them especially close together. But the attraction to soccer is more than this. When Josh talks about his son's soccer career his voice deepens and his stance changes. He clenches his fist when he says "ball guy," as the masculine image of athletics appears to especially appeal to him.

Given their "multiple-muscles" theory, it is not surprising that Josh and Marla have chosen activities to provide complementary skills for their son. "The team aspect in soccer is essential," Josh notes. "People work together [on the field]. . . . And it's not at all like that in chess because when you're competing as a chess player, you're not working with other teammates, you're essentially working on your own."

Marla listed a different set of skills she thinks Jeremiah derives from competitive chess: "Chess really helps with and reinforces the capacity to focus and concentrate. It's also amazing in terms of what it imbues a child with—strategic thinking, advance planning, and awareness of consequences."

Josh and Marla think that these skills—teamwork, focus, and strategic thinking—are of great value in adult life. Even though the biggest tournament of all, the college admissions process, is ten years off for Jeremiah, they think about it frequently. Jeremiah's prospects are good, Josh reflects: "[Our daughter] got someplace good, so even more I feel like Jeremiah will get something good because he's going to be a high achiever or an overachiever."

"I'm realizing I have very high expectations for Jeremiah," Marla adds. "I mean I'm his mom, but he's really, really smart, and he excels at school." She went on, "He's very self-driven, and so I feel like that's going to propel him through life and if he's lucky, and remains well, I could imagine him pursuing college and then a graduate degree, and some kind of exceptional work in whatever career he chooses."

They know just how competitive the world can be because Marla and Josh are the survivors of many tournaments themselves. "Well, I mean I'm a Baby Boomer kid," Marla notes. "There's just such a [huge] population. Then my kids are Baby Boom-lets, so there's just a crunch of less resources and a lot of people. So that's partly the reason for the competition." She continued, "You know, as I got older there was always a sense that you've got to have a lot of stuff you're doing, your extracurriculars were meant to be strong. *But it just didn't start as young.*"

THE COMPETITIVENESS OF AMERICAN FAMILY LIFE

Why have competition and "extracurriculars" taken hold for such *young* children, and why are busy families, like Jeremiah's, devoting so much time to them? Like the other middle- and upper-middle-class parents behind the swinging doors of the chess tournaments, Josh and Marla are affluent and educated, working full-time jobs while also shuttling their kids to tryouts for all-star teams, regional and national tournaments, and countless evening and weekend practices. Many of these families need to outsource to keep up—Marla and Josh have had a nanny for years—especially since they live far away from grandparents and other family members. Family meals take place on the go, in the backseat of moving cars, or not at all.[3] As the parental "second shift" continues to grow,[4] alongside it a second shift for children has emerged, which is suffused with competition rather than mere participation.

That American families are busy is not surprising. A book by a team of anthropologists, *Busier Than Ever!*, makes the case that American families, especially those with two working parents, have never before had so many obligations outside of the home.[5] Time-use studies yield similar results, finding that parents work more hours outside of the home and children spend more time in organized settings than in previous American generations.[6] More children than ever are also "hurried," participating in three or more organized activities per week or in a single activity for four hours or more over two days.[7]

Ethnographic work on family life affirms this finding, documenting, in particular, middle-class families racing from work to children's classes and practices to home, repeating this cycle day after day. Sociologist Julia Wrigley found that "children had no friends to play with in the neighborhood, because [the other] children were all off at classes."[8] Anthropologist Marjorie Goodwin explains, "Increasingly middle class parents are going to extraordinary lengths to foster their children's talents through maintaining a hectic schedule of organized leisure activities."[9]

But it's not just that middle-class children spend their time in organized activities. What is critical, and rarely discussed, is the *competitive* nature of their extracurricular lives. The Tallingers, one of the case studies in Annette Lareau's seminal work on childhood socialization that finds that class trumps race in terms of parenting strategies, had sons who were members of several travel and elite soccer teams.[10] Lareau highlights the organized and interactive experiences middle-class parents construct for their children, such as constantly talking with them and encouraging them to question adults in a variety of institutional settings. She calls this parenting style "concerted cultivation."

But little is made of this competitive element in Lareau's *Unequal Childhoods*. She does not discuss the powerful presence of competition in children's lives or the emphasis their parents place on acquiring a competitive spirit.[11] *Playing to Win* both updates Lareau's findings and extends them, looking deeply at an important but previously unexamined component of concerted cultivation by examining one of the most intriguing examples of today's intensive parenting: competitive after-school activities for elementary school–age children.

The popular media have certainly picked up on the increase in competition for young children, and the conflicts that often ensue. Recall the Disney Pixar movie *The Incredibles* and the media coverage of it, focused on deconstructing the line "Everyone's special. . . . Which is another way of saying no one is," along with numerous news stories on parents' sometimes criminal misbehavior on the sidelines of kids' sporting activities. But no one has systematically examined the structure, content, and potential consequences of competition, particularly for young children.

I argue that it is this organized, competitive element, outside of the home, that is key to understanding middle- and upper-middle-class family life. Parents worry that if their children do not participate in childhood tournaments they will fall behind in the tournament of life. While it's not clear if the parents are correct, what matters is that they believe that they are and act accordingly. Their beliefs about the future shape their actions in the present when it comes to their children's competitive after-school activities.

STUDYING KIDS AND COMPETITION

What exactly do I mean by "competitive childhood activities"? In *Playing to Win* competitive children's activities are defined as organized activities run by adults, where records are kept and prizes are given out. There is a continuum of competitive experiences in childhood. For instance, sandbox play is at one extreme, on the left-hand side of the continuum. The activities featured in *Playing to Win* are to the right of center for sure. But they are not at the right-hand extreme, as these kids, for the most part, are not elites; in fact most of their parents explicitly don't want their children to be "professionals" in chess, dance, or soccer.

Children's competitive activities can be classified into one of the following types: athletic, artistic, or academic. My case studies consist of one of each: soccer, dance,[12] and chess. As one of the most popular youth team sports, with over 3 million children registered each year by U.S. Youth Soccer, soccer was a natural choice. Competitive dance has also grown by leaps and bounds, with competitive dance numbers estimated to be in the mid-six figures.[13] Dance has experienced a resurgence since the rebirth of dance on television with such shows as *So You Think You Can Dance* (which highlights many "competition kids") and *Dancing with the Stars* (with a few seasons featuring a "ballroom kids" competition). Finally, each winter and spring thousands of elementary school–age students sign up for the national chess championships, in addition to competing at local weekend tournaments. In the past decade scholastic membership in the United States Chess Federation (USCF) has nearly doubled in size, now accounting for a little more than half of all memberships, or about forty thousand kids.[14]

Each case study activity varies in the extent to which it emphasizes individual versus team competition. Soccer relies on a strong team structure, while dance develops a slightly weaker but identifiable team element, and chess involves the least amount of team competition. Chess and soccer are inherently competitive, meaning there is almost always a "winner" and a "loser" when a game is played, while dance is inherently expressive, so a competitive structure is imposed on the activity. Finally, the gender makeup of the cases varies. Soccer tends to have the same number of teams for both sexes by age group. Dance is dominated by girls, but there are some boys who participate. Chess, on the other hand, is dominated by boys, though there is a minority of girls as well.

For each activity I had two field sites: one urban, in and around Metro, and one suburban, in West County. Both chess sites—Metro Chess and West County Chess—have organizations that offer group classes, private lessons, chess camps, and regular chess tournaments; but Metro Chess is far more competitive, serious, and developed than West County Chess.

The dance field sites, Metroville Elite Dance Academy and Westbrook Let's Dance Studio, follow a similar pattern, as the Elite Dance Academy is in an urban setting and is much more competitive than the Let's Dance Studio in the suburbs. Both offer classes, competition rehearsals, and group competition. Finally, the soccer field sites of Westfield Soccer Club and Metro Soccer Co-op offer a different picture, with the former being in a suburban location and highly competitive and the latter being in an urban setting with a greater emphasis on cooperation than competition. Both have nonprofit status and organize travel soccer teams that play in various regional soccer leagues and travel to regional and national tournaments.[15]

I engaged in six to nine months of intensive observation with each activity, talking informally with those involved, attending tournaments, and taking extensive field notes. During that time I conducted a series of semi-structured interviews with some of the parents, coaches, and children I met. I completed 172 interviews—ninety-five with parents, thirty-seven with children, and the rest with teachers, coaches, and administrators—to explore how competition shapes the lives of these contemporary American families.

As will be discussed, the group of families I met is diverse, though almost all belong to the broadly defined middle class. But variations exist within the middle class, particularly when it comes to education and income, as reflected in the *Playing to Win* families. On these measures the soccer parents are the most affluent, and the chess and soccer parents are the most educated. The dance parents are the most diverse group in terms of race/ethnicity (a little more than 50 percent are white), while the soccer parents I met are almost universally white (94 percent).

COMPETITION AND EDUCATIONAL CREDENTIALS IN THE UNITED STATES

America is frequently called a competitive country that focuses on achievement, as discussed in the preface. In this context achievement is often exemplified by the acquisition of credentials.[16] The scholars Randall Collins and James English explain how this increasingly competitive environment has affected various realms in contemporary America—including the corporate world and the arts—as the focus on credentials becomes ever more dominant.[17] In particular, as credentials grew ever more important throughout the twentieth century, the educational system became a screening system.

Max Weber, in some of his foundational work in sociology, argues that in a bureaucratic and hierarchical society, social prestige and status are based on credentials. As a consequence, performance on examinations and possession of degrees from particular institutions became centrally important.[18] The need to perform well in school and to compete in order to secure a spot when only a limited number are available becomes a high priority. Parents, recognizing the need for their children to be prepared to acquire credentials, have grown to favor "a protected adolescence, curbing any turbulence or independence that might distract their sons [or daughters] from a steady preparation for success."[19]

Credentialing tournaments were once limited to adolescence and high school. Outside the classroom, students entered athletic contests, joined debate teams, built "careers" as high school newspaper editors, and in hundreds of other ways sought to distinguish themselves in adolescence. But today it would seem that for millions of middle-class, twenty-first-century American children, waiting until high school to prove one's mettle is a mistake because the credentials bottlenecks these kids will face require much more advanced preparation.

Even the preschool set is busily trying to stand out from the crowd.[20] Journalist and editor Pamela Paul explains, "Entry into a high-quality preschool (and thereby, the theory goes, a good elementary school, high school, and college) has become cutthroat."[21] In 2011 one mother sued a preschool for destroying her four-year-old daughter's chances at an Ivy League education.[22] While the suit was widely ridiculed, its existence illustrates the extreme parental anxiety that exists today, especially in upper-middle-class communities.

It is tempting to denounce these behaviors and preoccupations as the hyperfixations of neurotic parents who are living through their children. Many pundits are not hesitant to invoke analyses that are just shy of pathology. These parents are labeled "helicopter parents" who hover over their kids from infancy through college graduation, even until children secure employment after college.[23]

Are these parents crazy? Have they lost their grip? No. Their children face very real gates and gatekeepers through which they need to pass if they are going to achieve in ways similar to their parents. And the probability of that outcome appears to their parents—with good reason given the economic crises of the first decade of the twenty-first century—to be less than it once was. Demographics only heighten this demand, which has spiked in areas where there have been "baby boom-lets," such as the Northeast.[24]

Parental concern over future academic options for their children may seem absurd since Baby Boomers and their children, the Echo Boomers, are thus far the best-educated and wealthiest generations ever seen in the United States. But Baby Boomers faced unusual levels of competition for scarce educational resources due both to their numbers and their coming of age when women first entered college in a significant way.[25] Hence the cultural experience of competition, of an insufficient supply of spots for the size of the group seeking them, has predisposed these Boomers to see life as a series of contests,[26] as Marla explained.

Pamela Druckerman, in her headline-making book claiming that the French raise their children better than Americans do, attributes part of the stress of American parents to changes that started in the 1980s linked to developing inequality: "Around the same period, the gap between rich and poor Americans began getting much wider. Suddenly, it seemed that parents needed to groom their children to join the new elite. Exposing kids to the right stuff early on—and perhaps ahead of other children the same age—started to seem more urgent."[27]

Also, because the Echo Boom is large and has a higher rate of college attendance than ever before, that particular competitive landscape is even more crowded. Popular press coverage of the low college acceptance rates, lower than ever of late at elite private and public universities,[28] only fuels parents' anxiety, buttressing existing anxiety over credentials, and hence contributing to an even more competitive childhood culture. Recent books, such as *Crazy U: One Dad's Crash Course in Getting His Kid into*

College and *The Neurotic Parent's Guide to College Admissions,* capture parental feelings about the college admissions process.[29]

MOTIVATION FOR AN EARLY START IN THE COLLEGE ADMISSIONS RACE

Parents are working early on to ensure their children get into good colleges and pursue advanced degrees. College is especially important in the United States, where it plays "a pivotal role in shaping future class destinations."[30] The degree of instability that has become an unwelcome staple in the lives of millions of educated, professional workers has reinforced the importance of educational prestige as perhaps the only protection, dicey as it may be, against future family downward mobility.[31] Most middle- and upper-middle-class families no longer pass on the family firm, so the ability to boost the succeeding generation into a better, or even the same, class is largely dependent on the next generation's credentialing success.

Middle- and upper-middle-class parents are willing to invest large sums of money and time to make this a reality. In her work on the upper-middle class, Michèle Lamont explains that most "American upper-middle class men spend a considerable part of their life savings for the education of their children."[32] Families are willing to make such a large investment because higher education is at the heart of social reproduction.

But that money is not only spent on tuition. Parents are savvier than ever, investing both time and money so that their children get specialized instruction outside of the classroom.[33] For many kids, extracurricular life is focused on athletics and other organized games. And those extracurricular activities, specifically sports, *can* offer an admissions boost, particularly at the most elite colleges and universities.[34] Even though this boost is far from guaranteed, parents are willing to hedge their bets.

Participation in competitive activities is especially appealing in honing skills that will matter in the more weighty tournaments to come, because these proving grounds look like recreation. While parents in many Asian countries encourage their kids to spend countless hours hitting the books in English schools abroad or in cram schools at home,[35] many American parents prefer to shroud the honing process in activities that can be—and are generally experienced as—fun. It is crucial to the American ethos of competition that it should not look too much like work, especially for children, even if the competitive experience clearly has work-like elements.[36]

At the same time it would be a mistake to think that parents of kids as young as Jeremiah fixate on specific college admissions offices every Saturday out on the soccer field. Instead they understand the grooming of their child as producing a certain kind of character and a track record of success in the more proximate tournaments of sports or dance or chess.

But were parents to think in directly instrumental terms about that thick admissions envelope, they would not be far off the mark. Activity participation, particularly athletics, does indeed confer an admissions advantage, through either athletic scholarships or an admissions "boost," giving students an edge when applying to elite schools.[37]

A 2005 *New York Times* article on the growing popularity of lacrosse explained, "Families see lacrosse as an opportunity for their sons and daughters to shine in the equally competitive arenas of college admissions and athletic scholarships."[38] One parent is quoted in the article saying, "From what I hear on the coaches' side in Division III [lacrosse participation is] worth a couple hundred points on the SAT." (Participation in sports like lacrosse also provides a social class signifier in an era of needs-blind admissions.)

All of the *Playing to Win* parents were realistic about their children's very slim chances of earning an NCAA scholarship, especially to a Division I school.[39] Instead what the parents I met are looking for is what lacrosse is thought to provide: an admissions boost. This boost is strongest at Ivy League schools, where students are not awarded athletic scholarships, and at top liberal arts colleges, where sometimes more than half of the smaller student bodies are collegiate athletes.

Higher education admissions systems are certainly "tied to Little League and high school sports and [are] related as well to the shared sports values of our national culture."[40] While we don't know with certainty that it is these specific activities that help children succeed in the college admissions race and beyond—because kids were not randomly assigned to competitive after-school activities—what matters is that parents *believe* participation in these activities is crucial and act accordingly while their children are still young.

That U.S. colleges and universities consider admissions categories other than academic merit is rooted in history and is uniquely American. Jerome Karabel shows how the "Big Three" of Harvard, Princeton, and Yale developed new admissions criteria in the 1920s to keep out "undesirables," namely Jews and immigrants.[41] This new system valued the "all-around man," who was naturally involved in clubs and athletics. Karabel explains that the definition of admissions merit has continued to shift over time, and parents' concern with college admissions for their children is "not irrational, especially in a society in which the acquisition of educational credentials has taken its place alongside the direct inheritance of property as a major vehicle for the transmission of privilege from parent to child. And as the gap between winners and losers in American grows ever wider—as it has since the early 1970s—the desire to gain every possible edge has only grown stronger."[42]

While researching *Playing to Win* I met one father, who actually did not attend college himself, and he told me about his motivation for his third-grade daughter's participation in competitive chess: "Well, if this helps her get into Harvard . . ." Another mother said that her son's achievements "might help him stand out and get into a good school." When I asked her to define a "good school" she replied, "Ivy League or equivalent, like Stanford"—though she had not attended any of these colleges.

While these parents had not attended the schools they were interested in for their children, that was not true for all the families I met. Karabel and the journalist Daniel Golden do find that at many institutions legacy status is powerful; Golden finds this to be especially true at the University of Notre Dame.[43]

We cannot know for sure that the way these affluent kids spend free time in their childhood will lead to their admission to these schools, which in turn will help maintain a class advantage. But we can say that the skills they acquire by participating in competitive childhood activities are certainly correlated.

In a society where a bachelor's degree has become common, and in many circles is expected, the institution at which a degree was earned becomes a distinguishing feature,[44] and many parents correctly believe these activities can help gain entry to more elite institutions. According to sociologist Mitchell Stevens, in his study of college admissions at an elite, private liberal arts college, "Families fashion an entire way of life organized around the production of measurable virtue in children."[45] Efforts to create this quantifiable virtue in children have led to the creation of a second shift for kids, which in turn has created what I call Competitive Kid Capital.

OVERCOMING CREDENTIALS BOTTLENECKS: THE ACQUISITION OF COMPETITIVE KID CAPITAL

Whenever children participate in activities, including unsupervised play or organized noncompetitive activities, they acquire skills through socialization.[46] This is also true of participation in organized activities that do not have an explicitly competitive element, as I have argued elsewhere.[47] But many activities that were previously noncompetitive have been transformed from environments that emphasized only learning skills, personal growth, and simple fun into competitive cauldrons in which only a few succeed: those who learn the skills necessary to compete and to *win*. Kids learn particular lessons from participation in competitive activities apart from normal childhood play.

There are two avenues by which parents think competitive activities can help children gain an edge: the specialist and the generalist avenues. Both pathways aid families in dealing with credentials bottlenecks because they help kids acquire skills and focus their time and energy. Parents think these activities help kids develop the kind of character that will be critical to success in the competitions that colleges, graduate schools, and employers pay attention to when making decisions.

The "specialist" avenue to the top has children competing to achieve national championships or awards for exceptional achievement. But this avenue requires specialization at an early age, professional coaching, high levels of raw talent, and substantial family resources, so only a few children can realistically pursue this path.

The "generalist" avenue is more common; it focuses on cultivating children into the all-around student who works "different muscles," as Jeremiah's parents put it. Generalist parents want their child to succeed in a variety of competitive endeavors, even though their child may not be the *top* competitor in one activity. Parents like Marla and Josh highlight particular skills that they think their children learn from participation in competitive activities, such as good sportsmanship, discipline and focus, and how to follow a schedule.

Often these generalist children try different activities in their youth, acquiring various skills from each before moving on to the next one, unless the kids really distinguish themselves in a particular activity and stick with it longer. As children get older there is often a transition from being a generalist to being a specialist, as the focus shifts from being well-rounded to attaining a special achievement, usually around high school.

Drawing upon Bourdieu's work on both cultural capital (defined as proficiency and familiarity with dominant practices, particularly with respect to adeptness in the educational system) and the *habitus* (defined as a system of dispositions that manifests in various types of taste, such as speech and dressing),[48] I label the lessons and skills that parents hope their children gain from participating in competitive activities "Competitive Kid Capital." The character associated with this Competitive Kid Capital that parents want their children to develop is based on the acquisition of five skills and lessons, which emerged in conversations with parents: (1) internalizing the importance of winning, (2) bouncing back from a loss to win in the future, (3) learning how to perform within time limits, (4) learning how to succeed in stressful situations, and (5) being able to perform under the gaze of others.

Internalizing the importance of winning is a primary goal in acquiring Competitive Kid Capital. One parent told me, "I think it's important for him to understand that [being competitive] is not going to just apply here, it's going to apply for the rest of his life. It's going to apply when he keeps growing up and he's playing sports, when he's competing for school admissions, for a job, for the next whatever."

Competitive children's activities reinforce winning, often at the expense of anything else, by awarding trophies and other prizes. Such an attitude appears to help bring success in winner-take-all settings like the school system and some labor markets.[49] Though many activities do award participation trophies, especially to younger children, the focus remains on who wins the biggest trophy and the most important title.

Linked to learning the importance of victory is learning from a loss to win in the future, another component of Competitive Kid Capital. This skill involves perseverance and focus; the emphasis is on how to bounce back from a loss to win the next time. A mom explained, "The winning and losing is phenomenal. I wish it was something that I learned because life is really bumpy. You're not going to win all the time and you have to be able to reach inside and come back. Come back and start fresh and they are able to. I'm not saying he doesn't cry once in a while. But it's really such a fantastic skill."

Because competitive activities belong to organizations that keep records, the stakes are higher than in recreational leagues, and children can see that it matters that there is a record of success. These childhood competitive activities can also help kids learn how to recover from public failures and how to apply themselves and work hard in order to be long-term winners. Kids learn the identity of being a winner only by suffering a loss. This father summarizes the sentiment, trying to raise a son to be a winner in life:

> This is what I'm trying to get him to see: that he's not going to always win. And then from a competitive point of view, with him it's like I want him to see that life is, in certain circumstances, about winning and losing. And do you want to be a winner or do you want to be a loser? You want to be a winner! There's a certain lifestyle that you have to lead to be a winner, and it requires this, this, this and this. And if you do this, this, this and this, more than likely you'll have a successful outcome.

Learning how to succeed given time limits is a critical skill as well—one of the "this" things you have to do to be a winner—and a critical component of Competitive Kid Capital. There are time limits for games, tournaments, and routines, and the competition schedule is also demanding, cramming many events into a weekend or short week. On top of that children need to learn how to manage their own schedules, which they might have to do someday as busy consultants and CEOs. One boy revealed how busy his young life is when he told me what soccer teaches him: "Dodging everything—like when we have to catch a train, and there are only a few more minutes, we have to run and dodge everyone. So, soccer teaches that."

Children also learn how to perform and compete in environments that require adaptation, a fourth ingredient in the Competitive Kid Capital recipe. These environments may be louder, more distracting, colder, hotter, larger, or smaller than anticipated in preparations, but competitors, and especially winners, learn how to adapt. The adaptation requires focus on the part of children—to focus only on their performance and eventual success. The following quote by a mom of a fourth-grader links this to performing well on standardized tests:

> It's that ability to keep your concentration focused, while there's stuff going on around you. As you go into older age groups, where people are coming in and out, the ability to maintain that concentration, a connection with what's going on, on the board in front of you, and still be functional in a room of people, it's a big thing. I mean to see those large tournaments, in the convention centers, I know it is hard. I did that to take the bar exam, and the LSAT I took for law school, and GREs. You do that in a large setting, but some people are thrown by that, just by being in such a setting. Well that's a skill, and it's a skill and it's an ability to transfer that skill. It's not just a chess skill. It's a coping-with-your-environment skill.

Finally, in this pressure-filled competitive environment children's performances are judged and assessed in a very public setting by strangers— the final component to Competitive Kid Capital. This dance mom explains:

> I think it definitely teaches you awareness of your body and gives you a definite different stance and confidence that you wouldn't have. For example, you're told to stand a certain way in ballet, which definitely helps down the road. When she has to go to a job interview, she's going

to stand up straight because she's got ballet training; she's not going to hunch and she's going to have her chin up and have a more confident appearance. The fact that it is not easy to get up on a stage and perform in front of hundreds or thousands of people, strangers, and to know that you're being judged besides, definitely gives you a level of self-confidence that can be taken to other areas so again if she has to be judged by a teacher or when she's applying for a job she'll have more of that confidence, which helps you focus.

Children are ranked, both in relation to others' performance in a particular competition and in relation to participants their age. These appraisals are public and often face-to-face, as opposed to standardized tests which take place anonymously and privately. Being able to perform under the gaze of others toughens children to shield their feelings of disappointment or elation, to present themselves as competent and confident competitors.

While all of the parents I met believe their children need to develop this Competitive Kid Capital to succeed later in life, most were also concerned that their kids lack free time to play or to "just be kids." What is remarkable is that despite sometimes deep ambivalence, families keep their children involved in competitive activities. Even when the specific activity may change (for example, a child leaves soccer for lacrosse, or gymnastics for dance), children I met remain actively engaged in competition and in their second-shift activities after school. Their parents want to ensure they are giving their young children every possible opportunity to succeed in the future, in an often unpredictable world, by encouraging them to acquire and stockpile Competitive Kid Capital.

A PREVIEW OF THE COMPETITION

The following six chapters further contextualize how and why parents want their children to acquire Competitive Kid Capital by analyzing the roots and perceived benefits of participation in competitive children's activities. Each chapter answers some overarching questions: Why have these competitive activities developed over time? How is the competition structured now, and in each research site? Why do parents believe these competitive activities and Competitive Kid Capital to be so important in their children's lives? How do parents make decisions about the specific competitive activities for their children? In what ways is there an industry behind these organized competitive activities? What do the children think about their participation in these competitive activities?

Chapter 1 is a historical analysis of competitive activities for American children. Here I ask: What are the social forces that have shaped the evolution of children's competitive activities from roughly the turn of the twentieth century up to the present? I show that organized, competitive children's activities developed for elementary school–age kids but then became more prevalent among middle-class children than among their lower-class counterparts due to major changes in three social institutions: the family, the educational system, and the organization of competition and prizes in the United States. I trace the history of the development of competitive children's activities in general and then offer a brief history of competitive chess, dance, and soccer.

Chapter 2 describes the contemporary structure of these activities and my field sites, drawing on mixed methods and triangulated data from fieldwork observations, adult interviews, and child interviews. Chapter 3 turns to the parents themselves, presenting descriptive data on the parents I studied in each activity and analyzing the beliefs that motivate the parents to enroll their children in these activities. We see striking similarities among all the parents, mainly in their narratives about how their children got started in their particular activities and the ways they talk about the benefits they think their children acquire through participation. Their narratives are well-developed, suggesting a shared worldview about the future by both generalist and specialist parents. The components of Competitive Kid Capital that parents want their children to acquire are described in detail in this chapter.

Chapter 4 turns to the differences that demarcate chess, dance, and soccer, particularly when it comes to gender. For example, why do some parents strategically select soccer rather than dance for their daughters? I argue that divergent gender scripts explain the pathways parents are choosing for their kids. Parents of dancers have more traditional gender ideas, emphasizing gracefulness and appearance, while soccer parents with daughters want to raise aggressive, or "alpha,"[50] girls. I make the case that this distinction reveals forms of classed femininity, one of the most provocative arguments in *Playing to Win*. As the soccer parents can largely be thought of as upper-middle class and the dance parents as middle and lower-middle class, this shows an emerging gender divide within the middle class around aspirations for girls.

Chapter 5 delves deeper into the organizational context that surrounds parental decision making. Many of the parenting practices I observed are embedded in institutions, and these institutions offer a critical mediating level between individual choice and societal "culture." I argue that there is a world of competitive childhood, designed to maximize acquisition of Competitive Kid Capital—and ordered to make money off parents who are focused on its acquisition. I discuss similarities in the way the activities are organized, including the reward structures, organization of competitions, selection processes, and conflicts among competitive children's activities. I also identify processes such as the "carving up of honor" and the "problem of the high-achieving child." Understanding that there is a business world organized to convince parents of the benefits of competitive kids' activities helps us better contextualize parents' motivations. They no longer get information just from other parents at the school bus stop.

Chapter 6 places the attention on those kids at the bus stop by investigating their own daily lives and beliefs. What do *they* think about their participation in competitive activities, and in what ways do their conceptions differ from adults'? Children have definite views about their activities. This raises the question of whether children are actually acquiring the Competitive Kid Capital that their parents want them to have or are learning different kinds of skills and lessons, some of which may be unintended, such as being more social and cooperative than focused on winning at all costs. I highlight three main themes that consistently emerged from interactions with children: dealing with nerves and mistakes while being judged, comparing individual versus team success, and the role that trophies, ribbons, and other material rewards play in children's continued participation in these competitive activities. Overall kids find their participation in these competitive activities fun, even as they work hard to acquire the Competitive Kid Capital their parents want them to have, along with a few other lessons along the way. Children's own quite strong and divisive ideas about gender are also discussed.

Combined with a conclusion and an appendix, these six chapters represent a contribution to a cultural sociology of inequality by studying the daily lives of mostly middle-class American families as the parents work to develop the Competitive Kid Capital that they think will help guarantee their children's future success (note that the diversity of the middle class is represented here with some families falling in the upper-middle class, defined as having at least one parent who has earned an advanced postgraduate degree and is working in a professional or managerial occupation and both parents having earned a four-year college degree, and lower-middle-class families, defined as only one parent having a college degree and/or neither parent working in a professional or managerial occupation). Though only a snapshot, the intensity of what we see here reveals the outlines of a major feature of childhood today and illustrates the ways competition is now a central aspect of American childhood, showing that countless boys and girls no longer simply play—they play to win.

ONE Outside Class

A HISTORY OF AMERICAN CHILDREN'S
COMPETITIVE ACTIVITIES

Middle-class children's lives are filled with adult-organized activities, while working-class and poor children fill their days with free play and television watching.[1] This is one of the central observations of Annette Lareau's ethnographic study of families raising third-grade children around Philadelphia.[2] Lareau's findings about the way children from middle-class families use their time is consistent with popular conceptions of overscheduled American kids who are chauffeured and schlepped from activity to activity on a daily basis.[3]

Of course the overscheduled children of the middle class not only participate in myriad after-school activities; they also compete. These elementary school–age kids try out for all-star teams, travel to regional and national tournaments, and clear off bookshelves to hold all of the trophies they have won. It has not always been this way. About a hundred years ago, it would have been the lower-class children competing under nonparental adult supervision while their upper-class counterparts participated in noncompetitive activities, often in their homes. Children's tournaments, especially athletic ones, came first to poor children—often immigrants—living in big cities.

Not until after World War II did these competitive endeavors begin to be dominated by children from the middle and upper-middle classes. In the 1970s American children witnessed an explosion of growth in both the number of participants and the types of competitive opportunities available to them. This growth crowded out many who could not pay to play.

Today it costs a lot to participate in a diverse set of competitive circuits and tournaments that are now big business. For future Michelle Wies there is a youth PGA; for future Dale Earnhardts there is a kids' NASCAR circuit; and for future Davy Crocketts there are shooting contests.[4] There is even a Junior Bull Riders circuit that starts children as young as three in mutton-busting contests, trying to stay on a lamb as long as possible. These competitive activities charge participant fees and give out ranked awards at events where young kids risk injury to be number one.[5] The forces that have led to increasing inequality in education, the workplace, and other spheres have come to the world of play. This means that Competitive Kid Capital is unequally distributed.

What are the social forces that have shaped the evolution of these children's competitive activities from roughly the turn of the twentieth century up to the present? The answer is linked to major changes in three social institutions: the family, the educational system, and the organization of competition and prizes. This chapter provides a history of the development of competitive children's activities in the United States. To illustrate this history, I examine the evolution of the three case study activities: chess, soccer, and dance.

COMPETITIVE AFTER-SCHOOL HOURS OVER TIME

Beginning in the late nineteenth century compulsory education had important consequences for families and the economy. With the institution of mandatory schooling children experienced a profound shift in the structure of their daily lives, especially in the social organization of their time. Compulsory education brought leisure time into focus; since "school time" was delineated as obligatory, "free time" could now be identified as well.[6]

What to do with this free time? The question was on the minds of parents, social workers, and "experts" who doled out advice on child rearing. The answer lay partly in competitive sports leagues, which started to evolve to hold the interest of children, the first phase in the development of children's competitive activities. Overall we can identify three key periods of development: the first runs from the Progressive Era through World War II; the second moves from the postwar period to the 1970s; and the third takes us from the 1980s into the present.[7]

Seeds of Competition: Progressive Era to World War II

The Progressive Era, with its organizational and reform impulses, inevitably focused on children's lives.[8] These impulses gave rise to some of the earliest organized competitive events among American children. For example, reformers concerned about the health of babies started "better baby" contests in 1908 as a way to teach primarily immigrant and lower-class mothers the values of hygiene and nutrition.[9] The contests were often held at state fairs, where judges evaluated children along several dimensions, including measurements and appearance, in order to find the "healthiest" or the "most beautiful" baby.[10] These contests required little more of the baby than to submit to being poked, prodded, and put on display; the competition was really among adults.[11]

Reformers didn't forget older children. With the simultaneous rise of mandatory schooling and laws restricting child labor,[12] worry mounted over the idle hours of children, which many assumed would be filled with delinquent or self-destructive activities. Urban reformers were particularly preoccupied with poor immigrant boys who, because of overcrowding in tenements, were often on the streets.[13]

Reformers' focus was less on age-specific activities and more generally on "removing urban children from city streets."[14] Initial efforts focused

on the establishment of parks and playgrounds, and powerful, organized playground movements developed in New York City and Boston.[15] But because adults "did not trust city boys to play unsupervised,"
attention soon shifted to organized sports.[16]

Sports were seen as important in teaching the "American" values of
cooperation, hard work, and respect for authority. Progressive reformers
thought athletic activities could prepare children for the "new industrial
society that was emerging,"[17] which would require them to be physical
laborers. Organized youth groups such as the YMCA took on the responsibility of providing children with sports activities.

In 1903 New York City's Public School Athletic League for Boys (PSAL)
was established, and formal contests between children, organized by
adults, emerged as a way to keep the boys coming back to activities,
clubs, and school. Formal competition ensured the boys' continued participation since they wanted to defend their team's record and honor.
Luther Gulick, founder of the PSAL, thought, "Group loyalty becomes
team loyalty, and team loyalty enhances school loyalty, for the spirit of
loyalty and morality demonstrated publicly spreads to all the students,
not just those who compete."[18]

A girls' league within the PSAL was founded in 1905, though many of
the combative and competitive elements present in the boys' league were
eliminated.[19] In 1914 the New York version became part of the city's Board
of Education. By 1910 seventeen other cities across the United States had
formed their own competitive athletic leagues modeled after New York
City's PSAL. Settlement houses and ethnic clubs soon followed suit. The
number of these boys' clubs grew rapidly through the 1920s, working in
parallel with school leagues.

The national spelling bee, a nonathletic competitive activity for children, also grew in popularity at this time. Spelling bees, known historically as spelling fights or spelling parties, are an American folk tradition.
Throughout the eighteenth century they were part of the typical Colonial
education, and by the nineteenth century they had developed into community social events.[20] By the turn of the twentieth century spelling bees
had evolved into a competitive educational tool. In her history of American childhood from 1850 to 1950 Priscilla Ferguson Clement explains,

"Individual competition was also a constant in [late] nineteenth-century schools. In rural areas, teachers held weekly spelling bees in which youngsters stood in a line before the teacher (toed the line) and vied to be at the head of the line rather than at the foot."[21]

Around the turn of the twentieth century a social movement formed to promote a national student-only bee. The first nationwide student bee was held on June 29, 1908. But due to racial tensions (after a young black girl won), the next national student spelling bee was not held again until the 1920s. By 1925 the national student spelling bee as we know it, complete with corporate sponsorship, had taken shape.[22]

Other community-based competitions, such as Music Memory Contests and mouth organ contests, were also popular at this time.[23] Additionally, in 1934 the organization that would become the National Guild of Piano Teachers' National Piano Playing Tournament was formed.[24]

During this time children from wealthier families generally received a variety of lessons thought to enhance their social skills and prospects. In a history of children from different class backgrounds in the United States, Harvey Graff wrote of one new upper-middle-class, turn-of-the-century family, the Spencers: "The Spencer children went to dancing school, dressing the part and meeting their peers of the opposite sex. The girls were given music lessons, with varying degrees of success."[25] These activities were organized and overseen by adults but were not yet competitive. (This was especially true for dance, as I discuss below.)

By the 1930s this pattern began to shift as a consequence of the Great Depression and as educational philosophies changed. During the Depression, many clubs with competitive leagues suffered financially and had to close, so poorer children from urban areas began to lose sites for competitive athletic contests organized by adults. Fee-based groups, such as the YMCA, began to fill the void, but usually only middle-class kids could afford to participate.[26]

At roughly the same historical moment athletic organizations were founded that would soon formally institute national competitive tournaments for young kids, for a price. National pay-to-play organizations, such as Pop Warner Football and Little League Baseball, came into being in 1929 and 1939, respectively.

At the same time, many physical education professionals stopped supporting athletic competition for children because of worries that leagues supported competition only for the best athletes, leaving the others behind. Concerns about focusing on only the most talented athletes developed into questions about the harmfulness of competition. Historian Susan Miller explains: "Basketball, like all team sports, came under fire for a flaw that no amount of rule changes could rectify; critics charged that they inherently encouraged unnecessary and potentially harmful competition. . . . Critics argued that team sports put too much focus on winning at the expense of good sportsmanship and thus encouraged the rise of star athletes instead of fostering full participation by all team members."[27]

In the end this meant that much of the organized youth competition left the school system. But it did not leave American childhood. "By allowing highly organized children's sport to leave the educational context," Jack Berryman, a medical historian, explains, "professional educators presented a golden opportunity to the many voluntary youth-related groups in America."[28] The concatenation of concerns about competition and the financial realities of the Depression created an environment wherein organized, competitive, pay-to-play activities for kids would flourish outside of the school system in places like Pop Warner and Little League.

Overall during this "seeds of competition" period a transformation occurred both in the time spent in organized competition and in the types of children who participated in these activities. Earlier in the century, affluent children participated in personal growth activities where they did not encounter much organized competition, as the activities were more than anything a form of social grooming. But with the development of national compulsory schooling there had to be a way to distinguish the achievements of children from different classes. (Not surprisingly the 1930s also saw the development of gifted programs, and in 1941 the Hunter College Campus for the Gifted was founded in New York City.)[29] As school became more competitive, so too did the time children spent outside of school—particularly for those from upwardly mobile families.

Growth of Competition: Postwar to the 1970s

During this period competitive children's activities experienced "explosive growth" in terms of the number of activities available and the number of participants.[30] In the decades following World War II a variety of competitive activities began to be dominated by children of the middle class. As the activities became more organized, competition intensified within the middle class.

One of the first children's activities to become nationally organized in a competitive way, and certainly one of the most well-known and successful youth sports programs, is Little League Baseball. After its creation in 1939 the League held its first World Series only a decade later, in 1949. In the ensuing years Little League experienced a big expansion in the number of participants, including participants from around the world. As this model of children's membership in a national league organization developed, fees to play increased.[31]

With the success of these fee-based national programs it became more difficult to sustain free programs. Most elementary schools no longer sponsored their own leagues due to concerns over the effects of competition on children, similar to concerns voiced in the 1930s. The desire to dampen overt competition in school classrooms was part of the self-esteem movement that started in the 1960s.[32]

The self-esteem movement focused on building up children's confidence and talents without being negative or comparing them to others. As the movement did not reach outside activities, such as sports, private organizations rushed to fill the void. Parents increasingly wanted more competitive opportunities for their children and were willing to pay for it.

By the 1960s more adults had become involved in these organizations, especially parents. Parents and kids spent time together at practices for sports that were part of a national structure: Biddy basketball, Pee Wee hockey, and Pop Warner football. Even nonteam sports were growing and developing their own formal, national-level organizations run by adults. For example, Double Dutch jump-roping started on playgrounds in the 1930s; in 1975 the American Double Dutch League was formed to set formal rules and sponsor competitions.[33]

An often overlooked event in the history of children's sports, and especially competitive sports, is the passage of the Amateur Sports Act in 1978. This congressional bill established the U.S. Olympic Committee, largely taking away the function of the Amateur Athletic Union (AAU). Born out of the Cold War and the desire to defeat the USSR in sports, the U.S. Olympic Committee brought together the national governing bodies for each Olympic sport.[34] The AAU had to find a new function; over the next two decades they transformed themselves into a powerful force in the organization of children's competitive sports, serving as a national organization overseeing a variety of children's competitive sports, such as swimming and volleyball.

Nonathletic competitions for children also began to take off in this time period. One example is child beauty pageants. The oldest continuously running child beauty pageant in the United States, Our Little Miss, started in 1961. This pageant was modeled on an adult system, the Miss America Pageant, with local and regional competitions followed by a national contest. Throughout the 1960s and 1970s child beauty pageants began "mushrooming at an unbelievably fast rate."[35] By the late 1970s there was even a media-recognized "pageant circuit." A 1977 *Chicago Tribune* story reported, "Youngsters who travel the circuit learn how to fill the bill wherever they are, acting naïve and spontaneous here and knocking them dead with vampiness there."[36]

Whether the yardstick was academics, athletics, or appearance, by the 1970s parents (mostly those who were educated and upwardly mobile) wanted their children to "be better than average in all things, so they tried to provide them with professionally run activities that would enrich their minds, tone their bodies, inculcate physical skills, and enhance their self-esteem."[37] National organizations went along with this impulse to be better than average by instituting national guidelines and contests. Even programs that had a philosophy of "everyone plays," such as the American Youth Soccer Organization (discussed more below), joined the competitive fray by hosting elimination tournaments where there was only one victor. These competitions began to be geared to children of younger and younger ages.[38]

Some observers have argued that the rise of these adult-organized competitive activities for children can partly be explained by the decrease

in safe areas for children to play on their own.[39] While there is some validity to this argument, as safe play space for children in both urban and
suburban areas was declining, this argument does not explain the trend
toward increased competition because there was an alternative to the
competitive path. As upwardly mobile parents clamored to have their
children involved in competitive activities that would brand them as
"above average," adults involved with less advantaged children focused
on inclusiveness. Those involved with "preventing such youngsters from
being lured into gangs, drug use, and other antisocial behavior, steered
children into organized activities sponsored by churches, schools, YMCAs
and YWCAs, and Boys' and Girls' clubs."[40] In these inclusive clubs, participation and not competition was the norm.

So the same YMCAs and Boys' clubs that had been the first movers in
organized competition several decades before now moved in the opposite direction. The activities provided were still organized by adults, but
little of the tournament impulse remained. Instead, these children's better-
off peers were now the competitive ones, working to ensure their privi-
leged positions in numerous activities organized at a national level. As
the price of such competitive success continued to increase—even for
young children—many less advantaged children were pushed out of the
competitive space.

EXPLOSION OF HYPERCOMPETITIVENESS:
1980S TO THE PRESENT

Since the 1980s it is not only the costs of participation in competitive children's activities that have grown, but also the level of professionalization.
As more children compete in more activities for more money at higher
levels, the result over the past three decades has been the growth of hypercompetition. In addition, the distance between middle-class children
and others continues to grow within the same activities as middle-class
families become ever more competitive.[41]

Many explanations for the continued growth of organized activities
during this time focus on increases in maternal employment: with both

parents outside of the home in the after-school hours, children need to be supervised. But competitive activities—particularly the most common ones for elementary school–age kids, which take place outside of the school system—actually create additional work for parents and take time away from other household tasks.[42] Parents have to make sure uniforms and other equipment are clean and ready and shuttle kids to various lessons, practices, and tournaments. (This is especially true in the suburbs, where children's play space is largely physically limited to areas reachable by car, but it is also true in many urban settings as parents worry about children's safety if they play alone, even though kidnapping rates are down.)[43]

Competitive activities not only produce more work for parents; they also create many work-like elements for children.[44] Parents and children often use work language to describe kids' participation. For example, it is common when a successful child quits an activity to say that he or she has "retired."

It is not a stretch to say that many young athletes and performers are now young professionals. There are three specific ways in which children's competitive youth sports have become professionalized since the 1980s:[45] (1) the development of highly hierarchical divisions within youth activities, (2) the rise of the full-time paid coach, and (3) the ascendancy of the year-round season.

The development of elite programs (which includes travel, select, premier, all-star, and Olympic development programs) across activities intensified during the 1990s.[46] There are now many stratified categories of organized play, ranging from recreational up to elite.[47] Children usually have to work their way up through these divisions, with the goal being the top level team or organization in their geographic area. This system often tries to model itself on professional sports leagues, with club owners seeing recreational leagues as farm systems for the development of elite or pro players. Needless to say, these programs exist outside of the school system. This is true even for activities like spelling bees, which would seem to have to exist within the school system, but between homeschooled children and kids looking for their version of mental athletics, private bees are beginning to develop as well.[48]

The AAU illustrates the recent development of more and more hierarchical, competitive activities. Currently there are over a million participants in AAU sports. In 1995 the AAU had about 100 national championships, most for kids over twelve. By 2008 it held more than 250 national championships in which "a total of 1900 group champions are crowned, starting around age 6. More often, these tournaments begin at age 8."[49] Less than twenty years ago eight was the age when kids started participating in recreational youth sports. Now kids routinely vie for national titles at that age.

Of course these kids need coaches with high levels of expertise to help them reach those national championships. Enter the paid youth sport coach and other specialized trainers, who reinforce the professionalization of youth sports and activities.[50] Parent and volunteer coaches now often exist only in recreational leagues, and some elite clubs and organizations explicitly forbid parents from having any coaching responsibilities. When a team must pay for full-time coaches or trainers, who often charge over $20,000 for a season, the costs outstrip the budgets of all but the wealthiest families. And of course, now that adults can make a living from youth sports, they must continue to justify their employment, so they strive to increase the number of professional markers for these children's activities.

One such marker is the third way youth sports have become professionalized: the rise of the year-round season.[51] In the past, for example, soccer dominated the fall, basketball the winter, and baseball the spring. Now, at the competitive level, teams practice all year—much like the pros—often requiring a permanent annual commitment from families.[52] With indoor training facilities and specialized camps held during school vacations, children are asked as early as age eight to commit to a single sport. This has the consequence of forcing children to specialize early.

At the same time the number of competitors at the highest levels has increased, especially in the 1980s and 1990s, as the rewards for winning have also increased. Gymnastics and figure skating are good examples, as detailed by Joan Ryan in her 2000 book *Little Girls in Pretty Boxes*, which describes the efforts of young girls and their families to fight time and puberty in an attempt to reach the Olympics in their respective sports.

Ryan details how more and more families pushed their daughters into elite competition, often moving across the country to work with particular coaches. She describes one father, Bill Bragg, who actually gave up custody of his daughter to her figure skating coach, hoping that would help young Hollie become an Olympic ice princess. Ryan explains his motivation:

> Bragg himself had been a swimming coach, but swimming held no magic. It couldn't turn milkmaids into princesses. To him, skating was more than a sport. To succeed in skating was to succeed in life. It was a road to riches and recognition, and perhaps more important, it was a road to respectability. Skating offered a life of restaurants with cloth napkins, hotels with marble lobbies, a life where a girl from the wrong side of the tracks could be somebody.[53]

Other competitive sports and activities also come with promises of riches and recognition, particularly in the form of endorsements. This is another reason hypercompetition has started to permeate children's activities and promoted competition for younger and younger children. A 2003 *New York Times Magazine* piece focused on four-year-old champion skateboarder Dylan, who already was being touted as the "next big little thing" by promoters, merchandisers, and his parents.[54]

Even in historically established sports, such as golf, young children who succeed competitively garner publicity, attention, and hence money. Twelve-year-old Alexis "Lexi" Thompson made headlines in the summer of 2007 when she became the youngest qualifier ever for the U.S. Women's Open in golf. Touted as the next "pre-teen prodigy," Alexis began fielding endorsement deals. At age sixteen, in December 2011, she became the youngest ever winner of an LPGA tournament—while wearing sponsor attire.

This proclivity for naming children prodigies, another element of hypercompetition, happens even more often in music. In a 2000 book that highlights the young string students who attend Julliard's Saturday precollege program, music writer Barbara Sand explains that parents and students are so anxious to get and keep a "prodigy" label that they will often lie about a child's age.[55] Being named a prodigy (defined as a child who displays "talents that are only supposed to be the province of gifted and highly trained adults") confers status, but also money and attention.[56]

With so many competitive circuits available, high performers almost expect to be declared prodigies. By the 1980s, middle-class parents presumed their children to be above average,[57] and expectations have only increased since then. Indeed since the 1980s we have seen the development of complex, competitive circuits in a variety of activities that previously had a much smaller competitive element.

Cheerleading is a good example of the growth of complex, competitive circuits. Cheerleading has a long history in this country, starting with men as the first participants in the late nineteenth century. Women became cheerleaders in the 1920s and have dominated the activity since then, with a few exceptions (for example, yell leaders at Texas A&M are still all male). Cheerleading has often been associated with small-town local pride, national patriotism, and school promotion.[58] A few scholastic-based competitions were held for older cheerleading squads—at the high school and collegiate level—in the growth-of-competition period. In 1981 a national organization, the United Cheer Association, organized its own private cheerleading competition.[59] But in the 1990s private, competition-only squads, tied to neither scholastic nor civic identities, began to emerge as a variety of private cheer competitions started. Now such teams as "The Hotties, The Firecrackers and The Flames . . . [compete] at [events like] the American Showdown, a giant, 'Bring It On'–style tournament where more than 60 of the top cheerleading teams from Kindergarten–12th grade vie for cash and prizes."[60]

Competitive cheer is but one example of the hypercompetition that began in the 1980s and 1990s and characterizes competitive kids' activities today, along with many other activities, such as skateboarding, golf, figure skating, and gymnastics. But what about the three case study activities of chess, soccer, and dance?

Chess

Chess prodigies have emerged fairly often over time, which is not surprising given the game's long history. Chess has been part of the Western repertoire of games since the eighth century, when Arabs brought it to southern Europe.[61] In the United States it's been played since Colonial times. The first American chess prodigy was Paul Morphy, who is said to have beaten General Winfield Scott twice as a nine-year-old. Morphy famously went crazy and died in a bathtub at age forty-seven in 1884— not exactly an auspicious precedent for American chess prodigies.

Despite Morphy's success as the unofficial World Champion, there was not much youth chess development in the United States in the early twentieth century. Instead growth in chess for children occurred in other parts of the world. The USSR, which focused on developing children's chess after the 1917 Revolution, was the real center of chess excellence. There chess became as popular as soccer and ice hockey. Clubs were formed and children as young as four were tutored in strategy.[62]

The United States Chess Federation (USCF) was not even founded until 1939, the same time as Little League (though the USCF was not limited to children). The organization soon began to sponsor tournaments and clubs, and in less than two decades it helped develop the best American chess player and the most famous chess prodigy: Bobby Fischer. Fischer taught himself how to play at age six and achieved the status of National Master at twelve. He won the U.S. Junior Chess Championship in 1956. A year later, at age fourteen, he became the youngest-ever U.S. champion (a record that still stands). Before Fischer, the USSR had been certain of its global dominance in chess, especially because it had started teaching chess in school classrooms in the 1950s.[63]

The idea of teaching children scholastic chess finally began to take hold in the United States in the 1960s, as Fischer's star rose. But it was not until the Fischer-Spassky match of 1972 that American scholastic chess really took off. The phenomenal success of Fischer during the World Championship inspired moms to pull their sons out of Little League that summer and enroll them in chess lessons.[64] After 1972 it became possible for some chess players to make a career out of teaching chess in the United States as parents eagerly signed their young children up for lessons.[65]

As with other competitive children's activities, chess grew steadily over the course of the twentieth century and then exploded in the 1970s. Over the next three decades scholastic chess became more organized and competitive. The first national chess championship run by the USCF specifically for young children, also known as the Elementary Championships, was held in 1976.

In the early 1990s, the book and movie *Searching for Bobby Fischer*, about another young chess prodigy, Josh Waitzkin (the book was written by his father, Fred), helped scholastic chess reach a bigger audience. Chess journalist Dan Heisman wrote that the movie "was a phenomenal success, and served as a catalyst for the growth of scholastic chess in North America. In 1990, only about 10 percent of tournament chess players in the U.S. were under 19; today [in 2002], over half are."[66] The depth of this chess mania is reflected in the fact that parents were banned from tournament rooms in the 1980s, as they were all too willing to help their kids cheat.

Along with *Searching for Bobby Fischer* another type of chess story garnered media attention in the late 1980s and 1990s. This narrative focused on the success of chess teams from poor, mostly African American urban communities like Harlem and the Bronx. In 1991, a school from an impoverished section of the Bronx won the national championships, showing that kids from all class backgrounds could compete in chess.[67]

Children from poor urban areas could not afford the private coaches used by children from private schools, like Waitzkin, but they did have nonprofits in their corner. The most prominent of these programs is Chess in the Schools, based in New York City. Founded in 1986 as the American Chess Foundation, Chess in the Schools provides chess teachers for schools in impoverished areas all around New York City. Another organization, The Right Move, sponsors free tournaments where children can play without paying a fee—and these are some of the most competitive events for children in New York City.

Competitive chess is unusual in that it has refocused itself on helping children from less-advantaged backgrounds, in much the same way that settlement houses and boys' clubs did in New York City at the turn of the last century. This is partly because of the game's low cost, but also because there are many perceived benefits to chess, including academic outcomes (some say math scores increase, though the scholarship in this area is difficult to accurately assess) and developing life lessons (such as learning to make a plan before making a move). Many major cities now have a chess program serving underprivileged youth, sponsored by a not-for-profit organization.

In addition to urban programs, the rise of Internet play has enabled children from rural areas to find regular chess competition and instruction. The development of better chess software has also made a difference. Grandmaster Maurice Ashley (the first, and only, African American Grandmaster) claims that there is "an accelerated growth of prodigies,"[68] clearly a phenomenon with which chess remains preoccupied. Scholastic chess has become so prominent and vital to the success of the USCF that in April 2006 they started a bimonthly chess magazine just for their scholastic members, entitled *Chess Life for Kids.*

Soccer

While scholastic chess has grown in the past two decades, it cannot match the explosion of youth soccer in America. Today, according to soccer experts, more kids play soccer than any other organized youth sport.[69] Of course, this has not always been true.

Soccer came to the United States from Europe, particularly the United Kingdom, during the nineteenth century as immigrants brought the game with them.[70] As there were already sports considered "American," particularly baseball and basketball, soccer did not garner much of a following in the United States for most of the first half of the twentieth century. The same immigrants who brought soccer here, and their children, are the ones who kept soccer "alive in the United States until the 1970s [through] ethnic leagues, private schools, and colleges."[71] Colleges began offering soccer scholarships in the 1960s, helping to establish the legitimacy of the sport.[72]

As more and more competitive athletic activities established their own youth leagues and national organizations after World War II, soccer followed suit with the American Youth Soccer Organization (AYSO) in 1964. AYSO's guiding philosophy of "everyone plays"—which is essentially noncompetitive—along with Pele's popularity during that time helped soccer become the fastest growing youth sport in the United States by 1967.[73]

But by the mid-1970s many families were frustrated by AYSO's egalitarian philosophy; they wanted to challenge their children to be above average. Resistance from AYSO and other recreational organizations to the increased competitive impulse spurred parents to develop their own private clubs. As these private clubs developed, with their higher participation fees, many children from the European immigrant and working-class families who had previously kept soccer alive in the United States, along with an increasing number of Latino immigrants, were excluded.

By the end of the 1970s there were about three thousand of these private clubs.[74] Most were connected to U.S. Youth Soccer (USYS), which was founded in 1975 as the competitive parallel to AYSO. USYS explicitly focused on organizing leagues and tournaments for what are known as elite or travel soccer club teams. Such teams are easily distinguishable from recreational, or "rec," teams that AYSO sponsors, as they have year-round seasons, they sometimes play multiple league games each week that require travel, and they almost always have paid trainers and/or coaches.[75] These traits are characteristic of the professionalization seen in various children's athletic activities.

Another way youth soccer has tried to professionalize, which is noteworthy among kids' activities, is that they require all coaches—even volunteer parent coaches in recreational leagues—to get a license to coach. This rule is mandated by the national organizations. Such licenses go from A to F, with A being the most advanced, certifying someone to coach at an international level. Most youth coaches have only an E or F license, the lowest, and while these licenses simply require a few hours of training, the fact that they are required highlights the professional attitude many within the world of soccer have toward youth programs in the United States.

Soccer America, the monthly publication for soccer fans in the United States, also devotes at least one article each month to issues affecting youth soccer, illustrating its salience in the wider soccer community. Jim Haner writes in his 2006 memoir on being a soccer dad and coach that soccer is now simply a part of American childhood, at least for those from a particular class: "Soccer is now one of the defining experiences of childhood in suburbia—like Boy Scouts or Little League two generations ago, only much bigger—but it barely existed in most places as recently as twenty years ago."[76]

While youth travel teams did exist in the 1980s, many soccer writers are quick to point out that they barely resemble the teams of today, with their names, uniforms, and "highly evolved infrastructure."[77] Given that organized competitive soccer developed so recently, it is all the more remarkable how professionalized and organized the competitive landscape already is for kids in the twenty-first century.

Dance

Dance has long been considered a classic childhood experience, the way soccer is for many kids today. And as with soccer, the contemporary dance landscape is quite different than it was thirty years ago. It is now filled with hundreds of dance competitions run by private companies. "Competitive dance" refers to for-profit dance competitions that organize regional and national competitions for all forms of dance, as opposed to dance that is competitive only for admission to companies and programs or for roles in specific productions.

The history of dance education in the United States spans the twentieth century, though formal instruction outside of the home began in the nineteenth century. Dancing academies, such as the Dodworth Academy, started in the 1840s in New York City.[78] These academies helped mold upper-class American children in the image of upper-class European children, teaching them social dances.[79] The Dodworth Academy reached the height of its popularity in the 1890s as the nouveau riche wanted their children to acquire the proper cultural capital; on Saturdays they offered classes to children as young age three. But by the 1920s the Dodworth Academy had closed due to economic difficulties and family politics.

By that time ballet schools had stepped in to fill the void in dance education. One of the first formal ballet schools opened in 1909; it was affiliated with the Metropolitan Opera in New York City. Before schools like this developed, teachers would hold lessons in their homes.[80] Dance schools and studios developed and expanded over the next few decades. Dance teachers' organizations, including Dance Masters of America (DMA), organized in 1948, helped to legitimate the field and promote dance education. In the 1960s these teachers' organizations began to hold national conventions where teachers could take workshops and bring their students to show off their skills and compete.

Dance competitions did not arise for the first time in the 1960s, however. They were preceded in the nineteenth century by a tradition of mostly informal dance competitions among children and adults. For example, "challenge dancing" was common in African American communities, and Irish step dancing competitions (at fairs, pubs, and even in homes) were common both in Ireland and in the Irish diaspora.[81] What distinguished the new competitions of the 1960s is that they were organized, and the organizers earned money for their efforts.

DMA held its first competition for individual dancers in 1963, and another dance teachers' organization, Dance Educators of America, also started competitions in the early 1960s. These competitions awarded scholarships to winning dancers, supporting them in their continuing dance education. Dance competition expert Pam Chancey explains that the goal of the competitions of the 1960s "was to challenge professionals and add prestige to the art of dance. At that time, many people criticized dance competitions for attempting to turn dance, an art form, into a 'sport.' "[82]

But comparisons to sport likely helped establish dance competitions, at least in terms of the way parents viewed the value of participating. Private competitions, eager to jump into this competitive space and thinking of dance competitions as a different form of athletic contest, started to pop up in the late 1970s.

Showstopper National Championships was one of the first to enter the field, and today it remains one of the largest competitions. Showstopper held its first event in 1978, claiming it was the first of its kind. The founder, Debbie Roberts, explained her motivation for starting the competition: "It was my son's participation in organized soccer that inspired me to start Showstopper. I saw how excited and challenged he was to play each week. When he would lose, he would leave the game saying, 'I'll try harder next week.' He learned to practice and work hard to achieve all he knew he was capable of accomplishing."[83]

Another form of competitive dance—though not the focus of this book—is ballroom dancing, which has also relied on similarities to athletics to aid growth. Social ballroom dancing had been popular since the time of academies like Dodworth. But social ballroom dancing steadily lost popularity through the first half of the twentieth century. By the time of Chubby Checker and nightclub dancing, social ballroom dancing was as its lowest point. Interestingly, this is the moment when the competition system for ballroom dancing started to develop in the United States, around the 1960s.[84] By the 1980s this style of competitive ballroom dancing had been labeled DanceSport to "designate a competitive and more athletic form of ballroom in order to set it apart from its more recreational and social counterpart, which is often stereotypically visualized as dancing by seniors."[85]

Just as ballroom dancing became more competitive from the 1960s to the 1980s, so too did the dance competitions that are the focus in *Playing to Win*. The early years of private competition were far less competitive than they are today. One dance teacher reflects, "My studio began competing around 1985. . . . Then probably in the early '90s, some of the stronger studios started coming alive."[86] This teacher went on to explain that today the costs of participation (entry fees, costume costs, etc.) is much, much higher than in the 1980s and 1990s and that in some areas of the country a lot of the camaraderie that used to exist between teachers and studios has been replaced by animosity. The proliferation of dance competitions, "sparse thirty years ago,"[87] has also fueled the proliferation of thousands of dance studios, which explicitly train students to participate in the competitive events.

There is continued growth in competitive dance in the twenty-first century as some of the major competitions attempt to organize themselves into a dance competition federation. Popularity and growth has been reinforced by such TV shows as *So You Think You Can Dance* and *Dance Moms*, which feature many "competition kids" and their tricks. These tricks, such as triple turns performed by nine-year-olds, are a sign of the hypercompetitive atmosphere. To win, children have to perform feats that were rare twenty years ago and certainly not expected of children of their age.

Also unimaginable twenty years ago is the behavior of some adults involved with dance competitions. For example, some teachers and parents have been known to lie about the age of the competitors. Because of such misbehavior competitions now often require proof of age. This type of misconduct by adults highlights the current state of children's competitive activities and how much is at stake for the adults who are involved.

CHANGES IN FAMILIES, EDUCATION, AND PRIZES

What factors explain why competitive activities like chess, dance, and soccer have developed in the way they have over the past century? In addition to the trends described above, I have identified three more macrohistorical trends to help clarify how we got to the point where adults lie about the age of children: changes in the America family, the American educational system, and the organization of prizes and competitions in American culture. Class is an important factor as well, overlaying the historical narrative and influencing the contemporary situation and its outcomes.

In *Busier Than Ever!*, their study of why American families are so busy in the early twenty-first century, anthropologists Darrah, Freeman, and English-Lueck suggest, "Smaller family sizes, the reluctance of parents to permit unsupervised children's play, and preferences for structured, formalized children's activities require adults to transport and supervise their children. Many parents have also become more involved in their children's education and recreational activities reflecting shifting norms of good parenting."[88] Embedded in these reasons for the increase in busyness are some of the reasons for the increase in competition in children's lives.

Demographic changes, such as fewer children in each family, profoundly affect the tenor of parenting. Parents can devote more time and attention to their children in smaller families; this also means that there is even more parental anxiety since there are fewer chances to see children succeed.[89] More mothers now work outside the home as well, which affects child care arrangements. For many mothers, employment can produce parental guilt, as some delegation of socialization tasks must occur. This in turn may lead parents to indulge children in their competitive or organized activities more than they might have otherwise or to overcompensate for less physical time at home by being overinvolved in other ways.

Likely the most significant demographic change that has affected competitive children's activities is the population booms: the Baby Boom and its Echo Boom. While Baby Boom parents have been the best-educated and wealthiest generation ever seen in the United States, that enormous cohort has overwhelmed every social-sorting institution it has come in contact with, from preschool classrooms to retirement homes.[90] Hence the cultural experience of competition, of an insufficient supply of spots for the size of the group seeking them, has predisposed Boomers to see life as a series of contests. With their children's cohort, the Echo Boom, if anything the competitive landscape is getting more crowded than it was in the Boomers' formative years, and the stakes are even higher.

This is especially true when it comes to higher education. The 1960s saw "a growing competitive frenzy over college admissions as a badge of parental fulfillment."[91] Parental anxiety reached a new level because the surge in attendance by Boomers had strained college facilities, and it became increasingly clear that the top schools could not keep up with the demand, meaning that students might not be admitted to the level of college they expected, given their class background. This became even more problematic with the rise of coeducation and the nationalization and democratization of the applicant pool,[92] fueled by the GI Bill, recruiting, and technology that produced better information for applicants. Parents took on the responsibility of ensuring that their children were successful in the college admissions process.

Interestingly, the competitive frenzy over college admissions did not abate in the 1970s and 1980s, when it was actually easier to gain admission to college, given the decline in application numbers after the

Baby Boomers. Instead, more aware of the stakes, families became more competitive.[93]

With the Echo Boom in the late 1990s and early 2000s, it once again became harder to get into a "top" college.[94] It is not just that there has been an increase in the college-age population, expected to have peaked in most areas by the end of the first decade of the twenty-first century,[95] but there have been record numbers of applications to the most elite colleges and universities. The years 2009–2013 brought record applicant pools for Harvard, Princeton, Yale, Dartmouth, and Brown.[96]

This reality, combined with the existing tension around college admissions, has created an incredibly competitive atmosphere for families, which starts at younger and younger ages now, as parents start earlier and earlier in their children's lives on the long march to college admission. How early one starts seems to be related to class position. In some parts of the country some parents with higher class standing start grooming their children for competitive preschool admissions, setting their children on an Ivy League track from early on.[97]

After-school activities are a crucial supplement to in-school achievement and test scores. Performing well in activities that many parents perceive as integral to, but not entirely synonymous with, the formal educational system is seen as crucial. Why? Children can develop Competitive Kid Capital through their participation, which can be translated into the currency of credentials. Certain sports, such as squash and fencing, are especially helpful, as they signal elite status in the college admissions process.[98]

For those who wonder just why competitive children's activities are so much more developed and organized in the United States than in other parts of the world, look no further than this admissions practice. While American society's cultural attitude toward competition is more developed as well, the best structural explanation is that universities take participation in organized activities into account when making admissions decisions. Most of the other top systems of higher education in the world (in Japan, South Korea, China, India, and France, for example) rely on standardized test scores to determine admissions. It is a purely numeric enterprise. Of course, this carries its own stresses and problems for students, but academic performance is the main focus.

Parents know that academic credentials matter. Sociologist Randall Collins explained their importance this way: "The rise of a competitive system for producing an abstract cultural currency in the form of educational credentials has been the major new force shaping stratification in twentieth-century America."[99] As I previously mentioned, this new stratification connected to existing inequalities based on class.

The rise of competitive activities for children is tied to another major change in the educational system: the rise of compulsory education. As Viviana Zelizer carefully details in the classic *Pricing the Priceless Child*, the rise of compulsory education coupled with the eradication of child labor coincided with a cultural shift in how children were viewed. Even as they became less economically vital to families, children became emotionally priceless.[100] Starting in the early twentieth century, parents began to invest more and more in their children, just as they started to have fewer kids, which made the children they did have even more important. This sacralization of childhood helped contribute to the fetishization of childhood and childhood accomplishments.

In many ways it is no coincidence that during this time America experienced a fetishization of awards and prizes in general. The winner-take-all prize frenzy that characterizes American culture started around the same time. For instance, the late nineteenth century saw the establishment of several different types of competitions that still exist today. In 1874 the first Kentucky Derby was held, and 1877 witnessed the inaugural Westminster dog show.[101] More than animals got in on the act: in 1913 the first rose competitions were held in the United States.[102]

The early twentieth century also saw the development of organized American sporting culture. The National Collegiate Athletic Association (NCAA) was established in 1910, and a variety of professional sports leagues grew during this time. Less popular sports also developed their organized, competitive infrastructures in this historical moment; for example, the first synchronized swimming competition in the United States took place in 1939.[103] Social scientists Andrei Markovits and Steven Hellerman note that sports foster Americans' predilection for rankings and quantifications, a huge part of the sporting culture: "America's fetishism and obsession with rankings have made two ostensibly conflicting, yet essential, American values comparable: that of competition and fairness."[104]

The emphasis on competition, and rankings in general, intensified in the second half of the twentieth century. James English describes the 1970s as the most intense period of prize creation, with tremendous growth in every field, including the addition of even more prizes to certain fields, as in film and literature.[105] Music competitions saw similar growth in this time period.[106] Even offbeat activities, such as competitive eating, developed their own competitions and award structures in the 1970s.[107]

Since the 1970s prizes have become increasingly fashionable. They are broadly publicized in a variety of fields, including sports and literary awards,[108] along with children's activities. Competitive children's activities need to be contextualized in the development of the broader organized, competitive spirit of the United States.

Today the sheer number of competitive opportunities for kids has implications for children's long-term development and for class inequality. Competitive children's activities have evolved since they began in late nineteenth-century America. Now there are more activities, a greater number of competitions, and a change in the class backgrounds of competitors. These changes can be understood in terms of changes in families, the educational system, and prizes.

While there is an opportunity to once again involve less advantaged children in competitive activities—as is occurring with scholastic chess in Harlem, the Bronx, and other urban centers that have nonprofits supporting gifted children financially so they can train and travel[109]—it is clear that the middle class still dominates these activities. As paid coaches and fees for participation in activities and competitions continue to proliferate, those who are not able to pay are largely pushed out of the system, especially when they are in elementary school. There are opportunities for participation in school-sponsored activities in middle school and high school, but without specialized training at a young age, it is difficult to compete with those who have had such training.

Understanding the historical evolution and context of these activities is a first step. But we must also understand how parents and children conceptualize the place of these activities in their contemporary lives as they develop the Competitive Kid Capital needed to succeed in various educational tournaments through childhood and early adulthood.

TWO More than Playing Around

"Do you want to play?"

I always dreaded that question. Not because I didn't want to play, but because I didn't really know how. I am a chess neophyte and a failed soccer player. There was simply no way I could keep up with the pint-size players I was studying—even though I tried, much to their delight.

During six to nine months of intensive observation of chess, then soccer, and finally dance, I learned how these activities and their competitions are organized, who is in charge, and why they are ordered the way that they are in the present day. I spent the better part of evenings and weekends over sixteen months on soccer fields, in dance studios and hotel ballrooms, and in school buildings and other spaces where chess is played. I talked informally with participants, attended tournaments, and often carved out a social role for myself (usually as an informal assistant to a teacher or coach). I then conducted 172 semistructured interviews with parents, coaches, and children in their homes or places of work or at a coffee shop, a library, or other public space.

While I never became an expert chess player, dancer, or soccer player— and, sadly, never will—I did become an expert on the organization of these worlds. For each activity I had two field sites, one urban and one suburban, in the greater metropolitan area of a major northeastern city in the United States.[1] Within each urban and suburban setting I had a field site for each activity in order to maximize comparability, so I had a total of six field sites across the three activities.

All of the urban settings are in the area I call "Metro," and the suburban settings are in "West County." The Metro location is extremely diverse, in terms of both income and race/ethnicity, while West County is far more homogeneous. West County contains several affluent suburbs with a mainly educated populace dominated by white and Asian families. There is economic diversity within the county, but the towns where I spent most of my time are the most affluent in the county.

Because I knew the least about chess when I began, I started there. I then moved onto soccer, which I once tried to play in grade school. (The fact that I played in skorts instead of shorts likely tells you all you need to know about my abilities on the field.) I closed my research with dance, as this was the activity I knew the most about, having attended dance competitions as a child—though as a spectator and not as a participant. I myself have never competed in a chess tournament, a soccer tournament, or a dance competition.

I learned about these activities from the ground up, and this chapter is a pocket guide on how each of them works. I have highlighted certain practices within each activity that are relevant to understanding various aspects of Competitive Kid Capital formation that I discuss in the next chapters. In the appendix I detail how I selected field sites and those I interviewed, how I presented myself in the field, and some of the unique methodological challenges this research presented (particularly as it relates to research with kids). If you already know how any of these competitive activities function, you may prefer to skip that activity's section and simply read about the organizations I worked with. For each of the three activities I begin with an overview of the competitive landscape and then describe the six field sites: Metro and West County Chess, Metro Soccer Co-op and Westfield Soccer Club, and Metroville Elite Dance Academy and Westbrook Let's Dance Studio.

SCHOLASTIC CHESS: THE GAME OF KINGS

Chess is an inherently competitive event. It pits one player in a contest against another, and it almost always produces a winner and a loser. The world of children's competitive chess, usually known as scholastic chess (though this does not mean that the chess is tied to the formal school system; it merely refers to the age of the participants), magnifies the intensity of this inherent rivalry and formalizes it into rankings and ratings at regional and national tournaments. The United States Chess Federation (USCF) plays a large part in creating and monitoring the competition in scholastic chess.

The USCF regulates scholastic tournaments.[2] Parents discover these tournaments through chess teachers, other parents, online, or from the most important grapevine: their own children, who come home from school and excitedly report on an upcoming event they heard about from friends or teachers. The USCF itself hosts annual national scholastic tournaments and certifies individuals to run tournaments around the country. A certified tournament director must oversee a tournament in order for it to be recognized as a USCF event.

In many ways, "scholastics" are at the heart of the USCF. Roughly thirty thousand participants under the age of fifteen make up the largest component of USCF membership.[3] In order to be rated in USCF tournaments, children must become USCF members and pay a small annual fee; during my fieldwork the charge for those twelve and under was $17. Enrollment brings a subscription to the bimonthly publication, *Chess Life for Kids!* This publication, which averages about twenty glossy pages, colorfully spotlights national tournaments, chess puzzles, and major winners (both kids and adults).[4]

Children who are not USCF members can play in some local tournaments, but they cannot earn a chess rating. These children are usually beginners, in kindergarten or first grade. Thus the total number of children playing tournament chess exceeds thirty thousand.

The USCF is more than a tournament planner and publisher. By issuing chess ratings, the USCF is the ultimate arbiter of quality in the world of scholastic chess. Ratings range from 100 to 2,800 and are calculated using a complicated mathematical rating formula that assigns each player a number based on past performance; the higher the number, the stronger the player.[5] In his guide for parents, chess coach Dan Heisman succinctly describes ratings: "Suffice it to say that when one wins, his rating goes up, and when one loses, his rating goes down. The higher the rating of the opponent beaten, the more it goes up; the lower the rating of the opponent lost to, the more it goes down."[6]

Tournament opponents are decided based upon a player's rating.[7] Pairings are announced before each round via wall charts, which are essentially pieces of paper taped to the wall or to poster boards. Children and parents crowd around these sheets of paper before preparing for the next round and quickly retreat to their own corners to discuss the implications of the match-ups. Wall charts announce each player's name, rating, and school and who will play with the black and white pieces in the round. The wall charts are divided by section. Sections separate children by age and ability. For example, there may be a K–3 section, and then separate sections for those with ratings under 1,000 and those over 1,000. (There may even be a K–3 under 1,000 section and a K–3 over 1,000 section.)

In later rounds wall charts also reveal the tournament standings. The child with the highest point total at the end of the tournament wins. A win equals 1 point, a loss 0, and a draw or a bye is worth .5.[8] Ties are decided using software programs that judge how hard opponents were based on participants' relative ratings, and reward those who bested more difficult challengers.

The USCF publishes ratings every three months. But once tournament results are reported, children and their parents can log on to the organization's website and see the updated rating, usually within a few days after a tournament. All tournament results are publicly available online. You can use the USCF's website to search for a specific child's name and to see the results from every USCF tournament he or she has ever played in.

Besides being public, the system is completely hierarchical; there is no-where to hide for children falling down the rating scale. Yet the system is open to manipulation, and parents who are in the know are aware of the ways they can stack the deck to advantage their child. Ratings used to determine opponents at tournaments lag behind actual competitions. Only the quarterly published ratings are used to structure tournament pairings. If a player has earned many rating points in the past few months, he or she is still officially rated lower because of the time gap and hence can play in lower-rated sections against weaker players he or she can eas-ily beat. Some parents deliberately avoid letting their kids play right be-fore a new published rating so they can "save" or "protect" a lower rating for an upcoming event.

When ratings are published, the USCF releases its Top 100 lists of play-ers by age, starting with those seven and under and then on to eight-year-olds, nine-year-olds, and so on. The USCF also awards chess titles, such as Master, to players based on their ratings. (Titles come into play once an individual goes over 2,000 rating points.)[9] Children who routinely top these lists and earn titles can make the All-America Chess team and represent the United States in international scholastic events, but these are truly the exceptional children.

Separate lists and titles for the highest rated girls are also released by USCF. Chess is dominated by boys, starting at the youngest ages, with greater numbers of boys entering the game at the lowest levels.[10] Special attention is paid to girls, especially those who are talented, to get them to stick with chess as they get older; hence the separate lists for top-performing females.

The cost to participate in tournaments in order to earn rating points and titles is fairly low, and some major cities have organizations that host free tournaments. Entry fees range from $30 to $50 for local tournaments and up to $80 for state and national tournaments. On average, children I met play in one tournament a month during the school year. These con-tests are usually in a school cafeteria or a gym, if they are local events, and in a hotel ballroom or a conference center, if they are regional or national.

Children do not need any special equipment to participate in a tourna-ment. The tournament itself almost always supplies chessboards and pieces. Children often are expected to bring their own paper and pencil so that they can annotate their games,[11] but some tournaments even provide these.

Most competitive children have a chess notebook in which they record their games sequentially so they can be dissected and studied after a tournament. Hardcover notebooks that hold annotations from one hundred games can be purchased for around $8, and spiral notebooks that hold fifty games cost around $3. Even though it is not necessary, children usually bring a chess set to tournaments so they can play and analyze between rounds. Supplies like these are often purchased at chess tournaments, where organizers set up a small store with other chess-related gear and books and software. Similar items are also available for purchase online. Kids often keep all of their chess supplies together in a chess bag, which can be bought for around $25.

A chess clock is an important additional piece of equipment because scholastic chess games are timed. In local tournaments the time control is usually "G30," or thirty minutes for each player, for a maximum of sixty minutes per game. After each move a child hits a button on the chess clock, which reveals the time he or she has remaining, and then records the move in his or her chess notebook. There are a variety of chess clocks available, some digital and some analog. Digital clocks cost more, but a chess clock can be purchased for as little as $30 (though the more expensive ones, often endorsed by chess stars like Gary Kasparov, cost upward of $200). The player who has the black pieces in a tournament game gets to use his or her own clock. Players who do not have a clock can use their opponent's.

There is some debate in the chess world about the "proper" length of time for children's games. A G30 game is considered short,[12] but it is preferred at one-day tournaments, mainly because parents do not want to spend twelve hours (or longer) indoors on a weekend. State and national tournaments, held over two to three days, have longer time controls, often G90. Some believe longer games promote deeper chess thinking and calculation, but other demands on family members' time usually prevail and G30 games are most common.

In order to prepare for tournaments and develop strategies for games of different length, many children take private chess lessons. These sometimes occur in small groups, but most often they are one-on-one and take place in the home. Private lessons via the Internet are growing in popularity as well.[13]

Parents find private coaches mainly through word of mouth, either through other parents or through the chess teacher at school. Lessons typically last one hour and can cost between $50 and $150, depending on the reputation of the teacher and the level of the student. Formal certification for chess teachers and coaches has not developed, and since it can be difficult to locate a great coach, parents are often left with Internet instruction as the option. But families usually prefer a personal and in-person connection, and they cultivate relationships with coaches with whom they share goals for the child—and a price point. The bonds between family and coach can become very strong. When the demands of competition require that children leave one mentor for another, bitter feelings may result, especially when a coach feels the new coach "stole" his or her student.

Summer and holiday chess camps provide another venue for intensive instruction. These camps are generally run by those who give private lessons and run their own chess tournaments, creating a one-stop-shopping chess experience. A day at a chess camp usually costs between $80 and $100. Camps are held at schools (though in theory they are open to children from any school), private clubs, or semipublic community spaces such as those owned by religious organizations.

Camps and lessons increase in frequency before major tournaments, such as the state and national championships. Anyone can compete in state events, regardless of where they live, but if the winner is not from that state, the next highest finisher from that state is declared state champion. The Nationals are run by the USCF, though there are actually two held for elementary school–age kids, one in December and one in May.[14] The December Nationals are "grade" Nationals, known as The National Scholastic K–12/Collegiate Championship, meaning participants only play opponents from their own scholastic grade level, regardless of rating. In this way there is a national first-grade champion, a national second-grade champion, and so on, up through twelfth grade (regardless of chronological age, so children who are old or young for their grade still compete against grade peers). The May Nationals, called the National Burt Lerner Elementary (K–6) Championship,[15] is based on both grade and rating. There are K–1, K–3, and K–5 designations, and within those designations there are separate sections for those whose ratings are under a certain level (for example, 1,000).

This means that there are many different trophies awarded—a huge focus of all chess tournaments. The top ten or twenty finishers in each section receive trophies, and there are special trophies awarded within sections, such as the best performance for players with a rating under 500. Almost everyone leaves a local chess tournament with a trophy or a ribbon or medal, though they vary significantly in size. Trophies for winners at Nationals are often bigger than the players themselves. Some local tournaments also award participation trophies to all the kids, though these are usually only for the youngest children. In certain sections all entrants might receive a medal, but those typically are phased out by middle school.

The local-state-national structure of scholastic chess implies that there is a progression upward and that players need to qualify to play in the Nationals. Not so. There are absolutely no qualifications to play at the national scholastic tournaments. If someone pays the entry fee, a child can play in the event. Sometimes even unrated players compete in Nationals.

Many schools do not have chess teams. In that case a child may represent his or her school, and the school may not even know. In most schools that have chess teams anyone can join. At a tournament the team in scholastic chess is usually the three or four top-scoring children from the same school in each section (though the school may have brought twenty children). Homeschooled children are able to participate based on their current age, and many do, but they are not able to compete for team prizes.

When children attend tournaments as a school team they benefit from companionship and also from having a team room. This is a rented conference room or hotel suite that parents pay for, or which the school covers, where everyone gets together to go over games. Often schools hire team coaches who stay in the team rooms during the tournament to analyze games and give the children pep talks between rounds. Such schools also often have the children wear team T-shirts, which helps build camaraderie.

While some schools go so far as to order food for families to eat in their private rooms, less advantaged schools do not have the funds to rent their own rooms. These teams and their families use spaces provided by tournament organizers, known as "skittles rooms." Skittling is a chess term for analyzing a game to look for areas of improvement, whether a child won or lost.

Parents and children involved with scholastic chess quickly learn about skittling and become conversant in speaking the language of ratings, reading wall charts, and annotating games. The 1984 book *Searching for Bobby Fisher* and the 1993 film of the same name still accurately portray the contemporary world of scholastic chess.[16] But the book and movie do not explain how the competition actually works. Private lessons, the rating system, and tournament structure and pairings are all integral to understanding how the highly organized world of kids' competitive chess is structured. Parents must get involved and learn about these practices if their child is to thrive in scholastic chess, as many of the Metro and West County chess parents have done.

Metro Chess and West County Chess

In general, chess attracts a diverse group of participants. This is largely attributable to the low basic costs of equipment and participation. There are also many opportunities to play in free tournaments, especially in areas like Metro. Metro is one of the historic centers of chess in the United States, and it is one of the hotspots for scholastic chess.[17] Many public and private schools in Metro offer curriculum chess on top of extracurricular opportunities.[18]

The scholastic chess scene in Metro is a small and connected, but divided, world. Coaches jealousy guard their turf, both schools and students, particularly in the more affluent pockets of the city. There are many organizations and teachers who try to control the scholastic chess scene. Outside of the affluent schools different coaches and teachers dominate.

I worked with two organizations in order to meet children and parents associated with Metro Chess: Uptown-Metro Chess and Charter-Metro Chess.

I met parents in Uptown-Metro Chess through a for-profit organization that offers curriculum chess classes, after-school classes, camps, tournaments, private lessons, and chess supplies. At that time the organization was based in four schools, a mix of public and private. Through camps and tournaments children from other schools are also part of this organization, and these events are held in a church basement and in school cafeterias and gyms.

Uptown-Metro Chess teaches several children who routinely appear on the Top 100 lists and have won national championships, but the majority of the children who play in their tournaments and attend their classes and workshops do not have exceptionally high ratings. Boys far outnumber girls here, but several girls are top performers. Families that can pay enroll their children in classes, private lessons, and tournaments. Many of these families go to city and state tournaments, and a substantial number attend at least one national event a year. Both mothers and fathers are involved with their children.

Charter-Metro Chess is quite different. Instead of being for-profit it is part of a nonprofit dedicated to bringing after-school programs to underprivileged children. The chess program is a highlight, as many of the children in the program have been very successful. During the school year classes are offered on Saturday mornings to children in the community; during the summer a half-day chess camp is also available. The camp is especially popular, as it is free. Parents push their children to continue with chess during the school year because they know that if the children do well, they may be selected to travel to attend tournaments—again, for free. Both the summer camp and the classes take place in schools, the former in a public elementary school and the latter in a nearby charter school for middle school and high school students, though the program focuses on elementary school–age children. Free snacks and lunches are part of the chess day.

All Charter-Metro chess children are welcome to attend free tournaments around the Metro area. Top-performing children are also invited (or they qualify at an internal tournament) to attend local tournaments that require an entry fee. The best players are invited to travel to attend the Nationals. This is a much smaller group since travel expenses for the children are covered by the organization. Girls are the top performers in Charter-Metro chess, and the number of girls and boys involved is far more equal than in Uptown-Metro Chess.

Charter-Metro parents do not often attend tournaments with the children; instead the chess teachers take kids to the events. For local tournaments, they meet up on weekend mornings at the school and take the subway together. Often the teacher has to take a child home after the tournament when the parent does not show up. Because Charter-Metro Chess parents are often not present, they are not well represented in my data. But through fieldwork at Charter-Metro events, including attending their summer camp, weekly weekend lessons, and tournaments with their group, I was able to study this part of the scholastic chess world.

My other chess field site, West County Chess, is more similar to Uptown-Metro than to Charter-Metro Chess. In fact some of the teachers in West County chess originally started teaching in Metro; a few continue to make the journey to West County once or twice a week to teach students. While parents often pay for private instruction, there are far fewer opportunities for chess tournaments, camps, and lessons in West County. Instead of multiple offerings there is usually only one local, for-profit tournament in an entire month. (Meanwhile Metro Chess has multiple for-profit tournaments each month, with two or three on any given weekend, and often three or four free tournaments a month.) Similarly, there is a chess camp available in West County Chess, but that is usually the only camp available in that area.

In addition to limited options for chess camps and tournaments, West County generally exhibits a different attitude toward scholastic chess; it chooses to be less intensely competitive. While the West County and Uptown-Metro parents have similar financial resources and the children themselves are no less capable, West County chooses to focus on group after-school chess classes and other types of after-school activities. Significantly, most of the overlap I found with chess and soccer comes from West County chess kids. The overwhelming majority of West County chess players are boys; I saw only three girls in a class and never saw any at tournaments.

Most of these West County boys have chess ratings, so they certainly do not eschew scholastic chess competition. Yet for most of them, the largest tournament they play in is at the state level and not Nationals. One or two West County parents a year choose to use some of the Metro Chess resources, such as tournaments and camps, but they usually decide to return to West County after being exposed to the more cutthroat city chess scene.

Across Metro and West County I attended fifteen tournaments (including one national tournament), in addition to classes and camps. Altogether I formally spoke with twenty-nine families with children who were competing in scholastic chess tournaments. (Given that Metro had more families who were quite competitive, I spoke with more Metro parents.) I also spoke with parents from eight families whose children used to compete in scholastic chess but had since dropped out of the competitive scene. Additionally, I interviewed fifteen chess-playing children and thirteen chess teachers. Eight families had children involved in both competitive chess and soccer, four of whom I met through chess and four through soccer.

SOCCER: GOAL!

Although the United States lags behind European, Latin American, and African countries in terms of devotion to soccer, the sport has grown rapidly among the youngest age groups. Soccer is a good introduction to team sports because children just need to be able to run; no specialized skills, such as hitting or catching a baseball, are required. Kids as young as two or three can begin to play soccer in organized programs.

But within a few years after the introduction of recreational soccer, or "rec," through the American Youth Soccer Organization or other local programs, many are ready for more soccer intensity. As kids get older, many decide that they want to play travel or elite soccer with a nearby soccer club.[19] If they don't opt for the more competitive route, kids typically leave the sport altogether because recreational opportunities for soccer begin to dry up around age eleven as travel becomes the only option. In writing about travel soccer, ESPN journalist Tom Farrey describes letting his third-grade son try out for the local club as a "conservative move, the preserving of an option [to try out for his high school team in the future]."[20]

Enter U.S. Youth Soccer, which oversees many of the travel soccer teams. With over 3 million registered children between the ages of five and nineteen—along with nearly 1 million adults—U.S. Youth Soccer is a large organization.[21] The travel soccer clubs that help make up U.S. Youth Soccer are almost always nonprofits and/or have 501(c)(3) status.

Parent volunteers make up the governance of the clubs, though some clubs have paid employees to handle the administrative details. The parents often form a governing body resembling an elected board of governors that sets policies and fees and hires employees. Clubs are affiliated with the national organization, but they are self-funded through dues and fees and sometimes through donations.

Travel soccer teams are organized within these clubs. Parents hear about tryouts and clubs through local advertising and word of mouth. Teams are organized first by sex, then age, and then ability. Children born in the same year are grouped together; for example, all girls born in 2002 form a team. Kids who are younger or older than their school classmates may not play with them, as the birth year is a strict standard. The purpose of these strict cutoff dates is to promote fair competition and to give children age-appropriate instruction.[22] Team names include the designation "U9" or "U10", as in U9 Tigers or U10 Sprites. The U means "under," so all girls on that team are under the age of nine or ten.

Although teams are organized by birth year, those who are younger can "play up" and be on an older team if they display exceptional talent and the club and coach allow it. For example, an eight-year-old can play on a team of ten-year-olds, but an eleven-year-old cannot. In order to prove the age of each player on a team an adult must "card" all of the kids, meaning that verified identification cards with a child's birth details must be on hand at all times at games and tournaments in order for the team to compete.

Within clubs there are often two teams, and sometimes more, within each birth year. This means that there is an "A" team and a "B" team. They are usually not called this, but everyone understands that one of them is the better team. Movement is possible between the teams, but typically only once a year, during tryouts.

Each club has its own tryout policies and rules. In general, tryouts are held in the spring so that teams can attend summer camps and tournaments together. Tryouts are often a multiday affair with more players than slots, which is why more than one team is usually formed for each age group. Outside evaluators are frequently brought in to oversee the process, a strategy that helps prevent parental interference and claims of bias.

Once a travel team has formed, the club leadership decides the league with which it will align. There are many soccer leagues available in each state and region; in one of my fieldwork sites (Westfield Soccer Club, described below) there were fifteen league options, and teams decided to play in one or two. This means that teams within the same club often play in different leagues.

Some leagues are more competitive than others. Within leagues there are internal rankings called "flights," sometimes labeled alphabetically, with "A" as the top flight. Decisions about a team's proper flight are made based on its performance in the previous season and on the recommendation of the club.

Like clubs, leagues are often run by parents. For the truly involved mothers and fathers who work on club and league boards, this commitment can often seem like a job. Leagues require that clubs show their legal existence (with an incorporation document, constitution, bylaws, or tax return), but the leagues themselves are not required to do the same, and it appears that most leagues do not have 501(c)(3) status. Leagues schedule games, help arrange for fields for these games, hire referees, and record and report the results of each game and the overall standings for a season. Games usually take place once a week, either on Saturday or Sunday. Some highly competitive teams join two leagues so that they can play games on both Saturdays and Sundays.

Highly competitive travel teams almost always forgo volunteer parent coaches and hire a soccer coach who earns a salary. Professionals provide more rigorous training; they often have a prestigious aura as well. Most of these coaches have an E-level soccer coaching certification, and many have higher qualifications. Coaches influence the league in which their team will play, how often the team will practice, who spends time on the playing field, and who spends time on the bench.

Coaches also decide which tournaments to attend, though for long-distance travel they tend to consult the parents, usually through a team manager or a designated parent, often called a "team mom," who has volunteered to be the liaison between the coach and the parents. The team manager also arranges such details as who will bring snacks to practices and games (an out-of-pocket expense for families a few times a year) and often configures a carpool schedule. In this way parents can volunteer for their child's team within the club.

In a given club paid coaches often have two teams, usually one girls' team and one boys' team. Teams are almost entirely sex-segregated, but girls can sometimes play on boys' teams. If only one boy joins a girls' team, though, that team is considered coed.

While the coach makes all of the soccer-related decisions for the team, such as who plays what position, the club handles all of the administrative details, including providing practice field space and organizing a practice schedule for all of the teams. Finding field space is often difficult because many soccer teams, and clubs from other sports, compete for the use of public fields. If a club is wealthy enough, it can buy and care for its own soccer fields, with lights so they can practice after dark, but most are not so fortunate. An additional obstacle is that fields used by younger children must be flat and free of holes and rocks to prevent injury, so upkeep can be costly.

Some clubs have scholarship programs to cover the fees associated with travel soccer.[23] Fees can be anywhere from $500 to $1,000 a year, depending on the number of travel tournaments a team attends; team fees range from $600 to $1,600 a year and club fees are about $100. Entry fees for teams in tournaments are usually about $450 (around $40 per team member). Travel and hotel costs are additional for each team member and family members. The basic team fee usually gets a team a paid coach, two uniforms, practice uniforms, and other perks such as team warm-up suits and backpacks, though some clubs charge a separate fee of around $250 for clothing.

Given the amount of practice time and game time each week, the overall basic price is quite low, especially compared to an activity like competitive dance. Even so, these costs are a hardship for many American families, especially when the fees have to be paid in a lump sum in the fall, when a child's other activities and events require payment as well. Parents must also buy soccer cleats, shin guards, and other personal items for their children, and these can cost several hundred dollars per year. Cleats cost about $20 to $30 for an outdoor pair and $30 to $40 for an indoor pair; shin guards cost about $18; and one pair of soccer socks to cover the shin guards cost about $10. Families are responsible for the upkeep of all team-related items.

Moreover travel soccer is not a one-season commitment for a family; it is a year-round obligation, with the main seasons being the fall and spring, when practices and games take place outdoors. Winter is an indoor season, and during the summer many team tournaments and camps that involve significant travel are held. Often coaches ask the children to commit to only one sport, and the year-round structure of travel soccer prevents many kids from engaging in other activities, either recreationally or competitively. Some kids can play more than one sport if the practices and game times do not conflict, but this gets more difficult when siblings are involved and as the distances required to travel to play games each week grow.

With such high stakes coaches and adults sometimes misbehave. One problem is the "poaching" of players. Unscrupulous coaches may try to coax a talented player to leave his or her travel team for another one, perhaps with the promise of more victories and more playing time. Some leagues have rules about poaching, with penalties in place to try to prevent it. But it certainly happens in areas where competition between clubs is fierce. Most poaching occurs over the summer or during tryouts (even though deals have already been struck and offers made, making the tryouts a rubber stamp). Poaching rarely occurs in the middle of the season, probably because the switch would be too obvious and would invite criticism or sanction from leagues. Tellingly, in some leagues where poaching was rampant and controversial in the past, team rosters cannot change at all during the season.

Competition is particularly fierce when a state cup tournament hangs in the balance. Each state is able to organize its own state tournament through U.S. Youth Soccer. These tournaments are run elimination-style and teams are seeded. Not every state has one, but in those that do these tournaments increase the competitive stakes. The label of being a state cup champion follows both a team and individual players as they age.[24]

Major victories for top travel clubs, such as state cups, fill the pages of *Soccer America*, a monthly magazine that prints a regular column on youth soccer. Such websites as www.Nationalsoccerranking.com rank teams beginning with U11 boys and girls. In order to be ranked, teams need to attend national and regional tournaments. Like other activities, soccer tournaments are not truly national, but they are prestigious nonetheless.

Local tournaments, the events in which most travel soccer teams compete, are not part of these rankings, and they are smaller than state cup tournaments. The hierarchy of tournament participation and wins matters less for elementary school–age kids and more for high school players, as part of college recruiting efforts, known as "showcases." Whatever their size, these tournaments matter greatly to coaches, kids, and parents, who want their child and team to win.

The prizes here, as with other activities, include trophies. These often go only to the winners, but all children receive a patch for participation, and they may receive a special patch for winning. Collecting as many patches as possible, and even swapping with other kids, is a pastime of many soccer kids. Kids often display these badges on their soccer backpacks, which carry their cleats and shin guards.

Overall, soccer is the largest of the three case study activities and also has the largest organizational structure to sort and rank the players and teams, with about six thousand soccer clubs nationwide. It is a popular activity in the United States, at both the recreational and competitive levels, especially in the suburbs and among the middle and upper middle classes (often parodied, as in Alan Black's nonfiction work *Kick the Balls*, fiction such as Nancy Star's *Carpool Diem*, and movies such as *Kicking and Screaming*).[25]

Metro Soccer Co-op and Westfield Soccer Club

In contrast to my findings for chess and dance, for soccer West County is more competitive than Metro. Also unlike the other activities, both soccer field sites were with organizations that are not-for-profits, though they still charge fees for children to participate. Metro Soccer Co-op and Westfield Soccer Club boast similar numbers of male and female participants, but boys have a slight edge in the numbers in both clubs among the elementary school–age teams.

Westfield Soccer Club is very competitive. The Club has several components to its program, including travel teams for children above age nine, a travel "training academy" for children age seven to eight, and recreational weekend games for those seven and under. They also organize summer camps and indoor soccer tournaments in the winter. Each program is designed to feed into the next, training the children to be accomplished soccer players. Each year several Westfield teams participate in the state cup tournament, and a handful of the teams win.

Despite creating many highly successful teams, Westfield Soccer Club does not own its own soccer fields. Instead they have to pay to use the fields of a nearby college for practices. For games they use municipal fields. But neither the college nor the municipal fields have lights, so teams cannot practice at night. This means Westfield cannot control its teams' schedules. The city or college may decide its fields are unusable due to weather. Moreover the Club has to entrust the upkeep of these fields to others. Given high property costs in this affluent area, they will not be able to afford their own fields in the near future unless they receive a sizable donation.

Competition is not restricted to the children within Westfield Soccer Club. Parents are also wrapped up in jockeying for influence and important roles. This clubby, or clique, atmosphere within the leadership of the Club encourages infighting among the parents. While the Soccer Club has paid, full-time staff members, the parents run the Club and control the careers of the employees, who also pick sides in the fractious disagreements. Because of this contentious atmosphere, many of the younger teams have not done well, losing families to other local soccer programs or to lacrosse, basketball, or other popular sports in the area.

Metro Soccer Co-op is also competitive on the field, sending a few teams to the state cup tournament each year, but there is a sense of cooperation among the upper-middle-class parents who run the club and its teams. Carpooling is common, and there is little fighting at either the leadership or the team level.

The Co-op offers only travel soccer team opportunities, though it is strongly linked to a popular and well-known noncompetitive recreational soccer league, which some of the leaders of the Co-op helped found. When these parents realized their children needed more competitive opportunities with soccer, they started their own club twelve years ago. To discourage the potential for fighting between parents, the Co-op's bylaws state that all teams must hire a nonparent coach.

In the past few years, a few of the Co-op's teams have garnered national distinction, as have many of its players, who have been awarded collegiate soccer scholarships. These successes fuel the Co-op parents' sense of purpose and cooperation. From what I observed, part of the reason the parents get along so well is that they are so similar.

Not only do most of them live in the same affluent, geographic area in Metro, but most of them have similar educational and income levels. The Co-op is full of well-off families both because the fees for participating in Metro Soccer are fairly high and because the municipal practice fields are not easily accessible by public transit, so most families need cars to get their kids there—a luxury in Metro. This means that there is not a lot of diversity in terms of race and ethnicity or in terms of class.[26] Opposing leagues are all located outside of Metro's center, so cars are needed to transport kids to weekend games that can be up to two hours away.

In total I spoke with parents from forty-one soccer families from Westfield and Metro; thirty-two of these families had children currently competing on a travel soccer team, and nine had children who had previously played. Consistent with the differing level of competition, I interviewed slightly more Westfield families with active soccer players and more Metro families with inactive soccer players. I also spoke with seventeen soccer kids and ten soccer coaches. Because of the extent of parental involvement I interviewed an additional eleven parents who were soccer leaders (usually for their clubs but also for leagues and the national organization). Due to this parental leadership I attended many board meetings for both the clubs, in addition to attending practices, weekend games, summer camps (both local and regional), a local tournament, and a state convention. (None of the elementary teams competed in national tournaments during my fieldwork.) Unlike chess and soccer, which had more overlap, only two families had daughters who participated in both competitive dance and soccer, both of whom I met not through soccer fieldwork but through dance fieldwork.

COMPETITIVE DANCE: AND FIVE, SIX, SEVEN, EIGHT . . .

Dance has recently experienced a television revival, thanks to such shows as *So You Think You Can Dance, Dancing with the Stars, Abby's Ultimate Dance Competition,* and *America's Best Dance Crew.* The reality show *Dance Moms*—featuring tween girls, their moms, and their dance teacher, who drags them across the country for dance competitions—has further spotlighted dance competitions, attracting interest and scrutiny. But what exactly is "competitive dance"?

Let me begin by saying what competitive dance is not: it is neither ballet nor ballroom dance. Ballet, the most classical form of dance, is highly competitive in terms of entrance into dance companies and productions, and there are ballet competitions, such as the USA International Ballet Competition held every four years in Jackson, Mississippi, spotlighted in the 2012 documentary *First Position.*[27] But these competitions focus on older dancers who have the requisite physical development to dance *en pointe.* Ballroom dance, which features a boy and a girl dancing together, is also a competitive endeavor, and there are competitions specifically for children. The documentary *Mad Hot Ballroom* featured the New York City–wide annual competition for fifth-graders.[28] *Dancing with the Stars* has featured a kids' competition, with children as young as six participating on live television.

The kind of competitive dance that is the focus in *Playing to Win* takes place in the context of for-profit competitions that incorporate a variety of dance styles. These styles may include ballet and ballroom, but the main styles are jazz, tap, and lyrical/contemporary (a mix between jazz, ballet, and modern techniques, usually performed to slower tempo songs). The closest type of professional dance style is Broadway. The dance competition television show that best represents competitive dance is *So You Think You Can Dance*. This show sometimes specifically refers to the "competition style" of dance, which features lots of "tricks," such as pirouettes, leaps, kicks, and even some acrobatics, prominently featured on *Dance Moms* (often at the expense of ballet).

Competitive dance is dominated by girls. This is especially apparent because, unlike ballroom and even ballet, couples' dances are not required. Routines can be performed in large groups (sometimes close to a hundred competitors in one routine), small groups (usually groups of fewer than ten dancers), duets, trios, or solos. Dance studios decide what types of groups to form, and they slot themselves into one of the existing competition categories. Similarly, each studio decides how to select its competition team, either through auditions or invitations to select students.

Dance studios also decide which competitions to participate in and how many of their students will attend. These competitions are for-profit events held on weekends during the spring and fall months, known as "regionals," and four- to seven-day events over the summer, known as "nationals." There is an entry fee charged for each routine *and* for each participant in each of those routines. For example, a soloist pays $80 to compete, but if she competes in four other group routines, she pays an additional $30 per routine, for a total of $200. If one of her routines has five people, the entry fee is $150 for the group, and if another routine has fifty people, the entry fee is $1,500, even though the time spent on stage is the same. All the routines are given a time slot, typically with three minutes to perform, though the time limits are not uniform from competition to competition.

Nationwide about two hundred companies run dance competitions. The individuals who own and/or run these competitions often have some dance training or background, but not always. Anyone can start a competition; no restrictions exist. Most are not accredited with the Better Business Bureau, although some competition locations (for example, schools and convention centers) require the competitions to carry insurance.[29]

Some competition companies, or "systems," as they are referred to, are quite large, running hundreds of competitions per year across the country. Others run only a few events in a limited geographic location. What all the systems have in common is that they charge competitors. Other details—time limits of routines, age categories and rules, and routine categories—are not standardized.

In 2007 an organization called the Federation of Dance Competitions was founded (as a nonprofit) by a competition owner to try to establish such guidelines. Apart from this Federation, which comprises only a handful of the hundreds of competition companies, no national organization exists that can rank dance competitors (at the studio or individual level). This means that there isn't an organization like the USCF which tracks the number of competitors and details about them, such as age and sex.[30] Consequently there is no reliable estimate of the total number of participants in dance competitions. Showstopper, a major national competition, claims that they host over 100,000 dancers at their competitions each year.[31] Given that there are two hundred other competitions, we can assume that the total number of dance competitors is significantly higher than the fifty thousand for scholastic chess but likely less than the millions who participate in travel soccer.

The Federation has tried to standardize the judging procedures among their members, which likely will impact other competition systems as well. There are usually three judges at each competition, but some systems have more and drop the lowest or highest score. Judges sometimes know the dance teachers, and even some of the competitors, whom they evaluate. Judges tend to be professional dancers, but at many competitions their names and qualifications are not printed in the program book or even announced at award ceremonies.

Competitions themselves are usually held in hotels, large high schools, or community spaces. There has to be at least one large ballroom, with enough space for a stage and seats for the audience. Ideally there is an auditorium with a built-in stage, but the stages used at competitions are not always a standard performance size or made of materials that are best for dancing. Some are on raised platforms, so they shake during routines; others are more makeshift, produced by rolling out a nonstick surface on concrete.

The judges sit at the base of the stage at a table, usually with some distance between the audience and themselves, so people behind them cannot read their scores or intimidate them. A tabulator sits at the end of the judges' table, entering scores after each routine so awards can be announced soon after the performances conclude.

Competition sites must also have a large space to act as a girls' dressing room and a smaller space for boys. Many studios bring dividers to carve out some private space for doing make-up and facilitating costume changes. Ideally there is another room for groups to warm up and rehearse, but this does not always happen. A group rate (usually $100 to $250 per night) at a nearby hotel for overnight accommodations is often arranged. Most competitors need to use this hotel even if they live within driving distance because of the early mornings and late nights at competitions.

Nationals are usually held in a family-friendly destination, such as Florida, California, South Carolina, where families can make the event a vacation. "Nationals" tend to be held during the summer in different parts of the country, often an East Coast, Midwest, and West Coast location. Many competitors spend their summer months traveling and competing in multiple "national" competitions.

Dance teachers select which competition(s) to attend by consulting a variety of dance magazines, such as *Dance Teacher, Dance Spirit, Dancer,* and *Dance Magazine,* which are filled with ads about upcoming competitions. Often these publications devote a full issue once a year to dance competitions. The Internet is another way to find upcoming competitions, mainly through dance message boards or Facebook. Studios that have been participating in competitions for years are also on regular mailing lists for particular competition systems and keep track of which ones they have liked in the past. Most teachers evaluate these competitions based on whether or not they run on time, if they give out the advertised prizes, if judges' scores are quickly made available, and if the competition results appear to be fair (meaning that the directors have not tampered with the outcome and the judges were as objective as possible).

While each system can develop its own rules and judging standards, there are similarities across all dance competitions. For instance, most competitions have age categories that typically span two years, such as seven to eight, nine to ten, and so on. In group dance routines the age is determined by taking the average age of the group members. Some teachers will deliberately include younger competitors, even if they appear only briefly in a routine, in order to bring down the average age and compete in a younger category where a higher skill level is more unexpected and thus rewarded.

For most competitions the age of a competitor is the age as of January 1 of the year of the competition. This is known as a "fallback age." Participants with early birthdays have an advantage since they get to compete as nine-year-olds, for example, when they are already ten. Some competitions ask for copies of birth certificates or request that copies be on hand in case an age is challenged. This seems to be lip service, however, as I never saw or heard of anyone having to produce the copies (though this did occur on an episode of *Dance Moms*). Again, because children are judged according to their age and the difficulty of their routine and technique, if a child registers with a false age, she is likely to be rated higher. This can be a problem, particularly when competitions give away prize money for performance in particular categories.

Jazz, ballet, tap, and lyrical are categories that appear at almost all competitions. From there the options grow. For example, there may be a "character" category, which could be any type of dance but, as the name implies, involves taking on a role. Another category is "open," which allows acrobatic tricks, such as aerial cartwheels, in the midst of a jazz or even a tap routine.

Within the categories and age levels, there is yet another subdivision: competition style. For example, those who practice dance a total of three hours per week or less are sometimes offered the option of registering in a "recreational" category. There are also competitive/elite, preprofessional, and professional categories, and each system lays out its own rules for each. The professional categories refer to earning money by dancing, and each system has its own monetary limits. It is nearly impossible for directors to investigate how truthful these self-selecting categories are, and this can lead to conflicts between studios that complain about one another.

Once a routine is properly categorized for an event, the system assigns it an individual entry number. All of the above options—including age, category, even the size of the group—enable both the competition owners and the teachers to maximize their chances of making money and keeping various actors happy. Both make money by entering more routines: teachers charge parents more for lessons and rehearsals, and competition owners make money from each entry. Both also get the added benefit that children will be happier—the more they dance, the more likely they are to get awards (and more first-place awards). This means their parents will be happier as well.

Competition owners organize the events to maximize the number of prizes awarded by using an adjudication system. Under an adjudication system each routine is first evaluated on the judges' score alone. It is then given an award based on the numeric category in which it falls. Most competitions evaluate routines out of a score of 100 from each judge (so, often the total score is out of 300) based on a combination of technique and presentation, which includes costume, make-up, and overall appearance. Those scores in the highest range, perhaps 290 to 300, will be awarded the top level. This has different names across different systems, but it is often called "diamond" or "platinum." From there routines are given high gold, gold, high silver, silver, and a bronze or honorable mention. It is worth noting that it is often difficult to determine evaluation standards because the systems do not publicize either the breakdown of judging categories or the numeric values.[32]

After all the routines are adjudicated, they are numerically compared to one another for ranked prizes within each age division, category, competition type, and routine size. Often there are only one or two entrants with such fine divisions, so they can "win" first or second place. Organizers try to schedule those routines back-to-back to facilitate comparison. But this does not always work if children are in multiple routines and need to change costumes. Bottom line: This is essentially a competitive system based on evaluation and not head-to-head match-ups.

For those studios that are very competitive, adjudications are of little importance until the "overalls," when all the entrants in a particular category are compared. Groups of like size are matched against one another (large groups, duet/trios, or solos). Awards are typically also lumped together in an age category, such as all those over fourteen or under ten. Cash is sometimes awarded to these overall winners. Studios distribute the money among the group members themselves, or the teachers keep it. The amount is often not announced ahead of time, as it depends on how many entries there are in a competition. Overall awards are most coveted in terms of both attention and potential money to be won. Winning an overall award is also a plus for those studios that want to attract new, high-quality students, as many students want to go to a studio that has a winning track record.

Technically, every routine at nationals should have "qualified" at regionals, based on its adjudication category. The standard is often low (for example, silver), which is another reason it is rare for a routine to receive a bronze. In order to encourage as many routines as possible to participate in nationals, competition owners often organize a half-day or full-day competition before the formal start of nationals. This qualification competition is open to routines that did not qualify at the regionals, which gives them a chance to enter nationals. Sometimes those routines compete again as soon as the next day.

During the competitions, awards ceremonies are typically held three times throughout the day. This offers another opportunity to award more prizes, since overalls are often awarded only for those performances since the last awards ceremony. At nationals, however, a running tally of overall high scores is kept and awarded at the end of the competition.

During the award ceremonies most of the children sit on stage and an announcer stands in the middle reading the results over a microphone. The announcer acknowledges every routine, through the adjudication process, by announcing its number, its name (often the name of the song), and the level it was awarded. After the adjudication announcement, a child representative picks up the ribbons for everyone in the routine. Many girls keep all of their ribbons together, hanging on a stuffed bear (sometimes a "dance" stuffed animal, wearing a tutu or similar garb), which their parents have typically purchased at a concession stand set up at a competition. After all the entrants in that session are adjudicated, overall winners are announced and trophies are distributed for those routines. Only one trophy per routine is given out, no matter the size of the group. The dance studios usually keep the trophy and disburse the ribbons to the competitors.

After the awards are over, teachers can pick up the judges' comments, which are either written out or spoken into a tape recording. Families often visit concession tables where various products are for sale. Parents are able to purchase trophies (if their child's routine won one), video recordings of the routines,[33] or other trinkets for their kids, such as a T-shirt that says the name of the competition or a dance-related tchotchke such as a dance shoe keychain.

I have alluded to costs and how much competition organizers can make, which is considerable. This means that the costs associated with dance competitions for individual families are also considerable. There are the entry fees for each routine ($30 to $90 per entry). Also, each routine requires its own costume (often custom-made), typically paired with custom dance shoes (painted to match a costume). On average, these can cost $200 per routine. With many competitors participating in three to four routines per competition, costs add up—especially if a child's feet grow and shoes have to be replaced in the middle of a competition season. Tap shoes are the costliest, at $40 to $60 for a pair, not including additional work, for instance, getting rubber added to the soles to prevent slipping. Jazz shoes are $40 to $50, and ballet shoes are around $20. Children often have a pair of practice shoes for each routine, so the competition shoes do not get scuffed from practice.

Many studios request that students wear matching studio shirts or warm-up outfits, which can cost around $100, and they also tell families which make-up products to use. All of these items are out-of-pocket expenses for dance families. Studios also often dictate how hair should be styled, and some families pay someone to perform this service for their daughters. On top of fees and appearance-related costs there is the cost of traveling to competitions and staying in hotels, which can cost several hundreds of dollars each weekend.

Of course, there are the usual tuition payments for class and then rehearsal and practice fees as well. For a single class, which meets for an hour each week, the yearly cost is around $450 a year. But most competition kids take five to six classes a week, in addition to paying for additional rehearsal time. Kids also need practice clothes, including leotards and tights, which cost $15 to $20 for a leotard (kids often wear three a week) and $10 for a pair of dance tights. Parents with whom I did fieldwork can easily spend between $5,000 and $10,000 each year for one child in competitive dance. This is obviously a lot of money, and it may be surprising to many unfamiliar with dance, but it is commensurate with, and even cheaper than, such similar activities as figure skating and gymnastics.[34]

Clearly, competitive dance is an expensive activity, and many families initially get involved unaware of the expenses and the unstandardized nature of the business. Having no national organizing body means there is a lack of uniformity and a lack of standards in the world of children's competitive dance. Yet despite the often confusing structure and rules, thousands of children, mainly girls, head to regional and national competitions with their dance studios year after year.

Metroville Elite Dance Academy and Westbrook Let's Dance Studio

Students from Metroville's Elite Dance Academy and Westbrook's Let's Dance Studio are some of the thousands who compete in dance competitions every year. Like chess, the Metro field site for dance, Metroville Elite Dance Academy, is far more competitive than the suburban, West County location, Westbrook's Let's Dance Studio. Both studios are for-profit businesses that specialize in dance lessons for children.

Metroville's Elite Dance Academy is located in an area geographically connected to Metro's city center, and it is similarly diverse. There is a smaller, wealthy area, dominated by ethnic whites, and an impoverished area that is rich in ethnic diversity, with many Hispanic, Asian, and African American families. Elite Dance Academy is about thirty years old.[35]

It has a strong national reputation and two studio locations (down from three locations just a few years ago). As on the show *Dance Moms*, some current moms were competitive dancers with Elite as children. The owner of the studio started teaching dance in the late 1970s and was part of the early wave of competitive dance in the 1980s. Many of her students go on to professional dancing careers, either as Rockettes or on Broadway, and she has had students compete in television dance shows as well.

As the name suggests, Elite Dance Academy's teachers, parents, and students liken the competitive program to a dance education. Elite students rehearse four to six days a week, depending on the time of year, but virtually year-round. Out of about seven hundred students, eighty are members of the dance "company," and only four of them are boys (though none of them are elementary school–age, I did interview three of their parents).

There is no formal audition process for the company: the students are continuously evaluated in class before selections are announced in the early winter in a letter. All members of the Elite company must sign a contract, along with their parents, committing to being at practices and events throughout the year. The teachers decide which students will be in which routines and who among them will be selected as a soloist, again via private letter, a high honor at Elite.

Elite's teachers choreograph about twelve to fifteen competitive group routines each annual competition season, along with about twenty solos. Those selected as soloists must sign a contract committing to attend private lessons for about two hours a week; the contract prohibits participation in sports during the competitive season. Each dancer has a costume handmade by studio designers and seamstresses for each routine.

All of the company members compete in three to four regional competitions a year, along with one national competition. The caliber of dancing is quite high, and they routinely win overalls at nationals. But because of the limited financial resources of many Elite families, the company attends only one national event per year. Some of the senior dancers have traveled to Asia and Europe to dance in the summer, which essentially substitutes for another national competition.

With so many competitive routines that need to be rehearsed, along with regular classes for Academy students, space is at a premium. While there are two studio locations—a ten- to fifteen-minute drive from one another—additional space is necessary, especially during competition season. Elite Academy rents space from religious and athletic organizations that have wood floors suitable for dancing in order to accommodate their needs for more space.

While Westbrook's Let's Dance Studio also has two locations, that is virtually the only similarity between the two. Let's Dance is much younger—barely five years old—and its competitive dance program is subsequently less developed. The studio owners, one a former professional dancer, opened their first studio in a suburban strip mall. The logic behind being in a strip mall with grocery and drug stores in the same complex was that parents could shop while their children are in dance lessons. Following the same strategy, the second, newer location is also located in a strip mall with a grocery store.

Let's Dance competes in the "recreational" level at competitions. The "dance team," as it is called, participates in three to four regional competitions a year, but it does not attend any nationals. Let's Dance hosts an open audition for its dance team each spring and fall, and almost everyone who tries out is accepted. The "junior" routines, for those twelve and under, have approximately twenty girls in them, with one boy participating as well. Each routine practices only once a week, and many students miss rehearsals from week to week without repercussions as the studio does not make students sign a contract.

Let's Dance students usually compete in one or two routines per year, mostly tap and jazz. Costumes are ordered from dance costume magazines, but the moms sometimes add a few decorative embellishments. There are a handful of soloists, but they have not been specially selected. Instead their mothers have asked the teacher to give their daughters private lessons. Essentially their daughters have solos because their families can pay for all the extras.

I interviewed twenty-six dance mothers. The dropout rate for dance is lower than for chess or soccer, so I met only two moms who had a daughter who dropped out of competitive dance during elementary school. I also interviewed eleven girls, the majority of whom compete with Elite Dance Academy. During fieldwork I attended three regional competitions and one national dance competition with these dancers and interviewed eight dance teachers.

Across all three activities I interviewed at least one parent from ninety-five families with competitive children. With many of these families I interviewed a second parent either separately or together with the primary caregiver, and a child from their family. In addition to formal interviews with close to fifty teachers or coaches and activity leaders, I spent hundreds of hours in the field at practices and competitive events. By triangulating formal interviews with ethnographic observations I was able to observe the people I spoke with in action. The result is a rich, original data source that paints a picture not only of individuals but also institutions. The next chapter delves into the details of Competitive Kid Capital: the importance of winning; the feeling of being evaluated and ranked; and performing under time pressure.

THREE Cultivating Competitive Kid Capital

GENERALIST AND SPECIALIST PARENTS SPEAK

"Did you interview the chess lady?"

Lois, aka the "chess lady," is well-known throughout the Metro chess community. But Lois isn't really a chess lady. She barely even knows how to play chess. Through her organizational prowess, battle-ax attitude, and devotion to her daughter's competitive success, she is appreciated by some and reviled by others—especially after she had a chess coach fired from her daughter's school based on his legal status in this country when she thought her daughter wasn't getting enough individualized attention from him.

Lois is in her early forties. She is married with two young girls, one in third grade and the other in kindergarten. Her husband is an ER doctor who is frequently on call, and she is a former banker who opted out of the workforce in order to get pregnant after struggling with infertility, which she attributed to stress from work. Lois often speaks loudly and energetically, her frizzy black curls bouncing around her face. She usually wears brightly colored Crocs shoes, has multiple large bags flung on each shoulder, and fiddles with the BlackBerry glued to her palm or ear as she arranges her daughters' classes, appointments, and play dates. Instead of managing employees and clients, Lois micromanages her daughters' lives.

Her older daughter, Charlotte (known as Lottie), began playing chess after Lois heard about a chess-playing child while sitting in the waiting room of a doctor's office. Lois immediately arranged for Lottie, who was not yet in kindergarten, to get private lessons. Once Lottie hit grade school, Lois stepped in to help with, and essentially take over, the school's team and competitive program. She explained:

> There were some kids that really liked chess and the school wasn't really providing the right support for it and so I became the parent who just took it on. This was partly for selfish reasons, but not the reasons that you think. The kids that play chess at our school are fantastic kids, but the school, in general, has a lot of very, very, very wealthy families. Now some are doing a good job of raising amazing kids, and some are not doing such a great job and there are some first graders with iPods and some first graders who know how many millions of dollars are in their trust funds. It's just very off-putting and I found that the kids who play chess are not like that, whatever their economic situation is, they are not like that—they are just smart, nice kids. And to me, developing this community within the larger school community has been great for me because it has made me feel much more at home at the school.

Lois takes the "devotion to family schema" very seriously.[1] She regularly attends a Parenting Mommy Group in an area that is not close to her home; she is willing to travel because she likes this particular group's discussions about childhood, competition, and activities. She also told me about her conversations with psychologists: "Raising kids is a big experiment and I won't know till later [if I did it right]. I have my own therapist . . . and she is very suspicious about chess in particular because it puts rewards on achieving things rather than on the experience of it." All these meetings and discussions occur in between shuttling Lottie and her younger sister from chess tournaments to figure skating lessons, tennis classes, and private Hebrew tutoring. (Lottie is too busy to attend Hebrew school, so a tutor comes to their home when it is convenient.)

Lois describes Lottie as being balanced and well-rounded: "My daughter, she's like a totally well-rounded kid who likes chess and tennis and skating and who also plays video games and is just a kid." Other parents expressed different opinions (unsolicited by me), saying that even at tournaments, during breaks, Lottie is "forced" to do math worksheets. (I did not personally witness her doing anything besides chess at tournaments.) Parents also report that Lottie gets extremely upset, crying and sometimes wailing, at tournaments when she loses a game, behavior I did observe. Some parents pointed out that Lottie gets especially upset when her mother is around. Lois picked up on this problem and hired a chess teacher to accompany Lottie to tournaments and go over her games and tactics in between rounds. Lois was willing to relinquish some control in order to help her daughter compete, and win.

When Lottie does well, Lois rewards her handsomely. Lois told me about her reward system, but it is so well-known that other parents described it to me as well. Basically Lottie can accumulate points for various things she does—hours she puts into chess study, practicing skating, doing well on a school assignment, not fighting with her sister—and in this complicated accounting system each activity gets a certain number of points. When Lottie has accumulated thousands of these points, she can get a "humongous" reward, such as a video game system. Lois devised this elaborate system with lavish rewards to teach Lottie about hard work and competition:

> She goes to school with people who have trust funds and you can kind of see that their parents don't really care if they do well in school. She knows she has to do well in school because she needs to be on a track that she's basically going to support herself. And I can see other girls in her class where their parents are raising them thinking someone else is going to support them, but that's not what's going on here. . . . Like, when she grows up she says she wants to be a litigator. . . . It's shocking to me but there are a lot of second grader mothers who are concerned with how fat their daughters are. Like at her birthday we got cupcakes and one of the mothers said, "Don't give my daughter cupcakes, she

already has a little tummy and it is important to look good in clothes."
And there are mothers who are more concerned about their daughter's
popularity and to me, that is not what my whole focus is on with Lottie,
which is learning to be competent. . . . I'm raising my kid to where she
can compete in the marketplace.

Later, Lois added thoughtfully, "I want her to be happy and balanced
and not neurotic like me, obviously."

What motivates mothers and fathers like Lois to get their children involved in competitive after-school activities, and how do they explain
and understand these motivations? While Lois is a bit extreme, her motivations and experiences as a credentialed mother are not unique. Parents like Lois are acting rationally, according to economist Richard
Frank, as they are "attempting to launch their children well in life [by
taking] a variety of steps to keep pace with or surpass their rivals."[2] Their
decisions are shaped by their own experiences and backgrounds, understood in the context of competitive childhoods that are shaped by both
history and entrepreneurial adults.

While parents cannot be 100 percent sure that these activities guarantee their children's success in either the short term or the long term, they
are hedging their bets. They want their children to be as prepared as
possible for both the education and the job market that they think their
offspring will face as they age. In many ways the specific activity they
choose for their kids is less important than participating in competitive
activities in general, mainly because of the particular skill set that participation in competitive children's activities can provide. Enter Competitive Kid Capital, a concept detailed in the following pages.

In this chapter I describe and analyze the narratives parents draw on
to explain their children's participation in the competitive activities of
chess, dance, and soccer. As this is a cultural analysis, these narratives
reveal the kinds of adult lives they *want* their children to have and what
they *think* their kids need to do to actually realize those visions. These
families may have different backgrounds and differ in the activities in
which their children participate, but they all share a competitive vision
of the world, and they are trying to give their kids the skills necessary to

succeed in it. Their views aren't just molded by their personal backgrounds; they are also situated in the current structure of competitive childhood, described in chapter 5, in which adults who make a living from Competitive Kid Capital have helped form parents' worldviews, emphasizing how important Competitive Kid Capital is to children's futures.

In this chapter I begin by briefly describing these families and how they entered the world of competitive children's activities. I then detail the skills that make up Competitive Kid Capital before presenting two strategies—breadth and specialization—that parents employ to raise their competitive children to succeed.

GETTING STARTED WITH COMPETITION

Parents sometimes cannot explain or recall exactly how their children got started in their activities on a recreational level. In their fuzzy recollections they often rely on luck to explain how they initially happened into certain activities and settings, not unlike how people explain how they seemingly randomly got their jobs.[3] Even hyperorganized Lois thought it was "lucky" that she met that parent in the doctor's waiting room, and that chance encounter basically launched Lottie's chess career.

It is much easier for parents to explain how their child became a *competitor*. In all of these activities this is a choice that requires significant investments of money and time beyond the recreational level. Rather than relying on luck, parents deliberately chose a competitive path for their children after the initial exposure to an activity.

Parents offer three general types of explanations as to why their children made the jump from recreational to competitive participation: (1) one of the parents had been a competitor in this activity or a related activity; (2) a sibling or other family member was or is a competitor; and (3) the child's friends or others in the community participate competitively, which provides exposure to the competitive world. These reasons are consistent with the findings of others who have studied children's involvement in structured activities; Hofferth, Kinney, and Dunn found that kids became involved in after-school activities either through a personal interest, a parental interest, or a desire to be with friends.[4]

This is not to say that some parents do not feel "dragged in" by other adults or even their children, as this chess mom's story illustrates:

> In our conversations, Sally [another mother] kind of pulled me along. Like she was the one who first told me there's a tournament. I always blame her because she told me about a tournament and she was like, "Why don't you try this tournament?" So we go to the tournament and my daughter wins first place. . . . And it was almost like a marketing gimmick, because now my daughter always wants to win, okay? [Laughs] So every time, like for the first couple years, I would turn to Sally at tournaments and say, "You got me in this!"

Chess kids generally become competitors earlier than soccer players and dancers. I saw a four-year-old compete at scholastic chess nationals, but usually kids start playing in tournaments around age six or seven.[5] Since most scholastic chess exposure starts at school, this makes it easier for the families I met to find a competitive path.

Competitive soccer begins later, after skills are mastered in recreational soccer. Metro Soccer Co-Op fielded a U8 team for boys and girls, but Westfield Soccer Club only offered a training academy for U8 kids (which still required tryouts), starting their traditional soccer teams at U9. Similarly most of the Let's Dance and Elite Dance Academy dancers started competing at around eight or nine, given the need to develop skills that often require more muscle strength that comes with maturity and growth. Only a handful started competing earlier, around age six.

Some of the kids from families I met who started competition at younger ages pushed their parents to let them compete. However, even when competitive participation is child-motivated, the final decision to participate is ultimately up to parents, who need to pay the bills and get their children to various practices and events. The parents I met did make that choice to compete (even including parents of eventual dropouts); other kids may have less supportive parents who never support their competitive ambitions, though no coaches, teachers, or other parents mentioned any thwarted kids like that to me.

Table 1. Descriptive Data on Families Interviewed with Children
Currently Competing (in percentages)

	Chess, 34% N=29	Dance, 29% N=25	Soccer, 37% N=32
Sex of Child(ren) Involved*			
Girl	14	88	47
Boy	76	8	47
Both boy and girl	10	4	6
Marital Status			
Married**	83	88	88
Not married	17	12	12
Parental Educational Attainment			
High school degree, both parents	7	20	3
One parent HS degree; other at least bachelor's	7	32	9
Both parents with bachelor's	10	28	16
One parent with graduate degree; other bachelor's	24	12	22
Both parents with graduate degree	52	8	50
Annual Family Income ($)			
Under 40,000	3	4	3
40,000–79,999	10	12	3
80,000–119,999	7	32	6
120,000–199,999	21	24	13
Over 200,000	59	28	75
Employment Status			
Both parents work full time	62	64	44
One parent full time, other part time	17	20	9
One parent full time, other not in the labor market	21	16	47
Race/Ethnicity of Child			
White	62	56	94
Black	7	20	3
Asian/Indian	0	4	0
Hispanic	17	12	0
Other/Mixed	14	8	3

(continued)

Table 1.   (continued)

	Chess, 34% N=29	Dance, 29% N=25	Soccer, 37% N=32
Immigrant Status			
Both parents born in U.S.	41	72	70
One parent born outside U.S.	35	4	15
Both parents born outside U.S.	24	24	15
Religious Affiliation			
Protestant	24	32	22
Catholic	7	56	31
Jewish	38	4	28
Other	31	8	19

*Two of the chess parents also have children who do competitive soccer; five soccer parents have children who do chess and dance (three do chess and two dance).

**I interviewed one gay couple with children, and I include them in the married category.

Table 1 presents descriptive data on the competitively supportive parents I interviewed. These families tend to be quite affluent and educated, though there is some variation across activity, which I discuss more fully in chapter 4. The urban and suburban areas in which they live also tend to be affluent communities. (The median household income in West County in 2009, even after the economic downturn, was over $106,000; in Metro it was slightly less, coming in at just under $100,000.) Families I met whose children are involved in competitive activities do tend to be doing slightly better financially than those in neighboring communities.

However, note that in the majority of these households, both parents work. These families are upper-middle class but not upper class—rubbing elbows with the 1 percent but definitely not part of that percentile. Parents must work to support the affluent lifestyles their families enjoy as they have few resources (i.e., trust funds or large savings) to fall back on otherwise. While these credentialed parents are doing well professionally and financially, there is constant worry about present and future stability, especially for the next generation. In the context of this largely upper-middle-class group of engaged and motivated parents, insecurity, education,[6] and competitive endeavors are entwined and take on a great deal of importance to worried parents.

LEARNING LESSONS RECREATIONALLY IN AFTER-SCHOOL ACTIVITIES

Whenever children participate in activities, including unsupervised play and organized noncompetitive activities, they acquire skills. It is common for adults involved with these kids' activities—including parents and those who run the activities—to highlight the lessons and benefits that they believe kids acquire through their participation. The content of this radio ad about youth golf that aired in June 2008 in the West County market is emblematic of the ways many adults think about kids' participation in after-school activities and how they are marketed to parents:

> Think golf is just a game with a little white ball? Think again. The Tee-Off of [West County] knows that golf teaches kids valuable life skills including courtesy, respect, judgment, responsibility, confidence, honesty, integrity, sportsmanship, perseverance, and so much more! More importantly, the Tee-Off of [West County] fulfills the need for positive character development in an educational environment that's challenging, exciting, enjoyable, and continuous throughout the year.

In previous research I highlighted the specific skills parents with kids involved in child beauty pageants and Kumon after-school learning centers wanted their kids to acquire through participation.[7] Pageant moms believe that child beauty pageants help teach children eight specific skills (listed in decreasing order of how often they were mentioned): confidence, being comfortable on stage and in front of strangers, poise, dressing and presenting oneself appropriately, appreciation of practice, good sportsmanship, being outgoing, and listening. The Kumon parents also emphasized learning confidence and the ability to practice, along with speed, discipline and focus, and schedule following.

While studying chess, dance, and soccer, I found parents discussed similar skills and lessons that their kids acquired from recreational participation. Many soccer and dance parents said that they thought their children could acquire these same skills from another team activity (basketball, lacrosse, and cheerleading were mentioned as alternative choices), though parents did think chess developed somewhat different skills.

Chess parents frequently mentioned two skills that they think distinguish chess from other pursuits: focus and concentration, and strategic thinking. Because chess is not a physical activity, many parents also emphasized that their kids can learn about the "joy of using their minds" from chess. One mom's statement captures how many spoke about the lessons, benefits, and skills their elementary school–age kids acquire simply by playing chess for fun:

> I think thinking ahead, organizing your thoughts, and I think learning good sportsmanship. I certainly do think that this [sportsmanship] is one of the things that they try to emphasize in chess. They shake hands and say, "Good game," after they play, even in class. And I think the problem-solving skills are key too. So overall I think that some of them [the skills from chess] are intellectual, some of them are social, and some of them are academic.

Soccer parents focused on a slightly different set of skills. They liked to discuss their children's learning about teamwork and discipline the most, while highlighting the physicality of the game and how it can encourage lifelong physical fitness and help kids to develop strong mind-body coordination. This mom's quote also shows how parents liken skills acquired from playing soccer to other activities, such as music lessons:

> I think you probably do learn how to work as a team, work to have goals, and work to figure out how to work to get what you want. I think that's sort of the same with something like violin too. The play and all of that teaches you all these things about working, sort of having a sense of what the end goal is and figuring out how to get there. And then a lot of it is working with others and listening to what they have to say. Especially in soccer, you know, you really have to coordinate with the other people on the field.

Dance moms similarly highlighted teamwork, discipline and making a commitment, and setting a goal. One mom said:

Well I think it helps because she has learned to be organized, to honor a commitment, which helped her learn teamwork and responsibility. You know she's responsible for her [dance] bag and making sure she has everything in it. Like, if she wants a drink, if she wants a snack, she's responsible. Also to make sure her homework is getting done and her grades are upheld. Back to teamwork, I mean they know if somebody is not performing or somebody doesn't show up, which they've had those issues, that everybody else is affected because it changes the formation of everything [in the routines].

Participation in activities like chess, dance, and soccer is part of the process of concerted cultivation practiced by many families, especially those in the middle class.[8] Athletics in particular are an "important element of the larger package of activities that go into the concerted cultivation" for those in the professional class.[9] But children can learn these skills by playing in organized settings, without formal competitions and record keeping. So why do so many of these families make the jump to *competitive* participation? And what do parents believe their children can learn from competitive participation that they cannot learn solely from recreational participation?

DEFINING COMPETITIVE KID CAPITAL

Many activities that were previously noncompetitive have been transformed from environments that only emphasized learning skills, personal growth, and simple fun to competitive environments. Parents believe that by participating in these competitive organized activities, children get a boost to their skill sets beyond mere recreational participation. Parents are trying to develop a particular type of character in their children, what some parents refer to as a "competitive spirit." This is associated with what I call the development of Competitive Kid Capital. Based on interviews with parents, I have identified five skills and lessons that parents want their children to acquire through participation in *competitive* activities and which form the basis for Competitive Kid Capital: (1) internalizing the importance of winning, (2) learning how to recover from a loss to win in the future, (3) managing time pressure, (4) performing in stressful environments, and (5) feeling comfortable being judged by others in public.

Competitive Kid Capital is associated with an intensive parenting model, described by sociologists such as Hays and Blair-Loy.[10] It is also associated with Lareau's model of concerted cultivation.[11] As such it can be thought of as a form of cultural capital. A term first used by Bourdieu and Passeron,[12] cultural capital captures the skills, knowledge, and education that confer advantage. It is a term often drawn upon in the literature on education, childhood, and class.[13]

Competitive Kid Capital also clearly contains elements of social capital, as it connects children and their families and helps them to network. Additionally it can be thought of as a form of symbolic capital, mainly because these children are earning honors and acclaim that can give them access to additional prestige.[14] Since Competitive Kid Capital encompasses these various elements it is quite useful to think of it as helping to establish a competitive *habitus*,[15] particularly because so much of the cultural capital associated with it is both embodied and institutionalized. For the sake of clarity, though, the term *Competitive Kid Capital* is used to capture the various elements of capital that parents hope to instill in their young children through participation in competitive after-school activities.

Internalizing the Importance of Winning

Winning is the name of the game in these competitive activities, and it is in learning how to be a successful competitor that winners are created. Parents often reward their children when they *win* and not when they *lose*, and the activities obviously reward winners, usually with large trophies and other prizes, as adults keep records of victories and losses. Many parents decide to leap from recreational activities with their elementary school–age children so that their kids can learn to compete, and eventually win, in life.

One mother explained why she has her noncompetitive daughter in chess tournaments: "I believe that my daughter is not doing well with competitions period. She feels threatened. She feels that she's not going to win. . . . In any case, Susie does not do well with competition. Now, what do we do? I mean she has to get prepared, because life is competition." Another mother similarly described her daughter: "She's not competitive by nature, so I thought this is a good thing to help her mature in a way that says, 'I want to win,' you know."

Parents often drew connections between competing in activities and competing in school. One mom told me, "She's competitive in school now too. They try to compete, see who is going to get the Honor Roll. She has that ability [to compete], that little extra push, from [competitive] dance."

Others see learning to win in childhood activities as a stepping stone for larger victories, beyond their daily school achievement. One father said, "I think it's important for him to understand that [being competitive] is not going to just apply here, it's going to apply for the rest of his life. It's going to apply when he keeps growing up and he's playing sports, when he's competing for school admissions, for a job, for the next whatever."

A mother I met, whose son often makes himself sick before a tournament due to nerves, draws an even clearer link to future jobs and professions and why she wants her fourth-grader to master his nerves now. She described her thought process to me:

> I started to think if you're becoming physically ill over an activity, due to the competition, then maybe we need to reevaluate this. But, on the other hand, maybe this is your personality and you manifest physical symptoms when you have anxiety and stress, and maybe this is something you should be overcoming and we should work on it that way. Because you don't want to be a litigator who goes to court and gets nauseated and stutters in front of the judge, or a surgeon who goes in and gets so nervous since it's not the same as the cadaver.

These parents clearly want to raise competitive children who are focused on winning and who will become high-achieving, credentialed, professional adults—even if their children may not understand all the nuances of the lessons they should glean from their current involvement. A mother and father of a first-grade boy described how they think this works:

FATHER: I think he knows who he can beat and who he can't beat, who he's better than and who he's not better than, who he's afraid of, who is better than [he is] so he can challenge them. He knows that.

MOTHER: So, he does not know the word *competitive* by its meaning in the dictionary, but he knows the feeling.

I saw and heard parents act in ways that help teach their child the meaning of competition and what it feels like to win. Some bribed their kids with cash, edible treats, or collectible items to get them to practice. One chess father told me, when talking about his son in first grade, "He does ask me, 'Oh, what if I win all my games?' So I say, 'Okay, you can have an extra Oreo or we'll get you an ice cream or something.' We don't get him like a Game Boy, Oreos will do it for now." Implicit in this statement is that while Oreos "will do it for now," something else, and something bigger, and likely electronic, will eventually replace Oreos.

This exchange I had with a mother and father of an older boy show how this transition happens:

FATHER: I don't want him thinking that if he wins a game, he's going to get something. I don't want him to try to do a move because he needs a baseball card, or whatever we're talking about. I don't even want him to think, "If I win this game, I make the top ten." I just want him to not focus on that at all.

MOTHER: But didn't you tell him you were going to get him a rookie card? That was the first time I heard of a specific [card] as opposed to a pack of cards.

FATHER: (Nodding) We talked about it. I *would* like him to come out of a tournament, and celebrate something as opposed to walk out and say I won.

By linking winning to material rewards—especially expensive ones like a rookie baseball card—their son learns that winning is rewarded.

It appears from the media that children often are competitive with one another and want to be winners, away from adult interference. Such movies as *The Sandlot,* or even *A Christmas Story,* portray kids trying to one-up each other in pursuit of a variety of rewards. Intense play on basketball courts is also common, away from adult organization, as shown notably in the documentary *Hoop Dreams* and the film *Finding Forrester.* More recently movies such as *Save the Last Dance, Step Up,* and *Honey* show high school students in dance-offs in public spaces but not in formal competitions. We can all probably recall informal, out-of-school competitions with peers, whether on playgrounds, sandlots, or campgrounds.

But the adult involvement and the formalization of a hierarchy of winners and losers through ratings and websites produces a different type of competition and imparts a more serious message to kids, especially younger children. I observed a father of twin fifth-grade boys tell them at a tournament, after one drew a game with a lower-rated player, "That's really a loss. You're losing ratings points. Never make a draw!"

While it is the parents' decision to escalate participation from the recreational to the competitive level, and to keep competing, those who run the activities know how to hook the kids to make them want to come back. Again, the link is between winning and prizes, such as trophies. One dad explained, "They [the organizers] know that winning is a big thing for these kids, so they distribute trophies by the pound. So we have a whole bunch of trophies." A mom sheepishly told me about her son's trophies, "I'm sad to say that he counts them and has a very clear running tab of how many there are."

Parents dislike the practice of giving out trophies willy-nilly, especially if they are only for participation. Some complained that these trophies take up space and just collect dust, but the deeper issue is that many parents feel that they debase a "real" win. Many of the parents are careful to say that they do not want their child to be rewarded just for showing up, especially when it is clear that there is a real winner in each event. One father summed up this sentiment: "I don't want to be Scrooge, but I was just sort of startled that it's just like hauling out the trophies, one trophy after another, and everybody has to have something. And, you know, one of them that I went to had medals for kids and then trophies, so that everybody got something. But then they called the kids up in order from lowest score to highest score and said what their score was."

Parents like this one correctly read the participation trophies as a cheap and transparent ploy to keep kids wanting to go back, though not all parents are so savvy. Clearly these participation awards do not change the fact that there are still winners at the end of the day and that all of the kids are ranked. Giving awards in a public way emphasizes how serious the competition, and winning, have become. That records are kept and posted online highlights the seriousness of competition for families and distinguishes the activities from other forms of childhood play.

Some chess and soccer parents reported going online to check their child's rating and standing in their age group, and also to consult websites that rank teams on a national level. One soccer dad easily rattled off his son's rankings to me: "You go U11 boys by state, by region (there's four or five regions), and by national. Right now Jared's team is second in [our state]—oh no, first [in our state]!—second in the region, seventh in the country."

Another soccer father told me of his son's experience at a three-day tournament, where they were rated high and slotted to play in the top division: "I looked at the teams who were playing and I went, 'Oh shit, we're really going to have our hands full.' I didn't say this to the kids, but the kids knew it. . . . I just went, 'Holy shit they have their work cut out for them this weekend.'" He knew about their opponents and the rankings because of his online reading.

Rating and ranking systems can give kids an incentive to win beyond the material reward of trophies, while also teaching them that being at the top of the list is the goal. They also can teach kids another important lesson about competition. One chess father is particularly blunt with his son:

> I don't like dwell on the rating thing. I point out to him that if he thinks that because he has 200 points higher than somebody that they can't kick his ass, he's wrong, and similarly, he shouldn't be intimidated by someone who has a higher rating. And I also tell him that he should never believe anybody about their ratings, because *everybody lies all the time* [emphasis added]. So, I try to play it down, but he likes the idea of points.

This dad knows his son is motivated by points, but he uses the opportunity to help him become a savvy competitor, sharing his experience that people sometimes aren't truthful about their abilities. To this family, and to many others I met, learning to be a winner means learning to decipher other people's lies and learning to fudge at times. Being a winner is complicated, and winning children know how to thrive within the competitive system by accruing ever more Competitive Kid Capital.

Parents decide for themselves when their kids should learn about the importance of winning in competitions. One mom takes a clear-cut view: "When you start getting to be eight, nine, ten years old, I think that being rewarded for mediocrity is wrong. I think you need to find each kid's talent and reward them [sic] for that. I'm not saying exclude a kid and tell him he can't do anything. But if he's not a good baseball player, but he's a good singer, that's fine, that's his talent, that's what he should be rewarded for. But not for being a mediocre baseball player!"

The reality is that these competitive children are rewarded in various ways when they win. Winning becomes the focus, along with learning how to be competitive in order to win. But when losing does occur, parents like to make this a part of the learning experience too.

Bouncing Back from a Loss to Win in the Future

As much as parents, and our society, values winners, we know there is usually only one person at the top. So just as it is important to win, it is important to learn to be a good sport and a gracious loser. Children in soccer and chess are often taught to shake hands after a game, a practice common in many sports. Obviously when kids independently play sports and other games for fun, even board games, they will lose. However, the public nature of a loss in competitive activities in front of family and friends, and the implicit announcement of a loss, give the experience a different character. Children need to learn to be able to deal with the loss of face in public and the feelings of failure or disappointment that may accompany the loss, and then overcome them in order to win again in the future.

Learning these lessons involves developing an appreciation for perseverance, hard work, and what one mother called "stick-to-itiveness": "I want him to learn, probably the most useful skill I can think of, the value of hard work. . . . Things don't always come easily and you can't give up when things don't come easily, and specifically sort of a stick-to-itiveness." This stick-to-itiveness is tested after an unsuccessful competition. Another mother explains, when talking about her son's involvement with chess:

> To be able to keep going back [after losses] is tough. I've seen him be discouraged at a lot of these tournaments where we break even. There're four rounds and he gets two. On a good one, we'll get three. And I tell him, "As long as you break even, I think 50–50 is good. That's 50 percent. That's fair. That's a lot more than a lot of people can do." He might get a little discouraged, but he still wants to go. So I think it does create some kind of an ability to face defeat and put your successes into some context.

Competitive chess, dance, and soccer are structured to encourage kids to get back out there even if they did not do their best or they experienced a loss. Chess tournaments have several rounds, soccer seasons have multiple games, and dance competitions have various regionals and nationals. Obviously kids can withdraw from an event, but with money invested in each one, or in a season, withdrawal is rare. Many parents told me that once their child has committed for a season or for a year, he or she must honor that commitment. A mother explained, "We've committed. I mean once we've paid the money, I feel that you should commit until at least to the end of what you signed up for, if you wanted to do it at the beginning. And then I'm not going to make them do it, in the future, if they don't want to do it."

Of course it's difficult for both the children and the parents when a child loses, or loses often. A mother of twins told me, "I'm happy, very happy for them when they win. It doesn't bother me so much when they lose, if it doesn't bother them, and sometimes it doesn't. But it is sort of horrible to see when they are furious at themselves. That's hard. But it's a necessary part of growing up, as well. It's a pretty safe context in which to make a mistake." This mom understands that mistakes happen in life and losses occur, so to learn how to deal with that in childhood is helpful within a "safe" environment.

Other parents expressed similar sentiments about the importance of learning about hard work and loss in childhood, highlighting the unpredictable nature of life: "The winning and losing is phenomenal. I wish it was something that I learned because life is really bumpy. You're not going to win all the time and you have to be able to reach inside and come back. Come back and start fresh and they are able to. I'm not saying he doesn't cry once in a while. But it's really such a fantastic skill."

Parents value these life lessons about persistence because of the way they view American society. Every single parent I interviewed stated that they find American society to be competitive. One dance mom exclaimed, "Hell, yeah, America is competitive! But the beauty of it is, if you're mentally strong and if you're prepared and if you are open to possibility, I think you can create your own destiny, whatever it is."

Another mother and I talked about her views of this competitive society and how perseverance in competitive dance can help in the long term:

MOM: Academically, they're so much more advanced than we were and that's better as far as what they can do with their lives. I think it has gotten much better as opposed to what we, you know compared to when I grew up, there are more opportunities. But it's hard. It's a competitive world, you know? It's a lot, it's hard for them.

HILARY: Do you see dance fitting into helping her navigate that competitive world?

MOM: You know what, I think it helps with rejection, it helps with being able to handle it. You know she wants to compete in jazz. Well, if you want to compete in jazz you have to try even harder. I feel it teaches her that being able to handle the idea that, like, well she's [another girl] better than you. And there's no question about it, so another girl is going to move on and you're not. I think that kind of helps, you know? She learns not everything comes easy and you're not going to always get what you might want, or maybe even you're not trying hard enough.

This serves as a reminder that "winning" occurs not just at competitions but on the path to the competitions as well. Children have to go through tryouts and selection procedures within their local settings, which can also be difficult, especially when they may not be placed with their friends. But even these situations are framed by parents as learning experiences about how to deal with loss and competition and emerge as a winner. One mother told me about her son's difficult experiences with travel soccer in their hometown:

> The thing that is hard is looking at your kid and saying, "Okay, well, so-and-so and so-and-so and so-and-so, who are not as good as you, made it." We had a problem with the baseball team where he didn't make the baseball team. And here's this little kid crying hysterically and his skills are definitely better than the other kids. You know, not at the very top, but in the range of being better than a lot of others. I had to turn around and tell him, it's not based upon your skill. I can't say, "The harder you practice, then you'll make the team." It's not like that at all. So we've told him, you know, the only lessons that we've come out of it with are that we will bring him to where he'll be judged fairly. And anything after that then is up to him.

In the end, parents want to raise kids who are winners, but they know that sometimes they will be losers, based either on their skills or on other political or personal factors within a particular competitive site. These competitive activities in childhood help kids learn how to recover from public failures and how to apply themselves and work hard in order to be long-term winners. This father summarizes the sentiment as he tries to raise his son to be a winner in life:

> This is what I'm trying to get him to see: that he's not going to always win. And then from a competitive point of view, with him it's like I want him to see that life is, in certain circumstances, about winning and losing. And do you want to be a winner or do you want to be a loser? You want to be a winner! There's a certain lifestyle that you have to lead to be a winner, and it requires this, this, this and this. And if you do this, this, this and this, more than likely you'll have a successful outcome.

Part of acquiring Competitive Kid Capital is acquiring the right "this and this" to be successful. The next skill is one of those "this"-es.

Learning How to Work Well under Time Pressure

In competitive activities, children have to deal with two types of time limits in order to succeed. Obviously the activities themselves build time restrictions and time pressure into competition, as detailed in chapter 2. But children also must learn to manage their own time within a packed schedule, handling their obligations to their family and school work alongside competitive obligations, such as practices. Parents see time management as a skill that helps prepare kids for both proximate events (for example, standardized tests) and longer-term goals (balancing careers and their own families).

A key part of dealing with time pressure is concentration and focus, skills the stressful situations inherent in competitive activities help develop. As one mother explains, "It's hard when you're sitting there in the same room with competitors all around, people right next to you, especially with the time pressure." A father explained, "He has to do it right. He has to concentrate. He can't play around in the middle because it's timed."

Time pressure is most intense in chess. After every move the child needs to hit his or her chess clock, so players are reminded constantly of the time limit. Several parents commented that experiencing this kind of pressure is good, as it can help their children better handle high-stakes timed tests later in life. One mom said, "Well, I guess they'll be ready for all those SATs and AP [Advanced Placement] tests."

Soccer also pushes kids to perform under time pressure. When the end of a game nears, especially an important one, the pressure intensifies to score a goal to win or to maintain a lead. When the score is tied, a soccer game will often end with penalty kicks, when it is just one player against the goalie, putting pressure on both of them as individuals. Sometimes it's easier for the kids to handle this type of pressure than for their parents, as one mom explained:

They went into double overtime at her state cup game, and if it had gone past that, it would have gone into penalty kicks. I said to her, if that had happened, I would have had to leave—I would have gone and sat in the car. I would have missed seeing that, or I would have like been peeking. I fractured my teeth from chewing gum, because I get, you know, so nervous! The kids rise to it, but it makes me nervous.

Children must also balance their participation in competitive activities with school work, other activities, and time with family and friends. Competitions require additional preparation—both practicing as part of a team and having to get all the right materials together at home in advance of an event—so the need for time management is heightened when compared to recreational events. Add in the nerves that come with a competitive environment and it is a stressful mix. It is often a delicate balance, as this mom explains, detailing how various schedules affect her son's participation on multiple travel teams:

My pet peeve is the games not starting on time. So Matt's game was supposed to be from 11:30 to 12:30, and it was about thirty minutes north of here. His baseball game was at 1:00 around here, so I emailed the coach and I said I don't think that we can get there before 1:30. Was the first game on time? No! It was half an hour late and I had told Matt, "Tell your coach that you have to leave at 12:30!" Well, 12:30 comes and the game was tied. I was like, "I can't really pull him out now, can I?" They ended up losing by one point! So we raced down to baseball, and Matt pitched those last two innings.

Dance parents also dislike competition delays, which can affect their children's performance: "I like the ones that are run pretty much on time. . . . There was this one that they were like an hour behind. . . . The kids stress out a little bit because they're anxious and nervous and who knows what can happen in that hour while they're ready to go!" As this mother alludes to, the children have to learn how to control their nerves and deal with timing that may not be what they expected. This means staying mentally and physically prepared to compete, including keeping the muscles warm to prevent injury. Since life is sometimes unpredictable, knowing how to deal with time pressure in a competitive setting is another element of building up Competitive Kid Capital.

Constant time pressure in their everyday lives means kids do need to learn to multitask. I never saw kids do homework during competitions because it's clear that a competitive environment requires more focus than the practice environment. But I did see many kids do homework in between classes at dance studios or while waiting for their parents to pick them up at chess lessons or soccer practices. One mom explained that balancing school and competitive activities helps her dancing daughter learn "to use [her] time wisely. You have to know you have to get your homework done between this and this time, because there is rehearsal at this time."

Just getting to and from school and practice can be a marathon in and of itself. Here's how one dancing family makes it work: "Like on a Friday, her class starts at 4:00, so I can't get her there [because I'm working]. My husband starts work at 4:30, so she runs out of school, gets in the car, does her hair in the car. He runs her to the studio, drops her right at the door, and he gets to work. He's always worried because if he's late he gets fired."

Wardrobe changes, even meals and homework in cars, are common occurrences. While some parents bemoan the loss of family dinner time, others embrace the hectic schedule and see it as training their kids to balance various obligations later in life, developing Competitive Kid Capital that will lead to later success. Despite the stress and unexpected problems, parents see these situations as part of the learning from participation in competitive activities.

Learning How to Perform in Stressful Situations

Children also learn to perform and compete in stressful environments that require adaptation. Stress comes not only from time pressure but also from the environment; it may be cold outside, hot inside, the space may be small, or it may be loud. Competition always presents surprises, and kids need to adapt in order to compete and win. In conversation, parents highlighted the roles of focus and concentration as essential to their children's success. But the end goal of that focus is winning, as opposed to developing the skill for its own sake, which some kids can do recreationally.

In scholastic chess, focus and concentration are especially useful because there is very little physical space that separates competitors from others, including spectators. People walk around all the time, even stopping to look at the game a child is playing; an opponent may even get up and go to the bathroom in the middle of a game.

One chess mom, mentioned in the introduction, explained how her son's experiences in large scholastic chess tournaments will help prepare him for important standardized tests later in life:

> It's that ability to keep your concentration focused, while there's stuff going on around you. As you go into older age groups, where people are coming in and out, the ability to maintain that concentration, a connection with what's going on, on the board in front of you, and still be functional in a room of people, it's a big thing. I mean to see those large tournaments, in the convention centers, I know it is hard. I did that to take the bar exam, and the LSAT I took for law school, and GREs. You do that in a large setting, but some people are thrown by that, just by being in such a setting. Well that's a skill, and it's a skill and it's an ability to transfer that skill. It's not just a chess skill. It's a coping-with-your-environment skill.

Some chess parents blamed spectators (sometimes even their opponent's parents) for deliberately distracting their child before tournament games. One mom (Marla, also from the introduction) described to me what happened to her son at his first big tournament. This is a long quote, delivered in monologue form, and Marla got noticeably upset as she recounted the encounter, even two years later. But as her comments show, Jeremiah was able to stay focused.

> So there was a dad who tried to psyche Jeremiah out before a game. The situation was that it was at the city-wide tournament in first grade which was Jeremiah's probably third or fourth tournament ever. It was about his fifth out of seven rounds and it's the end of a day. The kids were exhausted and the rating level that Jeremiah was at at that point, you either could or could not use a clock, and it wasn't mandatory. If your opponent wanted to use the clock, you had to. But if neither of you wanted to, that was fine. So Jeremiah had never played in a tournament with a clock, and we didn't know that this was part

of the tournament until we got there, and the first few rounds I guess nobody wanted the clock. Then we got to this round, and Jeremiah went to set up, go to his side of the board and set up, and this other dad came and said, "You're on the wrong side of the board." Jeremiah said, "Well, wait a minute, I'm white," or black, whatever he was. "Yes, but blacks all go on this side of the table and whites go over on that side of the table." We looked up and down the tables and, of course, that was not true. Black and white were alternating, wherever the kids happened to set themselves up. So I said, "Well, it doesn't really look that way, looking up and down." And then his kid came and took out his clock. Jeremiah said, "I prefer not to play with a clock." The kid kind of looked a little puzzled and said, "Well, I do play with a clock," and I said, "Well, you know, it's a choice. Would you be comfortable without the clock? Would it be okay to play without the clock?" And the father stepped in and said, "We play with the clock because he wins with the clock." And so I said, "Well, then," to Jeremiah, who was beginning to look a little bit upset, "Well, we have to play him and that's the rule. We have to play with the clock. We'll do the best we can and if you lose, you lose. But who knows? Maybe the clock will be helpful." And then he took out, he like showed the clock to us, and Jeremiah had never even seen a clock like this. I have never seen a clock like that since. I don't know where he got this clock. Jeremiah took one look at it and pulled me down to whisper in my ear, "I don't know how that clock works," and he was starting to well up with tears. I said to the father, "Well, my son has never seen this kind of clock and doesn't know how to work it," and the father said, "Well, this is the clock we have and this is what we play with." We didn't have another clock to say, "Well, let's use ours," or anything. So I said, "Let me speak with the tournament director, because I feel like maybe he could at least show Jeremiah how to use the clock." The tournament director came over, and took one look at the situation and Jeremiah's quivering lip, and Jeremiah said to him, in this kind of whispery voice, "I don't know how to use that clock and I've never played in a tournament with a clock." And so the tournament director tried to teach Jeremiah. He said to the guy, "Well, you're just going to have to wait then. We need to show this child for a few minutes how this clock works. You can't play a game where he doesn't know how to use the clock." And it was so clear that Jeremiah was honest about this, that he just didn't know how to use it, and he tried. The tournament director tried to show him, but I think Jeremiah was so far gone at that point. And the father stood there glaring at me, and then said something to his kid. Then the tournament director said, "I've given them a few minutes. We really have to get the game started," and I said, "Okay, that's fine." I joked a little bit with Jeremiah to try to lighten the mood, and then when we were leaving, I gave him a hug, and we were walking out and the father said to his kid, across the table, "Don't worry. You'll beat him." And we walked out and I was furious. Poor Jeremiah! He came out about 15 minutes later and I thought he had to go to the bathroom. He came and sat down in my lap. I thought, gee, I don't want to push him, but like, get to the bathroom and you're in the middle of a game. I wouldn't sit around on my lap for long. And then he leaned over and said, "I won." And the kid came out sobbing hysterically. The father said, "What happened in there?" I feel bad, I never feel this way, but I was happy Jeremiah won.

Soccer kids also face distraction from parents, mainly when they yell at soccer games. Other adults, including coaches, also often yell. I sometimes saw or heard about referees interceding to stop parents from distracting the kids. Neither Metro Soccer Co-op nor Westfield Soccer Club are involved with leagues who have "silent" games, where adults and especially parents are not allowed to shout, even encouraging words, from the sidelines, but these are common in other parts of the country.[16]

One especially inconvenient factor related to soccer is the weather. Parents often complained about weather-related scheduling issues. Both clubs (and their insurers) have very strict rules about playing in a thunderstorm. Additionally, since they do not own their own fields, others may decide that the fields are too wet or muddy to be playable. Often games and practices get rescheduled or even canceled halfway through. One Westfield Soccer Co-op team once drove two hours to a tournament in which only half of the girls played in half of one game before they returned home with the weather-shortened results recorded.

Stressful competitive circumstances affect families in dance as well. For example, at the nationals I attended with Elite Dance Academy one of the members of the younger girls' nineteen-person tap group had forgotten to bring part of her costume. The mother and daughter started fighting and crying, and the mother refused to tell the dance teachers, afraid of what they would say. Instead they planned to leave the competition. One of the other mothers intervened, saying that they could not leave; doing so would create an empty space on stage, which would affect the group's formations, and that would be unfair since all the girls had worked hard to compete at nationals. This same mother told the Elite teachers about the situation to see if they could get the competition organizers to push back the performance time for the routine so the girls could still compete. While the teachers were upset, and most of the kids and their moms were crying in the dressing area backstage, they did get the time switched, and within an hour a solution was devised for the costume problem.

After the incident one mom told me how she felt at the time: "We have nineteen girls that are on the verge of tears. They've worked hard all year, [and for] some of them this is their first nationals. Their heads were in the wrong place because they were all panicking that they're not going to go on and they're not going to win and what are they going to do because there's no costume for their friend?"

The teachers used this opportunity to teach the girls to check and recheck their costumes and their dance bags before each competition. After calming down, the girls competed, got a platinum award, won their division, and placed in the overalls for the entire national competition. In the end, the parents and teachers felt that the situation taught the girls to be more responsible and how to rebound after handling an unexpected situation—thereby also augmenting their Competitive Kid Capital.

One of the regional competitions I attended with Elite was held in a hotel ballroom with a stage that was basically a raised platform. Since it was not a full stage it did not have wings, which created a problem for a particular routine in which the dancers had planned to hide their props in a covered area offstage until they brought them out at as part of the choreography. In the end the teachers and dancers improvised a solution, and while it was not their best performance, they still received a platinum adjudication and an overall award.

At another regional competition I attended a different stage problem arose when the surface was more slippery than expected and a soloist fell in the middle of her routine. While she was not injured, she was embarrassed and nervous at the next competition. Her mom told me how her daughter dealt with that situation:

> She was nervous from the beginning and I really noticed that she was watching other performers before her turn. I told her don't watch them because you know, your confidence will be shaky and so that's why I told her just stay away from watching them. And so the next competition she was better and then the next one she was better. I think she's gaining confidence now and I think it's good because it's great to be a competitor.

This girl learned how to bounce back. The stressful situation created by her fall helped her learn how to succeed later, all while being judged by strangers.

Being Able to Perform under the Gaze of Others

In pressure-filled competitive environments children's performances are judged and assessed according to a set standard and in comparison to others. In chess, dance, and soccer, children are ranked both in relation to others' performance in a particular competition and in relation to participants their age. These appraisals are public and often face-to-face, as opposed to standardized tests, which take place anonymously and privately. Performing under the gaze of others—a vital component in Competitive Kid Capital—toughens a child to shield his or her feelings of disappointment or elation and to present himself or herself as a competent and confident competitor.

Because the judging in dance is subjective and is based on how one performs quite literally in front of judges, dance moms mentioned this skill most often among the three groups of parents. A dance mother explained to me how she sees this helping her daughter in her life:

> One thing that I think is neat about the competition is performing in front of judges and being critiqued on what they're doing. I think it's an important skill as they get older to feel comfortable to stand up in front of a group of people. Granted in the future it's going to be public

speaking or some sort of a presentation of something, but in general to have that confidence to get up in front of somebody and do something [is good]. I think that's a skill that's very important.

Another mother expressed a similar sentiment, emphasizing the fact that when one is being judged in dance, one's appearance is also assessed:

I think it definitely teaches you awareness of your body and gives you a definite different stance and confidence that you wouldn't have. For example, you're told to stand a certain way in ballet, which definitely helps down the road. When she has to go to a job interview, she's going to stand up straight because she's got ballet training; she's not going to hunch and she's going to have her chin up and have a more confident appearance. The fact that it is not easy to get up on a stage and perform in front of hundreds or thousands of people, strangers, and to know that you're being judged besides, definitely gives you a level of self-confidence that can be taken to other areas. So again if she has to be judged by a teacher or when she's applying for a job she'll have more of that confidence, which helps you focus.

Many of the moms discussed the importance of looking good when being judged. Here is another powerful quote on this subject:

Well, I think the whole idea that you have to get up on a stage and be your best—and put your best face forward and have a smile on your face—that's really important because unfortunately, in this world, you are judged on how you outwardly appear. Right or wrong or indifferent, that's the way that it is. So, I think that when they have to learn how to get up on stage and do that it does help them.

Parents also talked about how solo routines heighten the pressure because "everything has to be perfect because it's only you who's being judged."

Mothers also consider the ways in which negative interactions with judges can be learning experiences. For example, this mom told me how her daughter sometimes complains about the judges' reactions:

She'll say, "Oh, that judge was grumpy. She wouldn't smile at me." I say, "Well, you know what? It's hard when you have to perform in front of someone that's like that. But this is a good way for you to learn that when you get out there into the real world you may have to put on a presentation, you may have to deal with someone who is grumpy. If you're a teacher, you're going to be dealing with difficult parents. How are you going to maintain your emotions and how are you going to maintain your cool and your abilities to deal with difficult situations and so on and so forth?" So I always get into issues like that, so I take it as a learning experience.

In all three activities, parents want their children to learn to maintain their cool when performing and competing in front of others, a crucial element of developing Competitive Kid Capital. Parents encourage their children not to let others see them react or get upset. While I certainly saw tears at various events—and heard about even more—I also saw children struggling to hide their disappointment and often displaying good sportsmanship by congratulating others.

With soccer the biggest source of tears was not losing a game, but not making a team. This was especially difficult for kids whose friends made a team when they did not. Parents highlighted how difficult this was because every practice was a constant reminder of that failure. In these situations, performing under the gaze of others does not refer to unknown judges but to people who a child does know, such as friends and other adults.

This was also an issue for chess kids, especially when they had to play friends and classmates in tournaments. While some children were okay with losing to their friends (one father reported that his son said, "Well if I couldn't win, I'm glad he did!"), others were upset and embarrassed. One mother told me about the experience of her son, Daniel, at a local tournament when he had to play a friend and classmate:

> He was devastated. *He was devastated!* First he was shocked at the idea of having to play Mitchell and he was devastated at having lost to Mitchell. It didn't matter that he didn't get second place, and he got fifth. That was, whatever. The trophy thing was irrelevant, and he came home with a nice trophy anyway. In fact, it was the best he's ever done at that tournament. But he lost to Mitchell! The whole thing like tore him apart.

And the next day he didn't want to go to school, and he feigned illness and I let him.

Obviously some rivalries exist outside of a particular activity, such as in school or in another sport or activity. In this case Mitchell was not in a gifted classroom and Daniel was, so the loss felt to Daniel like a comment on his intelligence, even though Mitchell is his friend. Daniel was ashamed to face his other friends the next day. But the next time Daniel lost to Mitchell, his mom made him go to school. Daniel also participates in baseball, skateboarding, and language school, but he has only gotten that upset over a chess game, when the results were publicly announced at school and known among his group of friends. Like other soccer and dance kids, Daniel learned from this difficult experience, developing crucial Competitive Kid Capital, which will help them compete and succeed throughout their lives.

TWO STRATEGIES: THE GENERALIST AND THE SPECIALIST

Like Daniel, many kids participate in other competitive or recreational activities. A good number of parents I met strive to make their children "well-rounded." The idea of being a "whole person"—or as one parent put it, "finding one's passion"—is a very middle-class notion.[17] A smaller group of parents I met want their children to be extremely high achievers in just one area.

I identify two schools of thought among parents on how to best help their children achieve in the present and long term: the generalists and the specialists. Both generalist and specialist parents focus on their children's acquiring the five skills that are part of Competitive Kid Capital. But they have slightly different views of the best way to acquire those skills.

Generalists

The generalist path is the one most commonly taken among the elementary school–age kids I studied. This path focuses on cultivating children into the all-around person who works "different muscles," as Jeremiah's parents put it in the introduction. Generalist parents want their children to be exposed to and preferably succeed in a variety of competitive endeavors, even though their child may not be the top competitor in any one activity. This strategy helps children learn how to balance multiple commitments, manage a schedule, and perform in a variety of environments, which helps build additional Competitive Kid Capital.

One way parents do this is by making sure their kids cover all the bases by actively participating in different categories of activities. For example, many parents expressed sentiments similar to this one: "We read to the children what all their [after-school] choices are, but they have to take piano, and they have to do one athletic thing." Playing a musical instrument and doing something athletic was a common practice. Parents often see these activities—music and athletics—as working together:

> The idea is to build the individual. That's my idea. That's why she is in all of these things. She has all these different aspects to her that need to grow, and they need to grow together, so they help each other. . . . To be fit, to have strength, physical strength, is very important for music. You cannot be weak, with no muscles, just skin and bones and expect to play well at the piano. It doesn't work. It needs the body. So, yes, it all has to grow together.

The relevant idea here is building an individual who has multiple strengths. Parents most often called this having a "well-rounded" child, but since it was unclear what this phrase really meant to each parent, I probed further and received some interesting responses. For example, one mother told me that she would like her two sons to become "little Renaissance men" and be able to feel comfortable at any party anywhere in the world. To her, chess is an important skill to have because it transcends language boundaries and also is the mark of a cultivated person. But she also has her sons in soccer because that is an "international" game.

A father with two daughters told me that you can succeed anywhere if you know how to speak a foreign language, play a musical instrument, and ski. Chess also fits into the type of social world he envisions for his daughters (which to him seems to resemble a Vail ski lodge filled with educated, international people). His daughters also fence, which is their athletic activity, and they also compete as fencers.

Many parents explained that participating in multiple activities enables a "backup" option for their kids in case something goes wrong with one activity, such as an injury or a major failure. They expressed concern about, as one parent described it, "putting all of your eggs in one basket at this age." Through conversations and observations I came to understand that parents are trying to expose their children to multiple options so they can learn various skills and lessons. But note that they often move on within a year or two if the child does not demonstrate exceptional talent, a practice tied to the problem of the high-achieving child discussed in chapter 5.

Of course, during these discussions almost every parent prefaced his or her explanations with a statement such as "I just want my child to be happy" or "I just want her to find something she loves to do." In order to do this, they think kids have to try out several items from the menu of childhood activities. One dad explained, "Well, it's certainly a conscious decision to expand their horizons as broadly as possible, so that they can make their own informed choices."

It is because parents are concerned about the future that they emphasize the desire to see their kids live well-rounded adult lives. One mother introduced an evocative phrase—being a "sophisticated lady"—to describe why she has her fifth-grade daughter in multiple activities, some of them competitive: "Well, I hope she'll be a very sophisticated lady. I don't have a particular profession in mind. I don't want to tell her, 'You need to be a lawyer or doctor.' I see in her creativity, like, every day she says she is about to write a book. . . . But I hope she becomes a very sophisticated lady . . . doing something creative that would give her enough money to live a decent life."

A father, also focused on his daughter's future, emphasizes that being a generalist means becoming a specialist at some point in later childhood or early adolescence, but not at the exclusion of academic success. He explains:

I played college tennis in a Division I school, but I know that the guys who were top in the world were just better and that there was a big difference. Then again there was a big difference between me and somebody who was a decent Division III player. And so, I'm just realistic about it—if Suzanne could play college soccer, great. That would be a huge accomplishment, but it's not like she's ever going to make a career out of it. Let me put it this way: the odds are quite slim, if she'll ever make a career out of it. I just want her to be a well-rounded person. [But] you know, academics will be first.

This dad knows how hard it is to succeed as a specialist, especially in sports, so one must also pursue academics and other outside interests. But given the slim chances of being the best in the world, academic success coupled with extracurricular success is the goal (usually for college).[18]

As this father's comment implies, at some point, particularly as children get older, there is a transition from being a generalist to being a specialist. The focus often shifts around high school, from being well-rounded to attaining a special achievement, as families start focusing on standing out from the crowd during the college admissions process. Of course, some decide to specialize much younger, while their kids are still in elementary school.

Specialists

While some specialist parents may have started out as generalists, they have decided that while their children are still in elementary school it is best for them to specialize in a specific competitive activity. This may be because the parents think this is the best strategy or because their child directed them toward their strategy, mainly because he or she displays some exceptional talent. I never met any parents who decided what activity they wanted their child to excel at before the child tried it, but the popular press likes to spotlight parents who push their kids at a young age into particular pursuits (think golf, tennis, figure skating, gymnastics).

Not surprisingly specialist families are the most competitive, and their actions and attitudes tend to affect others in the activity by raising the bar for success for everyone. They are the primary cause of the problem of the high-achieving child. This happened mainly with chess and dance.

While it is difficult to find a single thread that unites this group of parents, I can say that about one-third of specialists tended to have at least one parent born outside of the United States. Given that being involved in competitive after-school activities seems to be an American phenomenon, this may be surprising. Immigrants, especially those from Asia, are known to place an emphasis on scholastic achievement. As discussed previously, many Asian nations emphasize national exams for university acceptance, while the schools in the United States tend to look at the whole candidate, making after-school activities very important. Choosing to channel substantial amounts of energy into certain after-school activities, such as chess, after a move to the United States is not surprising, as parents want to ensure their children have the best chance to succeed in the college admissions race.

Take as an example a first-grade chess player, Marco, who is so talented he won the spring nationals despite being nearly a year younger than his peers. Marco's father, Goutam, is from India and his mother is from Argentina. (They met while working in Japan). Goutam devotes much of his spare time to his son's chess career, as neither parent works full time outside of the home, since they can now live off of investments. Goutam told me, "I went to monitor all the classes. Whatever they taught, I'd extend. I'd go over whatever they taught and extend the lesson a little bit."

Marco does not do any other activities, both because they distract from his chess and because Goutam feels Marco is too small for his age to play soccer or swim with his classmates. He told me:

Yes, I do know that other people say, "He should go to this camp, this sport thing, this, that. You're not really giving him a proper childhood, he's not properly rounded. He should go to this for social reasons or something." I'm not really part of that world, to be honest, and so I don't feel any urge. I'm happy enough to have him at home and to spend time with him at home, rather than push him off onto this activity or that activity. I have the time, so I'm happy enough to do that [chess] with him.

Dance kids also specialize young, mainly because of the heavy time commitment that often accompanies competitive dance. Because there are so many classes and rehearsals after school, it is nearly impossible to pursue other activities, particularly as the children become more advanced. But parents spin this specialization as a good thing, saying that they have been told that sticking with one thing for so many years shows "the continuity and you sticking with the one thing and [the counselor] said it is going to get you tons of scholarships and tons of recognition."

Most generalist parents who are very competitive realize that eventually they will become specialist parents. One mother, who encourages her four kids to explore all of their interests at a young age, links this to the college admissions process:

When the kids are younger, more like elementary school age and younger, it's more like a general philosophy, explore lots of things. Build your confidence, feel like you can try anything and be comfortable with that, don't be afraid to fail, don't be afraid to lose. All that's okay. We have lots of experience with losing. And then towards the end of middle school, high school, you kind of sit back and specialize. Figure out which buckets are going to be yours. From a competitive point of view, if you don't have a strength, say, "Okay, that's not it." Our kids, each of them has a good strength. If you don't, say you're just kind of good at a lot of different things, then I would say then, if I were giving advice to a kid, I'd say find a niche. Make that your thing, because you need that. You can't be mediocre and be part of soccer, and what everybody else is doing, and find your way to Princeton, Harvard, Yale, if that's your goal. But if you have something that makes you stand out, it's a lot better. That's just like basic career counseling.

Of course, in some families, especially larger ones, the decision to specialize has less to do with a philosophy, talent, or long-term goals and more to do with logistics and having to balance the needs of various family members. Schedule and time restrictions often force children to make a choice and specialize. This mom explained to me how and why this happened to her daughter, at around nine:

> I tried to expose her to all different things, you know, with soccer and swimming and dance and you know, academic, extra academics, and things like that she liked to do. . . . When she started the dance team, I really had to draw the line and say something's got to give. She was doing softball and soccer and I said, "If you're doing the competition team, then you can't do this other stuff so you kind of have to start really focusing on what you really like." Which was probably a difficult question for someone who was like eight or nine. But she has two siblings and there is a limit to time. At first it wasn't so bad then because the little one [sister] wasn't involved in everything, she was just kind of a tag-along, but now that she's into her own things and play dates and her own social life and busy, it [sic] too hard.

As this mom says, siblings play a part in the lives of these competitive children, often limiting options since it is difficult to juggle multiple schedules and obligations. In general, though, most of the parents go out of their way to make sure each child develops his or her own talents and interests, accruing Competitive Kid Capital. Again, this is more of a middle-class notion, with each child learning to be self-directed; poorer families often have to put all of their resources in one child, whatever the birth order, to help the family.[19]

Lois told me how she handles her youngest daughter's presence at Lottie's activities:

> The younger sibling sitting underneath the stands at the gymnastics meet was a very powerful image to me, since I have a younger daughter. . . . And having a younger daughter, with both skating and chess, when she was three-ish, which was last year, she would go to these tournaments and she would sit in her stroller and be really miserable. Once she had a fever and because my husband works on weekends and I didn't have anything else to do with her, she came. I felt it was a little abusive to her—but she could eat whatever junk food she wanted! But ultimately, I felt it wasn't a great thing for her, so this year, I really made

an effort to not take her so she didn't go to any tournaments. . . . I try to
have a babysitter or my parents will take her. But she's starting to play
chess. Although, I see where the younger siblings are not into it and I
don't want her to be the kind that says, "Mom, I hate this." At the
moment, she's totally fine with it, and with chess, even if you never play
a tournament in your life, it's still good for you. So, I let her learn how to
play chess and it's similar with the skating. I figure as long as you're
there, you might as well get something out of it. . . . But I do feel that it's
important for her to have something of her own and not something that
her sister is competing with her and that's what we're trying to cultivate.
They're both starting to play tennis, but both are pretty good, so it's
more convenient.

Even though Lois is aware of her younger daughter's need to find her
own strengths and activities, the child is drawn into what her older sister does both because of convenience and because it is what she sees. Of
course, some kids decide they do not want to follow their older sibling.
One mom told me about her younger son, Chris, and his older brother,
John, and their relationship with travel soccer:

About three years ago Chris had started finding his own thing. But we
had to drag him to a lot of soccer games. You know, in hindsight I feel
like, "Why did we all need to go to John's soccer game?" I don't know,
but Chris seemed to have fun with the other siblings on the sidelines.
After I think really a year of that, we thought, you know, this isn't
really fair to Chris. So we would start juggling it and send John off
with the carpool so Chris could have a friend over.

Parents' talk about the merits of competition reveals some of their anxieties about their children's futures. Implicitly the generalists and the
specialists reveal the world for which they think they are preparing
their children. They are doing their best to find a way to prepare their
children for a seemingly more and more unpredictable adulthood for
which they hope that their children are acquiring the right amount of
Competitive Kid Capital in order to succeed.

Parents' talk sometimes revealed ambivalence about their decisions.
One father explained:

I'm concerned because in our desire to give them a well-rounded education and provide for them, what if we are just taking something away from them? What if the child needs to go to the backyard and just do nothing, kick the dirt, stuff that we did as children, have some imaginary play where she is the only actor, just on her own, or something like that? I don't see Sara doing that. I tell her, "Why don't you go to the backyard and be on your own for a while? Explore, look at the rocks." She doesn't want to do that. I'm not sure what can be done, but I do think about it. For example, she told me that in the car she gets bored. There's all this business of being bored. It's the catch phrase! Everything is "boring"! When she's not in one of those activities, she's bored. She says it's boring to sit in the car and do nothing. So I told her, "Sara, why don't you daydream when you are in the car?" . . . This is my concern, because I think you will end up wasting your time, some other time in your life, if you don't waste it now. There'll be some other time because I think we are just like that. We need down time. We need time to sort of reflect, slow down.

But note that even in his present concerns, this father thinks about the long-term consequences for his daughter. He frets about Sara wasting *future* time.

Like this dad, many parents emphasized the need for children to succeed both academically and in their extracurricular activities, particularly when it comes to future college admissions. Parents of eight-year-olds spoke of the SATs, AP Exams, and college counselors. Many were quite explicit about the direct link they perceive between these childhood competitive activities and elite college attendance. One father told me that his third-grade daughter's participation in chess is good, explaining, "If this helps her get into Harvard . . ." Another mother, mentioned earlier, said that her fourth-grade son's achievements "might help him stand out and get into a good school . . . Ivy League or equivalent, like Stanford."

But do parents of boys and girls jockey for their children's positions in similar ways? Earlier research on gender and after-school activities suggests that they do, and that boys make out better later in life because their organized play is more complex than girls'; consequently "these differences result in sex differences in the development of social skills useful in childhood and later life."[20] The next chapter explores how parents select activities for their sons and daughters to help them acquire Competitive Kid Capital, with a focus on decision making and its implications for girls.

FOUR Pink Girls and Ball Guys?

GENDER AND COMPETITIVE CHILDREN'S
ACTIVITIES

Up to now I have argued that the motivations of the families who in-habit the worlds of competitive chess, dance, and soccer are similar. Yet clearly there are differences, and most families choose just one of these competitive activities and do not simultaneously pursue all of them. Why do some parents select chess for their children instead of dance or soccer? Are these decisions based on the content of the activities themselves, other factors, or both?

Gender matters a great deal. Conversations with parents of boys and parents of girls in chess, dance, and soccer make it clear that the way they conceptualize the path to success differs depending on the gender of their child. Yet gender is not often a focus of contemporary studies on children and their activities. For example, in Lareau's *Unequal Childhoods* we do not get a sense of why some of the children in her study play soccer (for example, the boys of the Tallinger family), while other middle-class children do gymnastics (for example, Stacey Marshall, from the black middle-class family in Lareau's work).[1]

Girls today grow up in a world with an unprecedented set of educational and professional opportunities. More of them will graduate from college and earn advanced degrees than ever before, and all professions are open to them. Although the activities of girls and boys have converged over time, there are still distinctive paths for each sex, and many children's activities are still associated with particular aspects of feminine or masculine identity.

How do parents of girls navigate this often difficult terrain? To answer this question, most of this chapter focuses on the thirty-eight families I met who have at least one elementary school–age daughter currently involved in competitive chess, dance, or soccer. At the end, I turn to parents of boys, thinking about the implications of competitive childhood activities for young men.

FEMININE SOCIALIZATION, COMPETITION, AND SOCIAL CLASS

In their influential article "Doing Gender," Candace West and Don Zimmerman advance the notion that gender is an everyday performance for males and females.[2] But contemporary sociological studies that focus on femininity are not as prominent as studies of masculinity; even school ethnographies tend to focus "almost exclusively on the experiences and identities of boys."[3] Studies of after-school activities similarly have a male focus, such as Gary Alan Fine's and Sherri Grasmuck's work on youth baseball.[4]

Barrie Thorne's groundbreaking 1993 study of elementary school children, *Gender Play*, showed how both adults and children actively construct gender for girls and boys in schools through collective practices.[5] Much of this gender work occurs through teachers and other school personnel creating and maintaining separate physical spaces and cultures for boys and girls. In these settings, the norm is that girls are polite, follow rules, and hang together. Thorne found that tomboys, those who violated any of these norms, were sometimes ostracized both for playing with boys and not appearing as feminine as their classmates.

Looking feminine is strongly linked to what it means to be a good female. Donna Eder, Patricia and Peter Adler and other scholars show that in elementary and middle school much of female popularity depends on appearance, defined by physical development and having the "right" clothes and accessories.[6] Eder and her colleagues emphasize that girls are supposed to smile often.[7]

This body of research focuses on how the school system, broadly defined, outlines, promotes, and regulates the definition of girlhood today. But what of families, which are the other major source of socialization in children's lives? Little recent attention has focused on how families are involved in constructing girlhood as part of feminine socialization.[8] Decisions about where a girl goes to school and how she will spend her time are made behind closed doors within the home, so it is often difficult for researchers to gain access. Looking at organized after-school activities opens a window into this process.

About a century ago, organized team sports flourished only for males because of societal beliefs that women were physically inferior and mentally unable to handle competition.[9] Even when women were allowed to participate in after-school athletics, competition was off-limits, as it was seen as damaging.[10] When the Public Schools Athletic Girls League was founded in 1905, the director opposed keeping records, arguing that girls could easily injure themselves if they were too competitive and tried to break a record.[11] All-girls elite schools were among the first to break with this view of women and competition, though they called competitive organizations "associations" instead of "leagues," lest people complain a league was too masculine for young women.[12]

Sports are quite important in American upper-middle-class culture, "dramatizing and celebrating some of the values that are activated in upper-middle-class work environments—namely, competition, competence, male friendship, and masculinity."[13] Historically women from upper-class families were most focused on the arts;[14] today athletics have become especially important for these women. Two studies, one by the Women's Sports Foundation and the other by the Oppenheimer Foundation, found that 82 percent of executive businesswomen played organized sports in middle school and high school and that 80 percent of female executives in *Fortune* 500 companies identified themselves as competitive tomboys during childhood.[15] The Oppenheimer study also found that while 16 percent of women describe themselves as athletic, when you look at the responses of women who earn over $75,000 annually, the number rises to about 50 percent.

These findings are consistent with the work of academics like economist Betsy Stevenson. Stevenson's work on Title IX finds that participation in high school sports increases the likelihood that a girl will attend college, enter the labor market, and enter previously male-dominated occupations.[16] She suggests that sports develop such skills as learning how to compete and function as a team, which are especially important as women navigate the traditionally male-dominated labor market. Other researchers find that the ability to converse intelligently about sports can also be an advantage in the workplace, helping connect individuals across classes and social networks.[17]

But competition, athletic or otherwise, is still seen as more masculine than feminine. In 2010 *Sex Roles* published a study on high school boys and girls that found that "boys are 'trained' from an early age to be competitive. . . . Research suggests that girls are less comfortable than boys in competitive circumstances and that girls are socialized to mask overt competitiveness and aggressiveness more generally."[18] The authors, Hibbard and Buhrmester, argue that a mentality of competing to win is at odds with the ideal expected of nice girls, so girls who engage in head-to-head competition may have more social difficulties. McGuffey and Rich, in a qualitative study of a summer camp, find that boys are both more competitive than girls in everyday activities and more powerful in determining acceptable male and female behaviors in competitive situations.[19]

Sociologists do not explore the intersections of class and gender as often as other intersections, such as class and race or race and gender.[20] Early studies that looked at the relationship between gender and class tended to focus on men; Julie Bettie's research on working-class high school girls was a notable exception.[21]

I am especially interested in variations among the middle class and how these variations impact parents' child-rearing strategies. Karyn Lacy, in her work on the elite black middle class and the core black middle class, argues that scholars have not paid enough attention to variations in the middle class and how parents negotiate these varia-tions.[22] Studies that examine within-group identity and socialization patterns are not common, particularly when it comes to the middle class.

In the families I studied class plays a role in shaping parental deci-sions about specific activities, and I found significant variation within the middle class. Parental decisions result in differently classed forms of femininity for young girls, who learn to be either graceful girls in dance, aggressive girls in soccer, or pink warrior girls in chess. In par-ticular, upper-middle-class families (defined in this study as having at least one parent who has earned an advanced postgraduate degree and is working in a professional or managerial occupation, and both par-ents having earned a four-year college degree) and lower-middle-class families (defined as only one parent having a college degree and/or neither parent working in a professional or managerial occupation) encourage their daughters in specific ways in different after-school ac-tivities. Upper-middle-class parents promote an assertive type of femi-ninity, whereas lower-middle-class parents favor a more traditional type.

Among the thirty-eight families I met with competitive young girls, 92 percent of the soccer families are upper-middle (seven families) and mid-dle (five families) class. Dance is filled with middle-middle-class and lower-middle-class families (nine and five, respectively), and it is the only activity with any working-class participants (three families).[23] Chess fam-ilies with daughters who compete tend to look the most like soccer fami-lies, with four upper-middle-class families and two middle-middle-class families (86 percent total). These class variations set the stage for dif-ferent forms of femininity presented by each of the three competitive activities.

BATTEMENTS VERSUS CORNER KICKS: GIRLS
ACQUIRING COMPETITIVE KID CAPITAL

Consider the following explanations from two different families about
their decision to put their young daughters in a competitive activity:[24]

> The reason why I got her involved was . . . because I know that she liked
> to move a lot. She was very, very, very active. Not one of those toddlers,
> you know, who is kind of quiet every now and then. She's constantly
> active. So I said I needed some way to burn that excess energy.
>
> Mother of Alisa, a ten-year-old dancer

> She is of that disposition. She likes activities. She likes to run around.
> She has a lot of energy.
>
> Father of Dafna, a seven-year-old soccer player

Both parents emphasize that their girls are physical; they have a lot of
energy and they like to move their bodies. But the parents selected different activities for their daughters to burn off that energy. Alisa's mother
enrolled her in a dance studio; Dafna's father took her to the soccer field.
Why not the reverse, or the same?

On a basic level, the answer appears simple: parents simply choose
what is around them or what they know. One soccer mom told me,
"When she was four, they played the peewee soccer. But just out of convenience and exercise. Really, they 'have' to be doing something athletic
and [soccer] is what we know, I guess."

Some girls tried both soccer and dance and eventually settled on one.
This mom of a nine-year-old dancer explained, "Elizabeth used to always kind of dance around the house and, you know, with kids you
kind of always try different things with them. I mean, I tried soccer
with her. You know, you go down different avenues and you kind of
see what is their thing. And dance was always her thing, she was always dancing."

But how do families discern which activity is their daughter's "thing"?
Table 2 captures some of the similarities in the explanations parents give
about skill acquisition in competitive dance and soccer. It is clear that

Table 2. Similar Skills Parents Think Girls Acquire through Participation in Dance and Soccer

Skills	Dance	Soccer
Teamwork	I think she learns that whole being part of a team, you're only as strong as the weakest link. How to work in a group like that, when you really, truly need everybody. So I think that's just a good life experience. Because in a lot of school projects and stuff like that, you can compensate for somebody else. If you have a weak member of the team, you can just do their work. You know what I mean? In dance everybody needs to do it. You can't cover for somebody.	I think she can develop better social skills by learning to play with a team, as opposed to doing individual sports. . . . I think team sports are much more important, because they teach you group work, and how to go about being part of a group, and managing the skills to belong in that group and actually be harmonious with that goal. It's not an easy job. So, I think those are important skills to have.
Sportsmanship/ Winning and losing	I think the first thing is that you don't always win. And I think that's an important lesson. . . . You're not always the best. Part of me thinks when we grew up, there were twenty kids on the team. If forty tried out, only twenty made it. So twenty kids went home and cried. Okay, our kids today, fifty kids try out, fifty kids make the team and they all play for five minutes. There's a huge difference in what their expectations are. They try out, they expect to make it. So, I think it's really a good lesson for them to compete and	It could be any team sport, as far as how to lose, how to win, how to handle yourself appropriately when you have disappointments, how to work really hard even though you may not be feeling very good, all of that. It's really important because even in academics, or trying to get a job or anything like that—these are the kids that are going to know how to persevere, and they might not be doing well in the immediate time period, then they can kind of think more long term and stick with it.

(continued)

Table 2. (continued)

Skills	Dance	Soccer
	realize that they're not always gonna win. That there is always gonna be someone who is better than they are and that they can keep trying and they can make that second place or first place or whatever, they can move up and maybe someday they will be first but it's not so easy to be number one. It takes a lot of hard work and those are the kinds of lessons that I think that they end up learning [from dance team].	I think all these kinds of activities and things that the kids do, hopefully they'll all prepare them for whatever comes down the road. And I don't know that the soccer, the travel soccer, is better than doing regular soccer. I mean I think it probably is better, or different, because there's more commitment. So maybe that's the part of it that makes it different than rec. . . . She knows she can't just not go to practice or she can't miss games and go to a birthday party.
Dedication	I think motivation and dedication and she knows what it's like to be responsible, you know, like you have to get certain things done before you can move to the other. I think she does well with that through dance.	

parents see parallels between the two activities when it comes to team-work, sportsmanship, and dedication.

In addition to emphasizing particular skills, many of the dance and soccer parents also emphasize the need for children to exercise. This often starts at a young age, as one soccer mom explained: "Well, she was probably four or five when she started. And I only did it for exercise reasons. I didn't grow up exercising and now I exercise every day and I thought it was important that she at least be exposed to it."

While several parents mentioned lifelong fitness and health as a motivation, only dance moms mentioned obesity and appearance. This dance mom told me about her concerns about her daughter's future body:

> My short-term goal for her is to keep, believe it or not, physically fit. Because, she's an eater, across the board. . . . It keeps her at a nice weight. You know what I mean? And she struggles with that [weight], that's going to be her struggle, I told her, in life. . . . So I think my short-term goal for her is to stay physically fit.

Dance mothers' focus on physical appearance, and not just health, distinguished them from the other parents I met. With such similar narratives explaining participation in the activities, it is another set of scripts, about femininity, that help explain how soccer parents and dance mothers choose between the activities for their daughters. Dance, soccer, and chess parents are drawing from different gender scripts, which are shaped by class, when they make decisions about their daughters' participation in competitive after-school activities.

It is important to note that there are elements in each of the three activities that some say are inherently masculine or feminine, and these characteristics likely play a role in parental decision making as well. Adler, Kless, and Adler argue that traditional boys' activities, like soccer, emphasize masculine values of "achievement, toughness, endurance, competitiveness, and aggression," whereas girls' activities, like cheerleading and dance, foster "emotional management, glamour, and a concern with appearance."[25] With head-to-head competition and a focus on aggressive action, both in a physical and in a mental sense, soccer and chess are more similar to "hegemonic masculinity."[26] In Connell's work on hegemonic masculinity, an unmasculine situation includes "being peaceable rather than violent, conciliatory rather than dominating, hardly able to kick a football."[27] Dance instead presents an "emphasized femininity," with the lack of direct competition and the recognition of all competitors through the adjudication system.

The world of competitive dance can be thought of as a feminine form of a gendered organization not only because of its competitive style and the fact that the majority of participants are female, but also because of its focus on appearance.[28] Dancers are expected to wear make-up when they compete. While this has a practical purpose—to make sure the dancers' faces are not "washed out" by the stage lights—it also highlights the fact that the competitors are female, accentuating their feminine features with the use of lipstick, blush, and mascara.

Sociologist and gender scholar C. J. Pascoe would call these practices part of "normative femininity," which involves wearing make-up and dresses.[29] While sitting in the audience I often heard teachers and parents remark, "Wow, she looks beautiful up there" or "They look very good." In addition to make-up, costumes usually have sequins, rhinestones, ribbons, and other decorative embellishments that mark them as female. At most competitions, costume and appearance are evaluated as part of the final score.

In contrast, in chess and soccer, appearance does not matter at all when it comes to the outcome of the competition. Although girls' appearances are regulated in soccer, it is done in a way that de-emphasizes femininity. When playing soccer girls must remove all jewelry; this is for safety reasons, but the rule also strips many of them of feminine decorations they wear. Coaches also direct girls to make sure all of their hair is out of their faces; girls pull their hair back in ponytails and use headbands, or more often elastic bands (which have become a fashion and identity statement themselves—perhaps a way to assert femininity in a less-than-feminine environment), to keep shorter hair and bangs off the face. Again, this strips girls of a traditional marker of femininity: their hair. It is also noteworthy that female soccer uniforms are not easily distinguishable from male uniforms.

Chess is not a physical activity, so there are no physical requirements or restrictions based on appearance. Girls and boys wear comfortable clothes to tournaments, most often jeans, and they sometimes wear a school or team T-shirt. I can count on one hand the number of times I observed a girl wearing a dress while participating in a chess tournament.

THREE GENDER SCRIPTS: GRACEFUL, AGGRESSIVE, AND PINK WARRIOR GIRLS

Unlike masculinity, multiple forms of femininity are seen as acceptable by parents and by children,[30] so it's not surprising that different gender scripts emerged for each of the three activities. The names of these different gender scripts—"graceful," "aggressive," and "pink"—all came from language used by parents of girls in interviews. They help us understand how parents choose among different activities for their daughters.

Graceful Girls

When talking about why dance is good for their daughters, moms highlighted dance's ability to help their girls be graceful. One dance mom told me that dance produces good posture, which contributes to a more graceful appearance: "There are kids that you see in the studio and they walk in gracefully, there's just something about the way they hold themselves. If it gets her better posture then I've achieved something. But you know, if I see her slouched over, then I think, 'Well she's not pulling the whole dance experience with her through life.'"

Producing a graceful body also means producing a feminine body. Another mom explained, "When I started Brittany in dance I thought about grace, flexibility, and posture. A girl should be feminine and, you know, like refined. . . . And for girls I think it is good for them to have a little bit of that grace that you get from dance."

Even with their daughters still in elementary school, some of the mothers made an explicit connection between the importance of having a graceful body and attracting male attention. This mom explained how dance can help her daughter in the future: "It builds coordination, it builds confidence and I don't think there's anything worse than a girl that's in her teens that can't dance. You know? If nothing else, just knowing how to dance is important [at a school dance]." Dance has long been associated with preparing girls for various aspects of society life, such as etiquette and social grace,[31] usually implicit attempts to increase one's chances on the marriage market. Getting a good date at a school dance may be a first step along this particular path, and school dances are highly salient events in students' lives.[32]

However, the mothers I studied who promote this graceful girls gender script not only select dance for their daughters; they also promote a competitive dance experience. In this setting, how you look can help you be a more successful competitor. Additionally, the overlay of competition adds the other crucial element to the graceful girls script—which applies to both physical and emotional comportment—and that is being graceful in interactions at competitions.

One mother, a dance teacher, described her favorite dance competition:

> I think StarProducers is a wonderful competition. . . . Everyone is welcomed backstage. People say, "Hi, how are you? Good luck. I love your outfit. Your hair looks great! Oh, don't you look pretty?!" Even with the youngest dancers they did this, which really gives them a boost backstage, and 99 percent of the studios that went there were also the same way. Everyone would say, "Good job. Good luck on stage." It is just a very supportive atmosphere and they made sure to include everybody in the awards, even though it is an adjudicated system where more than one person can win gold or silver or whatever. Everybody got something and they gave out special awards to groups that maybe didn't win the platinum or the high score. . . . Maybe their costumes weren't custom or the greatest, or whatever, but they did focus on, for example, "Wow, that group had really great smiles," and they got a special award for that.

This quote captures the two ways in which graceful girls learn how to compete in a feminine way. First, in this competitive environment where competitors are being judged based on their talent, how the girls look plays a part. Costumes, hairstyles, and even smiles are complimented and may be a way to win special recognition. Girls learn that their feminine appearance is part of the evaluation and can earn its own reward, beyond the talent they have practiced. Second, girls also are expected to support their competitors. Wishing a competitor good luck, cheering for her, or telling her that she looks nice are seen as desirable in this competitive environment. Being supportive, traditionally seen as a feminine attribute, is also a way to demonstrate social graces. So the graceful girls are graceful both physically and socially.

The way that the competition itself is organized makes this easier, as everyone does get an award. While there is a high score, under the adjudication system all the competitors are recognized in some way, which helps facilitate an environment in which competitors can be supportive of one another. In addition to the adjudication system, the fact that the competitive experience itself is indirect in dance, without head-to-head match-ups, helps facilitate a more nurturing environment.

That said, dance parents and teachers strive to emphasize that competitive dance is a serious physical activity that should be thought of as having the same legitimacy as team sports. Comparisons to sport actually helped establish dance competitions, at least in terms of the way parents viewed the value of participating, as detailed in chapter 1. Following the model of a competitive athletic activity helped establish the competitive dance model by appealing to parents who wanted their girls to be athletes and learn to be more competitive, while still being feminine in terms of appearance and attitude.

Today's dance moms still embrace both the athletic and the artistic aspects of competitive dance. One mother, who is also a part-time dance teacher, explained:

> Well I mean it's an art form. But it's kind of an ongoing debate—why is dance not a sport when you have to be physically fit? I think it's both. I think it's a sport [because] anything that you have to train for is a sport. But because you're not really playing by any kind of rules—if you play football or you play baseball, there's a set way that you do it—and because dance involves an artistic eye and it is subjective, it's one person's opinion versus another, I guess that's where the art side of it comes in. Someday I'd like to see it considered both.

The link between dance and athleticism was also evident in my conversations with the two families who have daughters who dance and play soccer competitively. One of the mothers, whom I first met through competitive dance, provided the following response when I asked her what she thinks her daughter can learn from each activity: "From ballet she obviously gets poise and grace, which are very important because of balance. . . . I'm kind of surprised there isn't more of an overlap because most times dancers have both abilities and usually they're fairly graceful which makes you a better athlete and coordinated."

Despite this mom's seeing a productive link between athleticism and gracefulness, many soccer parents told me that dance is an activity for "girly girls," so they would not let their daughters (or sons) participate. One soccer mom I interviewed has a daughter who also takes ballet lessons, though she is a noncompetitive dancer. She said, "I think both activities require physical strength and dancing just adds an element of grace and femininity to it." This mom does not see soccer as promoting either grace or femininity for her daughter in the way that dance does.

The idea that dance is somehow just a "girl thing" and boys should not participate came up several times, especially when I asked dance moms who have sons why they did not have them in dance classes with their daughters. These women would often laugh or shake their heads, saying that either their son would not do it, their husband would not allow it, or "it's just a girl thing." One mom added a comment about her son when I followed up on a statement she made saying that exercise was a big reason for her daughter to dance:

HILARY: When she was four or five and you wanted her to get exercise, why did you choose dance and not a sport, something like soccer or softball [her son plays baseball]?

MOM: Because she was a girl. I think that's probably why. I mean, [dance] wouldn't have been something that my son did.

Overall the graceful girls strategy teaches girls that they need to be feminine, which means being graceful, looking good, and being supportive of competitors. While competitive dance does infuse dance, a traditionally feminine activity, with competition, it still keeps that competition indirect for girls. Yes, that competition can be fierce both between rival dance studios and within dance studios, as you might see on Lifetime's *Dance Moms*, but that show is purposely extreme, and you still see the girls supporting and cheering for one another. The dance girls I met do not get in the face of their competitors, as do the aggressive soccer girls, instead honing relational skills and their appearance, which are traditionally associated with femininity.

Aggressive Girls

While the graceful girls are taught to be kind competitors and value appearance, the aggressive girls are taught to be both physically and competitively forceful, actively subsuming aspects of their femininity. Many soccer parents define their daughters in opposition to those "girly girls" who dance. They employ the "aggressive girls" gender script when selecting competitive soccer for their daughters.

One father, whose older son plays travel soccer and whose seven-year-old daughter is already a member of a Westfield training academy team, captures the core elements of the aggressive girls gender script: de-emphasizing physical femininity, focusing on future career opportunities, and cultivating a winning attitude. He is concerned that his daughter has a tendency to be too feminine and not aggressive enough:

> I encourage her to be more aggressive because she's a cute little girl, but I don't like her to be a girly girl. . . . You know, I don't want her to be a cheerleader—nothing against that—but I want her to prepare to have the option, if she wants to be an executive in a company, that she can play on that turf. And if she's kind of a girly girl, maybe she'll be a secretary. [Pause] There's nothing wrong with that, but let her have the option of doing something else if she wants.

This dad clearly thinks that being a "girly-girl" subjects a girl to less desirable occupations, which are seen as traditionally feminine, like being a secretary. The images this father evokes related to being an executive, such as "play on that turf," suggests the importance that he places on athletics to help his daughter follow a selective, historically male career path.

In addition, he identifies cheerleading—which has much in common with competitive dance—as being too much of a girly-girl activity.

In general soccer parents told me that they want their daughters to be aggressive, "play like boys," and not worry about how they look. For example, one mom explained, "I think that girls who tend to gravitate towards sports are so not the girls who tend to obsess about their hair and their weight and their clothing. . . . When you're playing, you don't have to worry about your hair."

Hair was a theme in several soccer interviews. Another mom told me how her daughter got started in travel soccer and began to play more aggressively, like a boy: "[My older son] started and then my daughter saw how much fun he was having so she started. But she would run up to the goal, go to score the goal, know the goalie and go, 'Oh, hi! I like your hair.' Which is really funny, because now she plays goalie and she's the most cutthroat. Like, you put the girls out there and she goes head-to-head."

As the no–girly-girls soccer father suggested, many parents think being cutthroat and aggressive sets girls on a particular path, perhaps to the corner office as a company executive. In fact, every parent with a soccer-playing daughter I spoke with used the words *aggressive* or *assertive* in his or her interview. The focus on de-emphasizing appearance, as captured by these comments on hair and the fact that soccer girls wear androgynous uniforms and take off all of their jewelry, is especially important in this career race, as many parents know that being ladylike will not cut it in certain corner-office professions. This mom of a nine-year-old soccer girl said, "We have no illusions that our daughter is going to be a great athlete. But the team element [is important]. I worked for Morgan Stanley for ten years, and I interviewed applicants, and that ability to work on a team was a crucial part of our hiring process. So it's a skill that comes into play much later. It's not just about ball skills or hand-eye coordination." This same mom went on to explain, "When I was interviewing [job candidates] at Morgan Stanley, if I got a female candidate—because it's banking and you need to be aggressive, you need to be tough—if she played, like, ice hockey, *done*. My daughter's playing, and I'm just a big believer in kids learning to be confidently aggressive, and I think that plays out in life assertiveness."

As this quote suggests, being part of a team and being assertive are other skills aggressive girls can learn from competitive sports like soccer. Another mom powerfully explained, "I think when you play a sport, I think it teaches you assertiveness, because you can't just wait for the ball to come to you. You have to go for that ball."

Going after balls by getting in head-to-head match-ups and emerging as the only winner is definitely a different competitive experience than dance. One of the moms I met from dance has two daughters who do the dance team, one of whom also plays soccer for their local travel club (not for either of the soccer clubs I studied). She sees a difference in how parents behave at the different competitive events, and this behavior seems to map on to the different gender scripts they are employing while raising their daughters. She told me, "Other parents [at soccer games] tell their kids to be aggressive and push. They just act inappropriately and their mouths are swearing definitely through soccer. Not so much in dance!"

These aggressive and assertive girls are being raised to be women who will go after physical and metaphorical balls and tackle difficult and challenging environments throughout their lives. They are taught to be aggressive in various aspects of their lives, but without an emphasis on appearance, unlike the graceful girls in dance. Chess presents a slightly different picture; chess-playing girls are able to focus on their feminine appearance and be aggressive at the same time, if they so choose.

Pink Warrior Girls

Like soccer girls, chess girls are encouraged to be aggressive. But this aggression is slightly different because chess is not a physical game. Unlike dance and soccer, chess is primarily a mental competition, so physical femininity is not an issue at competitive events. With the lack of physicality, the femininity associated with chess is more inclusive. Chess promotes a hybrid gender script for the small group of girls who participate. These girls learn to be aggressive, but they also can focus on a feminine appearance if they so choose.

Chess allows girls to be what one mother of two sons described to me as a "pink girl": "These girls have princess T-shirts on. [They have] rhinestones and bows in their hair—and they beat boys. And the boys come out completely deflated. That's the kind of thing I think is so funny. That girl Carolyn, I call her the killer chess player. She has bows in her hair, wears dresses, everything is pink, Barbie backpack, and she plays killer chess."

That a winning girl can look so feminine has an especially strong effect on boys, and their parents. A chess mom described how a father reacted negatively when his son lost to her daughter: "The father came out and was shocked. He said, 'You let a girl beat you!'"

Most of the chess girls I met are not "pink girls" in the sense that they don't dress exactly like Carolyn. But in chess there is the chance to be both aggressive, like a warrior, and girly, embracing pink. The pink warrior gender script allows girls to be aggressive and assertive but still act in a normatively feminine way—if they want to do so.

For people affiliated with scholastic chess, it matters that the game is not physical. For example, when I spoke with Susan Polgar—the first female Grandmaster, a leading advocate for girls in chess, and an author on gender and chess—she said the fact that chess is not a physical game is important in its promoting gender equality: "Well, I think girls need to understand that, yes, they have equal potential to boys. I think that chess is a wonderful tool as an intellectual activity, where girls can prove that unlike in physical sports, because by nature maybe boys are stronger or faster, in chess women can prove equal."

Many parents actively use chess as a way to teach girls that they should have similar opportunities as boys. A chess mom explained, "We're raising her . . . to be feminist. And so she says she wants to be a Grandmaster or the president [of the United States]. She doesn't have any ideas about gender limitations and I think that's a good thing."

Despite its not being a physical game, there are more similarities between soccer and chess than between dance and chess because of the focus on aggression. With their head-to-head competitive match-ups, both chess and soccer are closer to hegemonic masculinity, hence the warrior component to the chess gender script. Those who write about chess often focus on this aggression and what it means for women. In the book *Chess Bitch: Women in the Ultimate Intellectual Sport*, the author, herself a chess master, explains that in chess the common epithet "playing like a girl" actually means playing with a lot of aggression.[33]

Despite, or perhaps because of, this aggression, girls are a distinct minority in scholastic chess. More elementary school–age girls participate in tournaments than at any other age, but they are far less than half the number of participants in coed tournaments. This is a problem that organizers seek to address by offering "girls only" tournaments, giving separate awards to the highest achieving girl and boy, and maintaining separate top-rating lists for girls and boys. Some feel this approach is negative, only reinforcing the feeling that girls can never be as good as boys, and advocate against it,[34] but many of the parents I met feel that the additional attention and success can keep girls involved.

By staying involved with chess, many girls who are not competitive by nature can learn to develop their competitive skills, finding their own place on the aggressive femininity continuum chess allows. I met Gabrielle, a second-grade girl with long blonde hair, at a chess class. She is often described as pretty or beautiful by the adults in her life. Gabrielle's mother, Ettie, grew up in rural France and told me that she finds the experience of raising children in the United States quite different from her own childhood: "I mean, just living here, if you breathe the air, you are going to be competitive by nature. . . . It's just a tough world." Ettie went on to explain why she thinks chess is particularly good for Gabrielle:

> We went in there to the class, and I sort of came early to see how it was going. When you have a little girl like Gabrielle, you don't want to trust her with two guys without really knowing them. So I sort of observed that too and really liked a few things about it. . . . I like the game itself. I realized that this was really something neat for a girl to do. It's also good for her IQ, good for her math, and for being competitive.

Gabrielle looks feminine and may even attract male attention while still in second grade. But her mother recognizes the importance of being competitive and honing skills often thought of as masculine, such as math skills. Chess allows Gabrielle to embrace her feminine side while also developing more "masculine" competitive skills, making her a pink warrior in chess.

However, one issue that Ettie sees as an impediment to Gabrielle's continuing to play is that not many of her girlfriends play chess, and the others who do are, in Ettie's opinion, "a little bit tomboy, so they're not the same type of girls." Ettie went on to describe more of the "feminine" aspects of Gabrielle's personality: "She's just a very happy flower, you know? She really is. . . . She has that, you know, 'everybody's beautiful and we should all be friends' attitude." Gabrielle, "the happy flower," can still be herself and learn to be more competitive and aggressive by playing chess because the pink warrior gender script can accommodate both femininity and aggressiveness.

Just as girls like Gabrielle can learn to be more competitive, chess accommodates the tomboys and can provide a space for them to find friends who are like them. Lois, the chess mom discussed at the beginning of chapter 3, explained,

> There are girls' mothers at [my daughter's school] who have said to me that girls really don't like [chess]. I think there is an attitude that for girls chess is not a feminine endeavor. . . . Lottie went to this crunchy preschool and she always played with boys and was into Pokemon and that sort of stuff. She never played with Barbie or American Girl dolls.

After Lois took over the leadership of the chess club at Lottie's school she recruited girls from Lottie's class so that the girls could hang out while playing at chess tournaments and events. Lois told me that they attended the all-girls national chess tournament "in part because [she] felt it was important to show solidarity with other girl players."

While not all girls who play chess will be aggressive, chess does provide an opportunity for those who want to be more competitive to do so in head-to-head pairings. Lois' comment captures the various forms of competitive femininity that can exist side-by-side in the pink warrior gender script and in girls' lives today: "Other girls, like her friend Donna, if she was playing a good friend of hers, she would figure out a way to have a draw so that there was no winner and no loser. Lottie never cared about that. She would play her grandmother, her best friend, anyone, even her four-year-old sister and she just wants to win. So, chess has seemed like a good fit for her."

AFTER-SCHOOL CLASSES IN FEMININITY

The graceful, aggressive, and pink warrior girl scripts generally vary by class, just as the class background of the majority of the families in each activity varies. Through these competitive activities we can see classed forms of femininity. Though nearly all of the families are part of the broadly defined middle class, parents higher up in the class hierarchy of the middle class promote a more aggressive femininity, and we see this in both soccer and chess families. Dance mothers, who generally have lower status than the chess and soccer parents, promote a femininity that is less competitively aggressive and prioritizes physical appearance. Middle- and lower-middle-class and working-class families place a greater emphasis on femininity. Working-class and lower-middle-class women have occupations that are typically more "front stage,"[35] "pink collar," and involve emotion work, like being secretaries, which require a focus on feminine traits such as friendliness and cleanliness.[36] Girls who are raised in these families are being taught that they will likely need to use their femininity in their future occupations; however, these occupations may be more competitive than they were in the past, which is why competitive dance is a useful socialization activity in these families.

Thinking in terms of occupations highlights parental occupations, in addition to parental aspirations for their children's occupations. Recall the soccer father who wants his daughter to be able to play on the turf of corporate executives and not be a secretary, and the soccer mother who previously worked at Morgan Stanley. The former is a lawyer, and the latter was an investment banker who recently stopped working to spend more time with her five children. Both of these parents attended elite universities as undergraduates. Most of the soccer parents had similar occupations or were professors or doctors. In short, these are parents who are highly credentialed and who have been through competitive credentialing processes themselves.

It is not surprising that these parents have similar occupational aspirations for their children, including their daughters, who will need to compete to get similar credentials. Parents like the Morgan Stanley mom are trying to impart particular skills and lessons to their daughters at a young age to help them succeed in the long term. They do not want their daughters to end up as secretaries, as the soccer father made clear. Participation in competitive activities, where aggression is taught, becomes a priority if the girls are to maintain their family's status in the future.

Upper-middle-class girls are being prepared much more strategically to help maintain their family's class position by entering what are traditionally hegemonically male worlds. This includes choosing after-school activities that will give these girls an advantage in college admissions.[37] Today there are three times more female soccer players than Girl Scouts in the United States.[38] The comparison to the traditionally female activity of Girl Scouts is indicative of the shift to using sports like soccer to train girls to succeed in the future. Those with strong financial, social, and cultural resources—associated with upper-middle-class families—are more likely to have access to and focus on travel and elite competitive experiences.

In contrast, the dance moms did not discuss future careers for their daughters that require lots of credentials and higher education. Some mentioned the possibility that their daughters would become a doctor or lawyer, and nearly all expect their daughters to attend college, even those who seriously consider a professional dance career for their daughters. But these moms routinely mentioned teaching as a career goal, while none of the soccer parents did (even the soccer mother who was herself a high school teacher). Being a dance teacher was specifically mentioned by several mothers, which has less status than teaching in a scholastic setting (because it does not require a licensing exam).

Parents' previous experience with these activities appears relevant here. Dance has the highest number of former parent participants. Six of the moms had done competitive dance as children; three of them had actually competed for Elite when they were younger. Three are currently dance teachers (two at Elite, one at a different studio). All the parents, but the dance mothers in particular, seem to be drawing on their own experiences, even as they apply these strategies to a more competitive environment for their daughters. While these mothers want their daughters to attend college, there is a focus on femininity that points them in the direction of an MRS. degree, not an MBA, which is what the soccer parents and many of the chess parents desire for their daughters. It is also possible that these women simply do not know what it takes to get that MBA, so the more achievement-focused among the dance moms may be steering their girls toward an MFA, which is a credential but still a very feminine one.[39]

The path to any of these credentials and careers is not easy. Aside from the difficulties of gaining admission to college and graduate programs, girls also need to deal with social pressures. They face difficulties in balancing aggression and athleticism with the more traditional notions of femininity emphasized in dance, like appearance.

A recent study of the long-term effects of sports participation on adolescent girls found that "many girls in sports continue to struggle to reconcile their athleticism with traditional standards of hegemonic femininity that emphasize maintaining a thin body ideal and adhering to a rigid definition of beauty."[40] In her work on female litigators, Jennifer Pierce found that successful women had to become either "very male" or "very caring." She describes this bind: "Whereas men are praised for using intimidation and strategic friendliness, women who are aggressive are censured for being too difficult to get along with, and women who are nice are considered 'not tough enough' to be good litigators."[41]

Aggressive and pink warrior girls, along with graceful girls, clearly face the triple bind of being supportive, competitive and successful, and effortlessly beautiful starting in childhood, continuing through adolescence, and into womanhood.[42] Their parents prepare them to deal with this triple bind in slightly different ways, shaped by their own backgrounds, but all are socializing their daughters to succeed to the best of their abilities in a competitive world.

These classed gender ideas have long-term implications for inequality, as girls from upper-middle-class families seem to be better prepared, and hence equipped with the skills they need to succeed in the credentialing processes that lead to more lucrative careers as adults. This reinforces the need for us to think about the middle class in more nuanced ways, as there are divisions in the broad middle class. It also reinforces the need to better understand everyday life and socialization practices at the upper end of the class structure.

Despite more opportunities than ever for girls today, different environments constrain and transform gender roles. We can see this in competitive after-school activities for children. Gender and class are being reproduced in these competitive activities, which will likely impact who ends up in that corner office and who ends up as the boss's assistant.

THE MASCULINE HIERARCHY: JOCKS, NERDS, AND "FAGS"

Femininity is only part of the gender story. So what about the boys?[43] Overall most of the boys I met receive very traditional advice about becoming men. A boy who plays with Charter-Metro Chess told me, "My dad will always say, 'Be a man. Don't cry over stuff like that [a loss].' So I'll always be a man about it and not cry."

Decisions made by parents about their boys' participation in competitive activities are somewhat predictable, which is not surprising given that parents push boys more than girls to conform to standard gender roles.[44] Dance is an unconventional choice for boys (across my field sites only four boys danced competitively),[45] soccer is normative, and chess is in the middle. The comparison between chess and soccer boys reveals what many would expect: "nerdy" boys are in chess, and "jocks" are in soccer. There is overlap, with some boys doing both soccer and chess, like Jeremiah of the "To Infinity and Beyond" family. But recall that his father, Josh, primarily described Jeremiah as a "ball guy," with no small amount of pride. Boys who dance are often assumed to be effeminate and gay.

Before describing these "nerds," "jocks," and "fags," it is important to note that there is one way in which the gender story for boys is different, and that is in terms of class. It is hard for me to determine whether there is a class story here, although I suspect there is, especially in terms of nonselection into particular activities. My sample has far less class diversity among boys than among girls, mainly because dance provided a group of lower-middle-class girls; because boys are not well represented in dance, I cannot assess the full class spectrum of boys among chess, dance, and soccer.

I can say that the socialization of boys seems not to have changed over time in the same way that it has for girls. Of course, girls can now attend college, whereas boys always could. Yet there have been significant changes in the labor market for men, in both white-collar and blue-collar jobs, so the lack of a shift in parenting strategies is somewhat remarkable.

Even without the clear presence of a class hierarchy for these boys, a hierarchy of masculinities is present, with athletic boys being at the top, nerdy boys below them, and effeminate boys at the lowest level. This is consistent with previous research, such as the work of Pascoe on masculinity in high school and the work of the Adlers on popularity in middle school.[46] Because athletics is at the top of this hierarchy of "male preserve,"[47] parents who chose other activities for their sons have to explain their sons' participation and justify why the activity is "masculine."

With chess boys, who are often described as "nerds" or "geeks," the sense of male companionship is often invoked as a reason for participation. One mom told me about her fourth-grade son: "I think he really likes the social aspect. It is very, very important to him to have his group of friends with whom he does this. As a matter of fact, we're planning a primarily chess birthday party with one of his other friends." Because the majority of the chess boys are not athletic, they are sometimes ostracized at school. Chess gives them a space where they are not social misfits, which is particularly important for adolescent boys who may otherwise not have a peer group.[48]

Another chess mother, whose sons are actually quite popular in school, explained, "The word has gotten around that chess is nerdy. But these are kids who pride themselves on being popular. I'm hoping that they'll take their popularity and take chess with them, but I don't know." But within a year the "popular" boys had dropped out of chess in favor of soccer and basketball, taking most of their third- and fourth-grade male friends with them.

I met a chess mom who really wanted her fourth-grade son to continue with chess into middle school. (In the end he did not.) When we met, her son was in a Talented and Gifted classroom and would soon be leaving the comfort of that small and nurturing environment for a larger and more competitive middle school. She envisioned chess as a way for him to keep a group of male friends but acknowledged that there would be obstacles:

It's funny, when we were at Nationals, I was checking out the other teams. I've been talking to him about how much he wants to do this, if he continues, as he gets older. And I said something like, "Well, there're those geeky middle school kids, but check out this team." It was this team from Texas and they had nice T-shirts on. They had sweatshirts. There were boys. There were girls. They looked good. By the time you get to high school, chess doesn't seem like such a bad thing, right? And I said, "I'll bet you there'll be more girls then. It'll be more social. You won't have all the parents going with you!"

In trying to convince her somewhat scrawny and nonathletic son to continue with chess, this mom acknowledges that there are many geeks in chess. But she went on to highlight that there are some girls as well—and such romantic relationships are another route to masculinity and popularity. For "nerdy" boys who are not at the top of a school's social hierarchy, chess can provide a different avenue to relationships with the opposite sex.

Being a geek or a nerd carries the association that a boy is not coordinated or athletic. A soccer mom told me why she has her three sons in travel soccer while still in elementary school, explaining that at her sons' private school athletics become quite important in middle school: "You can either play on a sports team or you can have gym—and only the really uncoordinated geeky kid will end up in gym in middle school. We wanted them to have another option."

This mom's fear for her sons' social reputations was common. But a vocal minority of parents of boys I met embrace "geekdom," as one father called it. As a tenured professor of theoretical physics, this dad proudly declared that he loves that his son loves chess: "You know, geek is good!"

It is worth noting that this father was the only parent I interviewed who is part of a same-sex marriage. Neither he nor his partner suspected that their son might be gay, but three other parents confided in me during our interviews that they had concerns that their sons might be gay.

Not one parent of a girl made a similar confession, and, notably, not one parent of a son who dances did either (though admittedly that pool of kids is smaller).

The "specter" of homosexuality does haunt dance. Just as Pascoe found in high schools that "dancing was another practice that put a boy at risk of being labeled a fag,"[49] this was true for the elementary school–age boys I met. One dance teacher told me:

> I think dance still holds that stigma. It is a girly thing. It is pink tutus and it is for fruity guys that swing to the right. I think that is mostly a society thing and I definitely think that So You Think You Can Dance and Dancing with the Stars and everything is really helping to bring a lot more boys in. I'm sure that is what brought a lot of our boys in and one can actually look and see strong men doing really awesome tricks and turns and leaps and throwing the girls around and doing these awesome things. Seeing, "Oh he is in a suit and he is dancing to that cool song that dad listens to. He is not in tights jumping around and swinging his arms around" and they actually have good role models now. Dads, a lot of times, are still old school and feel that dance is girly.

One of the ways to counter the "girly" and "fruity" stereotype for men who dance is to emphasize the strength of male dancers and the fact that they often dance with women.

Yet, the stigma remains. One mother of a seventh-grade boy who does competitive dance told me why she thinks her son's classmates do not participate: "Because I think people think if you dance you're gay or something. But they're not. They're just really good dancers!" Boys who dance do tend to be the best dancers in the group, as they can often jump higher and turn faster than many of the girls, though the girls tend to be more flexible. Even when a boy is not the best dancer, he is often spotlighted in routines by virtue of being the only male.

One mother who has a daughter who dances competitively and a son who plays competitive baseball (and who has never taken a dance class) tried to explain why her older son does not dance. This exchange was uncomfortable and slow, as the woman searched for words, and I finally jumped in to lessen the tension:

MOM: Oh, I just definitely think . . . uh, you know, people are stereotypic, like it's out there that like, oh you do dance, well, you know, there's something not right with you or you're not going down the right road. . . .

HILARY: They're gay?

MOM: (Smiles) You know what I'm saying? I'm not saying that's true, I mean like I said my son has two friends that tap dance and you know, and we've seen, we've watched guys tap dance and it can be really cool, you know what I'm saying. That's, but I do think, you know, unfortunately people look at them differently.

As I mentioned I did meet three parents who openly wondered about their sons' sexuality—though again, none of them were in dance. This father has five children—four boys and one girl—and his eldest, who dropped out of soccer, is interested in theater and the performing arts. He said:

Just based on stereotypes, in a prepuberty age, you would say that maybe he's gay. He's very effeminate. But I could be completely wrong, and the studies on that show that there's very little correlation between prepuberty and a person's actual sexual orientation. And like a lot of parents, I don't care if my son's gay. I want him to be happy. But I sort of take the attitude, it's just easier to succeed [if you're not]. I mean because he has great aspirations to do things, to have an impact on society and things like that, and certainly you can do that no matter what your sexual orientation. But I just find it's easier if you're more mainstream.

Again, the idea of "stereotypes" was invoked, showing the power of hegemonic masculinity. This father was most concerned about his eldest son's sexuality in contrast to his second eldest, who is quite athletic. Family members, such as siblings, certainly play a part in how parents socialize their kids and pick their activities, along with parents and their interactions with larger society outside of the home.

GENDER: A FAMILY AFFAIR

Children and their parents do not exist in a vacuum, particularly when it comes to gender, so it is important to consider other aspects of family life that can shape pink girls and ball guys. As might be expected, when I looked at families with both boys and girls, dance had the least amount of overlap, soccer had the most, and chess again was in the middle. Four of the soccer girls had older brothers in travel soccer, and none of them had brothers who did not play soccer. For dance it did not matter if a girl's brother was older or younger—he just did not dance.

For the three boys in dance, the story is slightly different. One of the boys has an older sister who is a prominent member of the company at Elite; the other has an older sister who took dance but did not participate competitively. It is likely that without the involvement of their older sisters, these boys would not have started dancing.[50] The third boy dancer has only older brothers; he discovered dance on his own, though not until high school, which is late for most competitive dancers due to the training required to perfect dance technique.

Three of the seven chess-playing girls have brothers. One of them is a twin, so they participate together; and the sister is the better player. Another girl has an older brother who is quite talented (he was a national champion), and she is barely rated; in this case, her older brother's involvement clearly has influenced her limited participation. The third girl also has a talented brother, though he is a year younger; she was exposed to chess first but did not start playing in tournaments until her brother's talent was identified.

Three chess families had boys who were quite talented in chess and had older sisters (in one case, a twin) who did not participate. This shows that having an older sibling of the opposite sex may not affect the younger chess child's involvement. One of the mothers claimed she did not know about chess for children when her two older daughters were younger, but she now regrets the fact that they did not learn to play:

> I had it to do all over again . . . I would have put my daughters in chess. I think I would have just liked them get some training at a young age. I think with their brother so successful it's a little disheartening to have

your brother move so quickly, when you're struggling. But if they had started when he wasn't interested in it, then maybe they would have continued.

As is evident from this quote, and many others, mothers tend to be the parents who are most involved with their children's extracurricular lives. While some fathers do get involved, they tend not to perform the more mundane tasks, like preparing snacks and washing clothes.[51] The title of Shona Thompson's book on boys and girls in elite tennis in Australia aptly summarizes women's roles in families where children compete in extracurriculars: *Mother's Taxi: Sport and Women's Labor*.[52] Essentially these mothers do the care work related to their children's competitive activities, while fathers take on the more celebrated positions of coach and trainer.

Yet these activities, particularly soccer and chess, provide an opportunity for fathers and daughters to interact in a way that previously was reserved for fathers and sons.[53] I saw fathers involved with both of these activities, and soccer dads would often take on a formal role as a volunteer coach or referee. None of the fathers I interviewed specifically mentioned his involvement with his athletic daughters as something unique, but this is clearly a change enabled by the passage and implementation of Title IX in the 1970s.

While fathers' involvement is likely a positive development, it can be problematic in two ways. The first is captured in a quote by a soccer father of two girls who helped found Metro Soccer Co-op. When I asked him if he saw differences in terms of how parents of boys and girls behave, he told me:

> With a typical yuppie Baby Boomer they always have one and another [baby]. Almost invariably it's one girl and one boy and if you see three it's because they had two boys and always wanted a girl. So it's hard to say about parents who have both a boy and a girl, but I would say they're more aggressive with their son's teams than the girl's teams, but not always and it's really not a tried and proven rule. For a guy like me where the girls are the only game in town we can be very aggressive.

This suggests that the father of a boy and a girl pushes the boy harder. But when he has only girls, the girls become more like sons and the father can be just as involved as he would have been with a son—and soccer provides that opportunity.

The second problem with fathers being more involved is that it creates more of a traditional gender role division between the parents, a problem to which I alluded earlier. Some moms complained to me that the dad would go to the field once or twice a week to coach, but it was the moms doing the daily work of making sure uniforms and practice gear were clean, snacks were prepared, carpools were organized, and the like. The fathers would swoop in and "take all the credit," as one mom put it, and the moms would labor invisibly. It is unclear what the children think about this division, and if they will reproduce this pattern someday as parents, but it is worth considering that fathers' increased attention to girls' competitive activities may only reinforce traditional gender roles instead of liberating women, as may have been the fathers' intentions when raising their aggressive girls.

In various ways these competitive activities constrain *and* transform gender roles for girls and boys. There seem to be more transformative effects for girls, likely because there was more room for growth, but these transformations appear to be differentially distributed by social class. Gender and class are implicated in the competitive structure and affect parental decisions about specific activities for their kids. Gender and class are also being reproduced in these activities, pulling some kids into activities that emphasize physicality or appearance—which could have real consequences for inequality, as some girls are strategically trained to end up in a corner office while others will end up as the boss's assistant.

One question that looms is whether or not the kids actually understand and will implement the skills that their parents want them to learn through their participation in these activities. Parents themselves admit that they do not always tell their children why they think certain activities are good for them. One mom said, "Do I communicate to her what I want her to learn? Actually, I don't really. Right now she only understands that I go to dance, I'm having fun. Like, I don't tell her anything else other than that. Just maybe I'll share it eventually." Statements like this, and the fact that children have strong opinions about their lives, make it clear that we must listen to the children themselves to hear what they think about their participation in competitive experiences and how it influences their future expectations. In the final chapter of *Playing to Win* I turn to the children themselves to hear what they think about these activities.

But first I further contextualize parental decision making about competitive after-school activities by showing how these activities are structured as businesses today and how this shapes the lives of the children who can pay to play outside class. The next chapter focuses on the similarities that exist across these activities, showing that there is a developed world of competitive childhood in American culture, and explaining how the institutionalized context of competitive children's activities creates and reinforces parental concerns about their children's future.

FIVE Carving Up Honor

ORGANIZING AND PROFITING FROM THE CREATION
OF COMPETITIVE KID CAPITAL

For the teachers and coaches affiliated with Metro and West County Chess, Metro Soccer Co-op and Westfield Soccer Club, Metroville Elite Dance Academy and Westbrook Let's Dance Studio, and many other programs, competitive kids' activities are a source of financial stability. They make a living by creating an environment to create Competitive Kid Capital and by creating and sustaining a base of families who believe that Competitive Kid Capital is essential to future success. Behind the culturally celebrated veil of competition is an elaborate infrastructure and industry that organizes, supports, and promotes organized children's activities while shaping the daily lives of many American families.

How are these social worlds organized? Who controls and profits from these children's activities? We actually know little about the business of these after-school programs. Using the results from my comparative study,

I show that while particular competitive activities have their own distinct features, overall these activities have internal structures that carve up time, money, and talent in similar ways.

This chapter describes the organized world of competitive childhood activities that profits from parents who are anxious about their children's future. Eight of the full-time teachers and coaches I met are parents of former competitors, so they know how to package their services to appeal to parents. But it's various actors, including teachers and coaches, who come together to create Competitive Kid Capital for their young charges.[1] Just as it takes an "art world" to create an artist or a piece of art, these individuals, organizations, and businesses play a role in producing child competitors.[2] I identify five structural similarities across chess, dance,[3] and soccer—their industries, their organizational practices, their reward systems, their selection processes, and their conflicts and scandals—which indicate that there is a larger structure of competitive childhood in the United States today.

ENTREPRENEURIALLY PROFITING FROM
COMPETITIVE CHILDHOODS

Adults make money from competitive children's activities in a variety of ways,[4] sometimes as part of the formal economy and sometimes as part of the informal economy. The majority of the forty-one teachers and coaches I met make a living by teaching children chess, dance, and soccer. This is their "day job." Many of them are small business owners, owning a dance studio, for example. Some can be thought of as independent contractors, for instance, coaching multiple soccer teams within a club or giving private chess lessons. Only a few are full-time employees of someone else, such as a dance studio or soccer club.

We should think of those who run organizations related to children's competitive activities, whether they are for-profit or not-for-profit,[5] as entrepreneurs. Because parents are willing to invest a lot of money in these activities, there is a lot of money to be made by those with an entrepreneurial spirit. Teachers and coaches can charge a lot since there are not many rival instructors in their areas of expertise. While some parents express discomfort that adults are making a living off of their children,[6] they still tend to pay up once they have gotten involved at the competitive level for fear of derailing their child's potential success.

These entrepreneurs are surrounded by constellations of other entrepreneurs who charge for additional services: those who publish magazines about the competitive activities, sell software to organize tournaments, or run the competitions themselves. Such trade publications as *Chess Life for Kids!*, *Dance Spirit*, and *Soccer America* feature articles and advertisements about improving performance. The writers, editors, and publishers of these magazines can be added to the list of adults who earn money from these children's activities.

Those who produce the goods and services that are advertised in those magazines and sold at concessions at competitive events—software programs that schedule lessons and help organize class lists and rosters, special clothing like uniforms, costumes, or customized team shirts and outfits—also profit from the big business of competitive children's activities. In her work on ballroom dancing, sociologist Julia Ericksen explains that "competitions spawn a cottage industry, with designers and sellers of dresses, shoes, and jewelry, and practice wear all hoping to attract the dancers' attention."[7] The term *cottage industry* aptly describes the constellation of businesses that surround children's competitive activities.

I was particularly struck by this when I attended a State Soccer Expo and saw vendors selling products I had not previously considered vital to the travel soccer enterprise. For example, there was a booth by a company that sold the paint used to paint the lines on soccer fields. Another booth featured a small business specializing in packaged cookies, popcorn, and other snacks that can then be sold by teams, at a marked-up price, as part of fundraising efforts. Yet another sold special headbands meant to help prevent concussions. Clearly such products are only sometimes necessary. But producers, looking for financial gain, advertise that the products will make participation more convenient or improve a child's performance and thus label a product "required." Some products, like the headbands, are successful because they prey on concerns of parents about their children's safety.

Of all those in the children's competitive cottage industry, those who organize tournaments appear to make the most money, particularly when it comes to dance and chess. Most dance competition owners try to include as many entries as possible in a competition, with many competitors on stage at any given time. Each entry and each member of a routine means more cash in their pockets.

Competition owners understand that those studios that bring the most contestants bring in the most money. Some dance teachers suggested to me that competition owners sometimes manipulate the judges' scores to make sure these studios get the top overall awards because if the teachers, parents, and kids are happy, they will come back the next year. It is harder for such manipulation to happen in chess and soccer since the outcome is more objective, but I saw tournament organizers make concessions for those families they knew well, for instance, allowing a child a bye if he or she had to arrive late at a tournament. Because these activities are at root businesses for many adults, owners strive to keep their clientele happy and satisfied.

At the same time, because these activities do occur in after-school hours and are run by individuals who are not teachers in a traditional academic setting, instructors and coaches often have to play many different roles to different people—and will do so to keep parents happy, even if it means sometimes skirting the law. For example, I saw parents ask for receipts for classes and lessons and the organization's tax identification number to submit reimbursements as part of their company's child care flexible spending accounts. This happens most often with chess, especially when classes are held at school and on school holidays, but it also occurs for soccer camps and dance classes. All but one of the teachers with whom I spoke willingly provide this information if asked and are not bothered that parents do this, essentially labeling their work as child care.[8]

Teachers sometimes skirt other rules related to taxes. Some do their teaching off the books. For example, I met chess teachers who ask for cash payments for private lessons so they do not have to report the income; this also happens at soccer camps and clinics.[9]

Not only do some teachers and coaches make money off the books, but many lack what might be regarded as the requisite training in their respective areas, especially when it comes to teaching. While there are no formal certification procedures for teachers in any of the activities, there is training available. (Soccer comes the closest, with licenses for different levels of coaching.) The dance studio owners I met dislike it when people simply start a dance studio without knowing proper teaching techniques because negative experiences can affect their potential clientele as well. Additionally, dance and soccer instructors who lack proper training may cause lasting damage to children's hips, knees, and ankles.

The ease with which someone can claim to be a coach or teacher became clear to me when I went to a summer sleep-away soccer camp. I met the owner of the Northeastern States Soccer Camp at the State Soccer Expo I attended. Whenever I walked by his booth he tried to get me to take one of his brochures to send my child to his camp.[10] Finally, not wanting to be rude, I explained that I did not have any children and that I was attending the Expo to do research. Being a graduate of one of my alma maters, he offered to help by inviting me to attend one of the camps to see how a soccer camp is run.

Over the next few months we spoke several times, and he asked if I would consider being a coach. I clearly explained on multiple occasions that I had no soccer skills but that I could be a counselor, living with the kids in their dorm and supervising them. When I arrived at the camp I discovered that I was supposed to be in charge of training a group of participants whose parents paid nearly $700 for the week under the impression that their children would receive top-of-the-line coaching and training. I immediately protested and again volunteered to help in other ways, such as doing registration and working in the camp store. But that week the camp was understaffed, so the director continued to try to convince me to run drills. Again I said I had no knowledge to run those drills or give corrections. The director was frustrated with my unwillingness to serve as a coach. After two days of feeling deeply uncomfortable, I decided to leave the camp. The experience showed me how easy it is for someone to pass herself off as a coach, even in a reputable program, when she has no knowledge of coaching.[11]

It is shockingly easy for individuals to go into business simply by applying a veneer of professionalism. Parents invest a great deal of money in their children's participation, and many teachers, coaches, and other entrepreneurs are there with their hands out, ready to accept whatever people can pay, and often asking for more. Legal scholar Laura Rosenbury has written about the unregulated space between school and family life, and competitive children's activities certainly occupy this space.[12]

When it comes to the unregulated nature of the cottage industries surrounding competitive chess, dance, and soccer, part of the reason for parental acquiescence is that competitive events are stressful experiences, setting nerves on edge. Parents understandably want their children to enjoy themselves and to succeed at these events. In the moment of competition, many parents feel pressured to comply with their children's requests, shaped by the temptations of various entrepreneurs. T-shirts, stuffed animals, books, and the like are real-time rewards for a performance. Tom Farrey, a sports journalist who has written about youth athletics, claims that one of the reasons national championships are available for younger kids is that organizers know that the younger the kids are, the more money gets spent on miscellaneous merchandise.[13]

The cottage industry of childhood competition captures families in a vulnerable moment and charges higher prices because they can, similar to what occurs in funeral markets.[14] Notably, the funeral industry, and some industries associated with children (for example, preschool), are regulated in an attempt to limit exploitation of vulnerable populations. What is problematic is that the industry of competitive children's afterschool activities has become so commodified and profit-oriented, with little to no regulation of their practices.

ORGANIZING COMPETITION IN TIME AND SPACE

On the way to creating Competitive Kid Capital, and turning a profit, teachers and coaches have limited time and space in which to organize training and tournaments. Regardless of the activity, competitive children's activities are organized in similar ways and deal with similar organizational challenges and dilemmas. How do organizers deal with logistical issues like time and space when running competitive kids' activities?

Given the time constraints created by school days, practices and lessons tend to take place in the late afternoon and evening.[15] Compared to the rest of the world American children in general spend far more time competing than practicing.[16] Competitions, tournaments, and games take place on the weekends. Larger tournaments and competitions, such as nationals, are held in the summer, either over a week or a long weekend, often in a family-friendly locale.

For all of the activities, the term *nationals* is misleading, for two reasons. First, very few of these events are national in the sense that competitors come from across the nation. National chess tournaments come the closest, with a continental representation among competitors; for example, at the 2007 spring national, competitors from forty-five states were present.[17] With dance and soccer most of their "national" events feature competitors who live near the event. While soccer teams may represent their state in some capacity at high-level tournaments, this never really happens with dance competitions.

The second way in which the term *national* is misleading is that there is no standard qualification process that goes into being a "national" competitor, as one may assume based on the Olympics and other athletic models. Those who can pay can easily "earn" a spot to play at the nationals. Many of these events—whether in chess, dance, or soccer—simply insert *national* into their name. Calling an event a national one means charging higher fees and attracting more competitors, particularly over the summer, when parents and teachers are faced with multiple choices of how their children will spend their time and where they will compete. As Tom Farrey explains, "The branding of the event as a 'national championship' is effectively a marketing gimmick."[18]

Because of the limited amount of out-of-school time available for many competitive activities—whether for national competitions, local events, or practices—time is at a premium.[19] The best way to organize this time is an issue. Parents often find it hard to deal with other adults controlling the entire family's schedule by establishing rehearsal and practice times, sometimes unexpectedly. As life revolves more and more around children's after-school schedules it seems that the calendar, often occupying a prominent place in the kitchen, has become the new family hearth. When I visited people's homes, family calendars occupied central locations in kitchens; in one home the family had installed a large white board that covered an entire wall so that they could leave notes for one another regarding their ever-changing schedules.

Time is also an issue for tournament organizers as they struggle to best schedule the competitive events themselves. Leaders in all three activities have active discussions about the proper length of time for events in competition. In chess the issue is about the length of games: whether thirty minutes for each player is enough time, even though it allows more games in a one-day tournament than would be possible with a longer game length. In soccer the main concerns are playing too many games in one weekend and how many members should constitute a team so as to maximize the experience for all team members (so whether or not games should be five or nine players on a side to promote more one-on-one time and contact with the ball during a game). With dance the amount of time available for each routine is not standard from competition to competition, and this makes it difficult for teachers to choreograph routines that will work at all of the competitions they attend in a given year or season.

Space limitations, particularly in the case of dance and soccer, add an additional constraint. The issue for dance is having the right kind of floor. In order to protect dancers' legs, they should dance on a wood floor or a Marley dance floor, which is slightly rubberized and has some spring. Dancers should not dance on concrete, as it does not have the give that is needed to protect legs and joints. Given the number of routines that require rehearsal for competitions, additional space is sometimes needed, and studios look for any wood flooring available in the surrounding areas. The dancers from Elite Dance Academy often rehearse on racquetball courts and in a religious center. If space for studios were not so expensive, the owners would open another studio, but because real estate costs so much and would drive up the price of lessons, the studio turns to the community.

Metro Soccer Co-op also has to rely on public spaces. The teams use public fields, accessible only by car, for space to practice and host home games. This means that the club and the coaches have little control over the maintenance of the fields (making sure rocks and other sharp objects, along with holes, will not affect players) or over whether the fields are deemed playable on any given day (a field might be unplayable if there has been a lot of rain, for example). They also compete with other sports organizations over how often and how long they can use the space.

Westfield too makes use of community fields for games and uses land from a local college for practices. But the practice fields do not have lights for evening practice, and they are not marked for standard soccer fields. Both clubs have tried to raise money to buy their own fields, but as with dance, the price of real estate is too high. Because soccer practices and games usually occur outdoors, the unpredictable weather can create further scheduling havoc if games or practices are cancelled and need to be rescheduled. Children are expected to attend rescheduled events even if they throw the delicate balance of a family's complex schedule into chaos.

Chess faces a similar problem when it comes to space, because it can be difficult to find large spaces for kids for a good price in the after-school hours. Classes and tournaments are often held in school classrooms, though getting enough space for chess tournaments even in schools is sometimes a problem, as many schools do not want to open their doors on the weekends. When schools are welcoming on the weekends, the chess organizations must pay security guards, a cost that is passed on to families in the form of increased entry fees.

Special workshops and camps during school breaks have to be held elsewhere. Sometimes they take place as group events in family apartments. Uptown-Metro Chess holds its events in a synagogue's basement. While it is not entirely surprising that many religious organizations provide space for children's activities, as they often rent space to various groups not connected to their religious community,[20] these spaces are not designed for use by children, let alone for use by any of these particular activities.

Overall, organizing these events is simultaneously straightforward and difficult. The general pattern is the same for all three activities, but space and time constraints complicate matters. Families must adjust their schedules to accommodate the demands of their children's activities. Competition organizers make decisions to maximize the number of participants, and ultimately their earnings.

REWARD STRUCTURES AND THE CARVING UP OF HONOR

The reward systems associated with these activities is part of the effort to maximize earnings. At chess, dance, and soccer competitions organizers give out prizes to those who participate. These prizes are awarded in public ceremonies that rank participants. Most often the prizes are trophies, but they are also sometimes ribbons, medals, and patches.

Awards are ubiquitous at the competitive events and in all of the activity surrounding the events. When I explained my research to people, I would often say that I study activities where a child "can win a trophy." You would not be wrong if you thought that every child seemed to get a trophy at an event. It is not uncommon for everyone to get something at every awards ceremony.

Children display the awards they win at competitions in various ways (even though they do understand the difference between participation awards and prizes they have earned, discussed more fully in chapter 6). Some do so in public, such as dance girls who hang their ribbons on their stuffed animals and soccer kids with their patches. Others display their awards in private, on bookshelves in their bedroom, and proudly point them out to visitors like me. Children sometimes bring trophies into school for show-and-tell. Some schools will display a chess trophy earned by a team that represents the school at a tournament. Kids also carry their awards through hotel lobbies, airports, and other spaces where people outside the activity can see the evidence of their skill and victory.

Sociologist William Goode has written on prizes and prestige. He explains that prizes are commonly awarded for both school and athletic achievements: "Prizes, ribbons, and medals are deemed so appropriate in athletic contests that it is difficult for most Westerners to imagine a competition . . . without such tokens of victory."[21] The trophy or ribbon is tangible proof of achievement.

Many parents I met complain that they are actually paying for this tangible evidence. In essence the entry fees pay for the award. Several joked that their son or daughter had "won" a $50 trophy.

With dance, trophies actually can be purchased. Only one trophy is awarded to a routine, even if there are fifty participants, and some children really want a trophy as opposed to "just" a ribbon. Since there are fewer trophies in dance, they seem to mean more when they are awarded—evidence that when more and more awards are given out it actually lowers the value of all prizes.

But in order to reward as many participants as possible, competition organizers use very narrow categories to distinguish participants. I call this *the carving up of honor.* Children are divided by age, then achievement (their rating or status in a flight, for example), and sometimes by the type of performance in their particular activity (jazz or tap for dance, for example). The smaller the categories, the more opportunities exist for prizes.

This is most evident in dance, where every entrant is adjudicated and receives a formal designation before being ranked.[22] Kids are still rated, and one child still gets the biggest trophy, but everyone often gets some tangible sign of their participation in a competitive event, even if it is just for the best character routine among eleven-year-olds who dance in a trio. That top or overall award is on top of receiving an adjudication ribbon.

The carving up of honor reflects two major trends, described in chapter 1. The first is the self-esteem movement, which wants everyone to feel as if they have achieved something, even though there are clear winners and losers.[23] The second is the general growth of prizes and awards in America over the twentieth century and into the twenty-first century.[24]

While it is true that awards in general help people set goals and practice diligently, it is also clear that they are a savvy business practice. Awards, and the accompanying carving up of honor, help ensure that clients return year after year. By keeping kids, parents, and teachers and coaches happy with lots of awards and recognition, the money keeps flowing.

This award structure and carving up of honor also applies to some activities past childhood. Ballroom dancing is a good example. In her study of American DanceSport professor of dance Juliet McMains explains, "Several Arthur Murray teachers recall that the importation of the English medal system in the early 1950s aided tremendously in this project to instill in their student body a regenerating desire to purchase more lessons. By dividing the syllabus into levels (bronze, silver, and gold) and specifying technical skills that had to be mastered to pass onto the next grade, teachers could more readily sell larger packages of dance lessons."[25]

A trend that is linked to the reward structures of these competitive children's activities is the growth of the commensuration process, especially in childhood. Commensuration processes rate and rank participants using numbers. Such numerical rankings have become more and more common and public in a variety of fields, from law schools to hospitals.[26] Sauder and Espeland describe a commensuration process in which "qualities are turned into quantities and difference is expressed as an interval. This commensuration produces and exposes hierarchy."[27] The tendency to produce hierarchies is surely related to the growth of prizes and competitions in American society, from dog shows to rose shows.

Commensuration of children in competitive after-school activities may be relatively new, but the practice itself is not new, even in childhood, though it does seem to be increasing. From the second a child is brought into this world he or she is labeled with a number. At birth this is the Apgar score, a score from zero to ten that a doctor uses to evaluate the health of a newborn child, and throughout early childhood it is percentiles associated with size. As a child enters the school system the identifiable number becomes a standardized test score, either an OLSAT (for entry into kindergarten) or an SAT score or a percentile (for entry into college). That this is now happening in after-school activities is a sign of the unrelenting ranking and quantifying in contemporary American childhood.

Chess, dance, and soccer numerically rank children as part of the process of determining winners. These rankings and rating structures are all public, and children and adults involved with each activity are intensely aware of where they and their friends and rivals fall in this hierarchical structure. Of the three activities chess is the most precise when it comes to commensuration, turning performance into a numeric measure, which is then used to rank children publicly according to their age, as in the Top 100 lists, described in greater detail in chapter 2. Many chess kids refer to themselves by their chess rating, for example, "I'm 850." Soccer also uses a form of commensuration, assigning children to A and B teams and then sorting them into flights within leagues based on their performance. Soccer insiders also rank teams on a national level on the Internet.[28] Dance too commensurates, separating out competitors who are "recreational" and "competitive" or "preprofessional" and "professional" and giving each routine at a competition a numeric label that then results in a categorization such as "gold" or "diamond."

There is continuous surveillance of these rankings by students, their families, and teachers, and within the local studios and clubs there is an annual evaluative process for selecting competitors that draws upon commensuration techniques. The carving up of honor can help soften the blow of a low ranking, but it doesn't hide the fact that there are micro and macro hierarchies in all competitive children's activities—and in most American kids' lives on a daily basis.

JUDGING THE SELECTION PROCESSES

Children in these competitive activities are judged and evaluated on an almost *daily* basis by those they know and by total strangers. At games and tournaments they are monitored and evaluated by judges, who may or may not be properly qualified to evaluate them. In soccer I saw referees as young as fourteen working at young kids' games. At dance competitions the qualifications of the judges are often unknown. It is somewhat strange that those who judge dog shows must have at least twelve years of experience with dogs to be considered an expert, but we don't have the same standards for those who evaluate children.[29]

In addition to formal evaluation by often dubiously credentialed judges at events, the competitive kids I met were judged on a daily basis by other adults, whom they tend to know (but who, as discussed, may have equally dubious qualifications themselves). This takes two major forms for all three activities: annual tryouts and ongoing decisions about who should participate and in what way. Such selection processes are often public, or eventually become public knowledge, adding an additional layer of internal stress and competition to children's activities. This process of internal evaluation is consistent across competitive activities.

Each year soccer and dance kids have to try out or audition to participate in their activities. This is true for many other activities, like baseball, which often has a public "draft" for selecting players.[30] Most soccer clubs hold their annual tryouts in the spring for teams that will start competing together the following fall. These are sequenced events, and parents need to know about them in advance if they want their children to have the opportunity to participate—knowledge that is often differentially distributed by class, with middle-class parents more likely to be aware of early deadlines and forms that need to be submitted than working-class parents.[31]

Both soccer clubs I worked with hold their tryouts over several days, and they bring in neutral adult evaluators to scrutinize particular skills and the overall performance of the children. There are almost always more children trying out than there are spots on a team. Coaches notify the children by phone or email whether they have been selected for the A or B team, or not at all.

Dance kids go through an arduous selection process as well. At Westbrook Let's Dance Studio the dancers have to attend an audition, similar to soccer tryouts, where they are evaluated by adults. In this case they most likely know their evaluators since they are usually their dance teachers. At the audition the girls perform a routine and get a chance to display any special dance skills they can do. Girls try out for specific routines, such as the jazz or tap routine for their age group, and they may have to try out three times to be on three different lines.

Selection procedures work differently at Elite Dance Academy. Elite does not hold an open audition for its dance company. Rather, all students are constantly under surveillance to see if they may be good enough to make the competitive team, or dance company. While this process is not nearly as torturous as the "pyramid" featured on *Dance Moms*, it is still stressful for the kids, making them feel like they exist in a panopticon, dancing under constant surveillance. At least one layer of surveillance is missing at Elite, as parents are not allowed to regularly watch classes through an observation window,[32] as on *Dance Moms*; this is an option at Let's Dance.

As described in chapter 2, at Elite teachers recommend students for the dance company based on their classroom performance and technique. Those who are invited receive a letter asking them if they would like to join the company. These letters, which also outline the requirements for participating in the dance company, are sent out in the late fall to new recruits. It is understood that previous company members will continue with the company unless there is a significant problem. However, returning company members at Elite are always being evaluated to decide which groups they will be asked to join. These decisions are communicated in a letter sent in December, before the following calendar year's competitive season. For those who want to be soloists or compete in a small group, this time is particularly stressful as they wait to hear the decision of their teachers.

Why are soccer tryouts often decided using external evaluators while dance uses an internal evaluation system? There are three related explanations. The first is that more kids try out for soccer teams, so there is a greater likelihood that a parent will complain about the process. Bringing in external evaluators who use set criteria to judge the children helps club administrators and coaches explain how decisions were made. Second, several soccer board members suggested that because the clubs have 501(c)(3) they can be sued if they do not select kids according to established guidelines. Third, because soccer itself is a more objective activity, while dance is more subjective and artistic their selection processes similarly vary.

The soccer kids not only have an intense tryout process once a year— either to make a new team or to keep a spot on their existing team—but they also compete with their teammates on a weekly basis to secure a starting position, which is more of a subjective decision on the part of the coach. On top of working to secure a starting position, they are trying to make sure that they play for as much of the game as possible. For younger kids, this is generally not for a particular position, like forward or midfielder, but the children do want to play as many minutes as possible in a game. The coaches make these decisions based on performance in practices and in previous games. If a child misses a practice, he or she may be prevented from starting a game that weekend; this was a widespread policy among the soccer coaches I interviewed.

Chess kids are also often under constant evaluation, particularly by their coaches with respect to ratings. Most chess programs do not have a formal selection procedure for including children on a team. In general, any child who can pay can enter a scholastic tournament, even those who are homeschooled.

An exception is Charter-Metro Chess, which does have a formal selection process because the program has limited resources and can send only a certain number of children to tournaments. This is not a problem for other chess programs, where families can cover expenses. Metro Chess has tournament-style games for children to compete for these positions, or they go by a child's current rating, choosing those with the highest rating in their section to decide who will participate in particular events.

On top of these formal and informal internal selection processes, there is an element of self-selection in the activities. Across all six field sites I observed what I call *the problem of the high-achieving child*. Basically, whenever there is a child who is very talented, this creates tension and jealousy among the parents of the other children. They are concerned that their own child is either just not good enough to participate or that their child will not get the same amount of attention as the extremely talented child. This leads many families to leave the activity completely or to seek a different team, teacher, or studio.

I witnessed this in a first-grade classroom affiliated with Uptown-Metro Chess. One kindergartener began performing extremely well in tournaments, starting with local and state events. At the spring nationals he was the only individual student from his school to earn a trophy, although the school team also did. By the end of the year his chess rating was over 1,000 even though he was only six years old. Fast-forward one year to the following spring nationals (which he won), and he was now the only first-grade student from his school playing competitively. The children he had played with the previous year dropped out and started other activities. It was clear from my conversations with their parents and with the coaches at that school that these families did not want to participate when their children could only ever be compared unfavorably with one of their peers. After this child won the national title at the spring chess nationals it signaled to other parents that they had made the right decision to withdraw their children from scholastic chess.

This was also an issue for Elite Dance when some of its students competed on a television show. Parents of other students from the studio left after the other dancers' success on TV. The studio owner reported that despite the dance school's public success, their enrollment did not go up because families worried that their own children were either not good enough to dance at Elite or that they would not be "stars" and receive enough of the teachers' attention. While many dance teachers want their students to be successful at dance competitions to increase their reputation and that of the studio,[33] when the scale becomes truly national, such as by being on a competitive reality television show, the stakes can change.

Soccer has similar problems related to high-achieving children, primarily with "ball hogs" and kids who score the most points. During my fieldwork Westfield could field only one team in the fifth-grade age division. The other, more advanced team in this age group had "imploded" over the summer when the top-performing boy on the team left to play on a more successful team. This led to a cascade effect, whereby many other kids left. The club and the coach could not get other kids to try out because their families assumed it was a "problem" team.

Given that many families leave when there are high-performing children in an organization, teachers and coaches, especially if they are business savvy, may be somewhat wary of producing a child or group that is *too* successful. This is because they lose immediate and future income if an entire age group leaves, which has a lasting effect over the years. While this is obviously a problem for only the most competitive organizations (and I witnessed it at only the three most competitive field sites for each activity), the possibility for conflicts around high-achieving children was apparent in chess, dance, and soccer.

CONFLICTS AND SCANDALS

Having conflicts is definitely not good for business, yet conflicts are commonplace in all of these competitive children's activities. From fights over poaching children to accusations of age manipulation, scandalous events are a fairly regular occurrence. Such controversies are not all negative, mainly because they show that these competitive children's activities are real communities made up of people who care, but they are unpleasant for those involved.[34] What's remarkable is how similar many of these controversies are across the activities.

Poaching is the source of many fights in soccer. A player is "poached" when a coach from another club's team promises the player more playing time or a position on a winning team, as discussed in chapter 2. This became so common at one point that some leagues implemented a no-transfer rule, saying that players could leave their current teams only after a season had concluded.[35] Of course, players are still poached, but at least not midseason.

Poaching also exists in dance and chess, though it is not called that by participants. Some dance studios approach dancers from nearby studios to join them. They try to lure them with reduced class rates, solos, and featured parts in group routines. A few Elite dancers have been approached by other studios, but none has left. Chess coaches sometimes tell parents that their child is playing the wrong opening or does not know the best endgame strategies, claiming they can teach the child better chess technique. This lays the groundwork to poach that student as their own.

Not surprisingly coaches and teachers fight over any perceived interference with their students, and these fights can sometimes include accusations of cheating. At a chess tournament I attended two coaches got into a shouting match (in front of the children) when one coach, who was also acting as a tournament director (TD) and referee, ruled in favor of his student and against the other child during a disagreement over a move. The coach of the other child intervened, insisting that the playing clock should be reset. Their argument escalated to the point that the non-TD coach was removed from the tournament room, causing many children to get upset. Parents whose children were students of that coach decided to stop attending those tournaments for the rest of the year as a protest against the TD, who they believed acted inappropriately.

Dance teachers also told me about teachers from other studios encouraging their students to move their competitors' costumes and props backstage so the kids would have trouble finding them. I never saw any direct confrontations during my fieldwork, but I heard about them. When complaints were made, they were lodged with the competition owners and directors, who were expected to act as intermediaries.

Conflicts of interest between judges and teachers are another common complaint voiced at dance competitions. A dance studio may have previously brought in a judge as a guest teacher or choreographer, only to be judged by them at a national event. No rules exist to have a judge abstain from judging students from a particular studio.

Another common charge is choreography theft. At competitions I heard teachers comment that a competitor's routine looked very similar to one of their previously successful dances. In general, choreography theft seems to be less of a problem than it once was, partly because personal video cameras are not allowed in competitions. (Of course this is hard to enforce now, with cell phone cameras, and I easily found copies of routines on YouTube.) Theft used to be rampant in competitive dance, one reason personal recording devices are not allowed; the other reason is based on profits: competitions mark up the cost of video recordings and make money on that service as well. To purchase a copy of a routine, a parent must obtain the signature of the dance teacher. Though the signature can be forged, this process seems to have stopped many of the theft issues, until YouTube came along.

A more frequent complaint across all three activities—and the basis of scandal when the accusations are founded—is about the alleged age of competitors. I never saw outright lying in any of these activities, though it definitely happens (as in the second episode of Season Two of *Dance Moms*). The stringent carding procedures in soccer to verify children's birth dates (described in chapter 2) were developed in response to parents placing older children on younger teams.[36]

Perhaps the most notorious case of a parent lying about the age of a child was not in chess, dance, or soccer, but in Little League baseball. In 2001, during the Little League World Series in Williamsport, Pennsylvania, Danny Almonte's father and coach forged the boy's identification papers, saying he was twelve. Danny was actually fourteen and hence ineligible to play Little League. After he pitched a no-hitter and led his team to a third-place finish, the deception was discovered and the team's placement was stripped.[37]

Other cases are less extreme, but do occur, and in a range of activities. In her work on girls' softball Jennifer Ring says that savvy parents try to schedule conception so that a child will be older than her peers in her birth year.[38] Other parents, like Almonte's, simply tamper with birth certificates to give them an edge because older children are more advanced physically, mentally, and emotionally, which helps them succeed in competitive arenas.

Giving children an edge in terms of age has the biggest effect in athletics (known as the "relative age effect"), but it also affects scholastics.[39] In a practice known as "academic red-shirting" children, especially boys, are held back by parents from entering kindergarten, sometimes at the suggestion of teachers but the decision is often made based on their own initiative.[40] A handful of the chess boys I met were red-shirted in preschool or prekindergarten, and one even in grade school. As with sports, some parents will report "timing the conception of their children with [academic] redshirting in mind."[41]

Notably, redshirting basically did not exist fifty years ago. This process would not exist today if there were not competitive consequences in being behind in the competitive hierarchy. This is additional evidence, on top of the presence of these competitive kids' activities and processes like commensuration, that there are now structures in place to help put kids in the best position to feed into a system of competitive positioning that is happening earlier and earlier in their lives.

Of course, redshirting is not cheating per se, but it is certainly gaming the system. Many of the parents and teachers I met have learned to manipulate competitive activity systems to maximize a child's chance of winning. For instance, some dance routines include younger children to bring down the average age of the group.

Others take advantage of competition fallbacks. Kids can compete in a younger age division based on their "fallback" age. Some events use January 1 has the age cutoff for an event; others use the child's age within thirty days of the competition. This means that a competitor who is seven years and thirty-one days may be competing against someone who is nine years and twenty-nine days—a big difference in physical and mental maturity at that life stage. To prevent an age advantage in dance competitions there is a uniform age cut-off, usually January 1, rather than one based on the date of the competition.

I also saw manipulation of the age and rating categories take place in chess. Some parents took advantage of a K–3 grouping rather than a K–5 grouping (especially meaningful when some boys were older than their third-grade peers due to redshirting). Several would manipulate a child's rating by not letting him or her play in tournaments before the three-month publication by the UCSF. This would help keep the children in a lower section, where they could play at a higher strength than their opponents, to increase their winning chances—quite common before a major tournament like Nationals. Other parents, even those from the same school, got upset about this manipulation because it affected the composition of the school's team, and hence their own child's ability to win a team award.

Parents' willingness to game the system across activities shows that they are sometimes more concerned with their children's winning record, even in a manipulated system, than getting a fair outcome. The focus is often on winning at any cost, a lesson that gets passed on to the children. Many teachers I met relate to this win-at-any-cost mentality, particularly those who emigrated from formerly communist countries. These teachers and coaches are used to a system that supports lying about a child's age, as many formerly communist countries were, and still are, willing to do.[42]

I had not expected, and was quite struck by, the presence of so many teachers and coaches in chess, dance, and soccer from formerly communist countries, particularly those from Eastern Europe. With all three activities I met adults who had come to the United States during the Cold War or right after who capitalized on the expertise they developed in their home countries. The Russian way of teaching ballet is of long standing, and Elite has had Russian teachers teach their students ballet. Chess too has also long been associated with Russia, so it was somewhat less surprising that many chess teachers were Russian or from the former Yugoslavia, where chess had been popular. Several soccer coaches I met also hail from Eastern Europe; the head coach of Westfield Soccer Club grew up in Romania, where he developed in a state-sponsored soccer academy.

Obviously the United States provides financial opportunities related to these activities not available in other countries, which helps explain why these teachers brought their talents and skills to America. While none of the parents I met said that they trusted these coaches' expertise more because of their countries of origin (in fact, the only comments made about their immigrant status were negative, when parents complained about misunderstandings due to the language barrier), the coaches themselves said that they felt they got more respect given what their accents signified. One soccer coach told me he felt his accent gave him instant authority as an expert. It makes sense that parents of the *Sputnik* generation, who saw the sports dominance of the USSR, are eager to combine the accomplishment-focused attitude of their American children with the expertise of coaches from the former communist bloc.[43]

But the communist system put an emphasis on the coach, not the parent, as the primary leader making decisions about a child's competitive career in an activity. Such a system also expects a near total commitment to one activity, which means not trying many different activities. Obviously things are very different in the contemporary United States. Unyielding allegiance to a coach is quite uncommon, as most parents believe they know best for their child, and they are not always shy about voicing their opinions. Children are also used to doing many different things and may be unwilling to specialize when their coach wants them to do so. So while some respect is accorded coaches based on their background, conflicts between parents and coaches easily and often arise.

Role confusion is a frequent source of this conflict. Because the position of coach or teacher is not professionalized when it comes to children's activities there is often debate about whether teachers are entrepreneurs, babysitters, or educators. Coaches and teachers often see themselves as professionals in their fields, but some parents see them as their employees, or as caretakers (as shown in their willingness to submit receipts for child care tax reimbursements). For example, I often heard about parents getting upset when a teacher or coach would not stay with a child when the parent was late in retrieving a child from a lesson or practice; I heard this described from both the parental and the teacher perspectives. Coaches found this behavior disrespectful and offensive, while parents believed that because they paid for lessons, the teacher should stay.

One Elite Dance Academy teacher recounted a story to me about a mother who arrived nearly an hour late to pick up her daughter from a solo rehearsal. The mother did not call to say she would be late. Despite the fact that the teacher lived nearly one hour away, she had to wait with the little girl since she did not feel she could leave her alone. By the time the mother finally arrived, with no apology or excuse, the teacher was livid and told the mom that this was unacceptable behavior. The mother reacted negatively and proceeded to write a letter of complaint to the owner of Elite Dance Academy. When I spoke with the mother she offered this incident on her own as evidence that the teachers at the dance studio are not understanding of parents' situations. This mother felt that given the money she pays in tuition, it was acceptable to make the teacher wait until she arrived.

I also saw parents become quite upset with teachers and coaches when they seemed to favor another child over their own. One situation I observed during my fieldwork became especially vicious. Lois, described in chapter 3, was very active in organizing the chess team in her daughter's school. She became quite upset when she thought the coach favored other students, both within her school and from other schools. Because this teacher was in the country illegally—from a formerly communist country—this mother convinced her daughter's private school to fire him by threatening to report the school for employing an illegal immigrant.

While this was an extreme case, during my time in the field I also saw many other coaches and teachers leave organizations or be fired because of conflicts with parents.

Conflicts between parents are less common (and less common than some reality television shows would have you believe based on my observations), but they do arise in all of these activities.[44] I saw parental conflict arise in the organizations that were controlled by a small, inner circle of parents. These groups of parents can be described as the "powers that be"[45]—or, more simply, cliques.

During my fieldwork the parent board members of Westfield Soccer Club got into a large argument about the best way to train kids, resulting in the resignation of about half of the board. (Recall from chapter 2 that the clubbiness of this group of parents was part of the reason I labeled this the "club" and not the "co-op" soccer field site.) Nasty emails were exchanged, and the tension at board meetings I attended was palpable.

While these parents were not motivated by money, as are coaches, they were motivated to make sure their children were in situations to maximize their chances of success, both in the short term with these specific activities and in the long term by applying the skills they learn from participating in these competitive activities and acquiring Competitive Kid Capital. Some of the parents, especially mothers, who had given up full-time careers to parent seemed particularly invested in these small-scale conflicts and were interested in gaining leadership positions. Because parental volunteers are needed in all three activities to help make the competitive process run smoothly teachers and coaches were often drawn into these conflicts in order to protect their financial interests.

It is remarkable that all of these competitive activities, which differ so much in content, are structured in similar ways in terms of their organization, awards, selection procedures, and even conflicts. The same can be said of a variety of other competitive activities, from music competitions to youth racecar driving and competitive cheer.[46] Other competitive children's activities that are similar to dance in terms of physical performance combined with an aesthetic dimension are ballroom dancing, child beauty pageants, figure skating, gymnastics, Irish dancing, and syn-chronized swimming.[47] Children's athletics—golf, football, Little League baseball, softball, tennis, and even mutton busting[48]—are also alike. Intel-lectual activities, such as competitive bridge, Scrabble, and spelling, aren't immune either.[49] All of these kids' activities share major structural elements that unite them, creating a subculture of competitive child-hood. If you have experience as a former competitor or competitive par-ent in these other activities, many of the descriptions of chess, dance, and soccer will strike a chord with you.

Competitive subcultures dominated by adults (for example, dog and ferret shows, competitive eating, and even competitive gardening) also share similar structures and scandals.[50] In America we can make any-thing competitive, even for the youngest participants. The carving up of honor knows no age limits.

While all of these activities remain largely unregulated, they strive for a veneer of professionalism by implementing rules. This is especially important when it comes to children's activities because of concerns about sexual and physical abuse.[51]

Given the stakes—including physical and emotional trauma—more must be done to protect kids in all after-school activities. Regulation of after-school coaches, mentors, and volunteers is so lax, and in some cases nonexistent, that many never undergo a routine background check to make sure they have never been convicted of child molestation. That means that some of the "professionals" paid to teach children in after-school activities may have previously been convicted, charged, or accused of child mo-lestation. At a minimum, all fifty states should require mandatory, na-tional, fingerprint-based background checks of all adults who interact with children (legally defined as those eighteen years and under).

But is that adequate? No. In addition to making sure that the basics are covered—like those background checks regarding child molestation and CPR certification—parents should make sure that coaches are experts in their area, with training in both the substantive subject matter (piano, chess, soccer, etc.) and instruction of children. State legislation that certi-fies youth activity coaches and organizations would make that process easier.

As I discovered, at present anyone can open a dance studio or a chess school or show up as a soccer camp counselor, and no one can stop him or her from charging fees for services. Essentially no formal certification procedures exist to make sure that the tap teacher, the oboe instructor, or the lacrosse coach who parents write a check to each month is qualified to instruct children in tap, the oboe, or lacrosse. Imagine if we ran schools this way.

While many of the teachers I met do want to professionalize their fields to give them more authority and gravitas, others resist. They assert that we should not live in a nanny state that tells parents what they should and should not do with their kids. But this used to be said about day care centers. After one too many accidents and one too many child molestation cases, this changed as the need to protect children and provide parents with safe options became more important.

This is also true of many summer camps. In her history of summer camps in the United States, Leslie Paris writes, "Camp leaders noted the ease with which anyone could start up a camp, regardless of qualifications."[52] Today summer camps, especially sleep-away camps, are better regulated (though they still lack strong state and national regulations when it comes to health and safety standards and what defines a camp counselor). When will better regulation come for children's after-school activities, especially competitive activities, where it is easier for some entrepreneurs to prey on parents' insecurities? Obviously not all teachers and coaches are like this, but parents need to be cautious and thoroughly investigate a program and its teachers' qualifications before writing any tuition checks as they seek to build their child's stock of competitive capital.

Until better regulations exist, competitions themselves can help establish the credibility of an instructor. They provide checks on the skills of teachers and coaches. In addition to helping support adults involved in the cottage industries surrounding children's competitive activities, competitions allow parents to discern whether their investment in the business of competitive children's activities is a sound one for their kids, at least in the short-term.

But parents are also very obviously concerned about the long term when it comes to their children's lives. Some are not aware of the elaborate structures around these competitive activities, which are designed to attract and keep parents by taking advantage of concerns about children's futures through advertisements and talk at events, while other parents know these are businesses and resist accordingly some of the upsell and pressure.

Whether or not parents understand the infrastructure behind competitive children's activities, it is clear, as I have demonstrated in previous chapters, that they see these activities as playing a crucial role in the overall development of their children through the cultivation of Competitive Kid Capital. While we don't have longitudinal data to see how these activities specifically impact kids over the long term, we can listen to what children think in the present. In the final chapter I discuss my interactions with the children themselves to see how their parents' decisions impact them and to assess how much Competitive Kid Capital they seem to be acquiring from the adults in their lives.

SIX Trophies, Triumphs, and Tears

COMPETITIVE KIDS IN ACTION

Outside the streets are covered in dirty slush, flecked with bits of the fresh, white snow that continues to fall on this cold March day.[1] Inside the office is warm, but the sound of car horns intruding on our conversation reminds us of the snowstorm clogging traffic twelve floors below. I am sitting this Friday afternoon talking about the career of the person sitting behind the large, wooden desk.

Max is white, Jewish, and nine years old, a fourth-grade student in the Talented and Gifted program at a public school in Metro. He is telling me about the evolution of his "chess career" with Uptown-Metro Chess. He sits in the large black swivel chair behind his dad's desk, and his voice sometimes fades in and out as he spins himself around in the chair while he lists all the chess tournaments he has played in since first grade.

"My first first-place win was at a Fox tournament, but in the kindergarten–first grade section, so it wasn't that hard."

"No, that's impressive," I respond, since Fox tournaments are some of the most difficult scholastic events in Metro.

Max modestly laughs and goes on, "And then I started to win other tournaments. What else did I win? Ummm, well, I went to PS 412, and this you wouldn't really say is a win. You wouldn't really call this a first-place win because I could have played in another section that would have been better for me. But I played in this easier section with six quick games and I easily won all of them. . . . I won that, but you wouldn't really call it a win."

"It's still a win," I respond.

"Yeah, but it wasn't really a great win," Max explains.

Over the next few minutes Max details the rest of his wins in the past three years, telling me about particular games in particular tournaments (for example: "In that game I started to play fast, so he started to play fast and I ended up winning that game and that's how I won the tournament"). As he nears the end of his "time," as he calls it, he points out that he has won a first-place trophy in a tournament every year since he has started competing. But Max is seriously worried about continuing this streak, which weighs heavily on him.

"Three straight years playing chess—first-place trophy—and I'm not sure it's going to be four."

"There's still time," I point out, since it is only mid-March.

Dejected, Max hangs his head, deeply uncertain about his prospects. He has reached the age when, in order to really progress in scholastic chess, a player has to study a few hours every day and usually have a weekly private lesson with a chess master. Max loves his school team, but it is clear that, to him, it is most important to have that first-place trophy that is only his.

Max's description of his competitive chess career and the themes he hit on—such as individual versus team success and the importance of a trophy—were echoed by the thirty-six other chess, dance, and soccer children I interviewed. I wanted to know what they think about their participation in competitive activities, how they experience competition in general (in addition to all the preparation for specific competitions), and if their experiences match up with what their parents want them to learn.

Examining these sorts of questions is in line with the paradigm shift in childhood studies, which says that researchers should take seriously what children think and not assume we always know what is best for them.[2] My findings are consistent with the body of work by scholars like Carol Dweck,[3] which argues that evaluative events and rewards have complex effects on children's motivation. Through conversations with kids like Max and observations at practice and at play, I discovered that children learn to accurately read between the lines of such parental exhortations as "Do your best!" and understand that their parents *actually* want them to win. It may surprise many, given negative conversations about overpressured children in the media, that I find most of the elementary school–age kids I met generally have fun while doing these activities with their friends, while still acquiring Competitive Kid Capital.

CONVERSATIONS WITH KIDS

As I did with their parents, I interviewed all thirty-seven children either in their home, a bookstore, the public library, or a parent's office.[4] Children were formally interviewed only after I had conducted formal interviews with one or both of their parents. For almost all of the interviews I first broached the subject of doing kid interviews, but three times a parent independently suggested I talk to his or her child. I rarely encountered resistance from parents about having their child interviewed; only one father explicitly said he was not comfortable with his son doing an interview.[5] Two parents told me that the children themselves declined to be interviewed after they had asked them to participate.[6]

The interviews with the children were much shorter than the adult interviews, both due to the number of questions I asked and the length of their responses. The child interviews lasted, on average, forty-one minutes (compared to a little over an hour and a half for parents), so they were about half as long. This is consistent with other researchers who find that adults tend to provide longer answers, sometimes as a monologue, and have an agenda for what they want to say or discuss in an interview, while children do not.[7] Consequently my children's quotes are, on the whole, shorter than adult quotes and in many cases are presented as exchanges. Notably, younger kids tended to give the shortest responses.

Table 3 summarizes some key characteristics of the children I interviewed. I interviewed an almost equal number of boys and girls. The majority of the children are part of middle-class or upper-middle-class families, and these characteristics are similar to the parents I formally

Table 3. Descriptive Data on Children Interviewed

	Children (%) N = 37
Sex	
Girls	51
Boys	49
Class	
Upper-middle	46
Middle-middle	38
Lower-middle	8
Working	8
Ethnicity of Child	
Caucasian	76
Other	24
Private School	
Yes	27
No (Attend public school)	73
Age	
6–7	16
8–9	46
10–12	38
Immigrant Status	
Both parents born in U.S.	68
At least one parent born outside U.S.	32

interviewed. The majority of the children I interviewed are non-Hispanic white; the rest are from a variety of minority groups, with three mixed-race children (twins who are black and Asian and one boy who is Hispanic and black), three Asian children, two African American children, and one Hispanic child. Included here are eight sets of siblings: the mixed-race twins, two sets of sisters, one brother and sister pair, and the rest sets of brothers (one a set of three brothers). Of these, thirteen of the children participate in chess, thirteen in soccer, and eleven in dance. Two dance girls also participate in travel soccer, two soccer boys also do competitive chess, and two chess boys also participate in travel soccer; note that there is no overlap between dance and chess.

REWARDS FOR WINNING: TROPHIES, RIBBONS, AND PATCHES, OH MY!

We know that parents of competitive children want their kids to internalize the importance of winning. One of the major ways this happens is at the award ceremonies at the end of competitions, when trophies, ribbons, patches, medals, plaques, and other celebratory totems are distributed. Often these items become an extrinsic reason for continued participation in an activity, as the various prizes teach the kids that when you win, you are rewarded—which makes winning their primary focus.

Trophies in particular are shiny, golden carrots for kids. These often ugly and cheap-looking pieces of plastic and metal are central to children's understanding of why they do an activity. Trophies are also often the number one reason the kids give to explain why they like participating in an activity. I asked one seven-year-old chess girl, "What do you like about chess?" and she replied straightforwardly, "Because I get the trophy!"

When I asked the child competitors what they like about trophies, most of them focused on the physical attributes of the trophies themselves. One boy told me, "They're beautiful. I like the gold, but they always use gold. The ones mixed with silver I really like." Another boy told me, "They are shiny, and you can bring them to show-and-tell." A girl explained succinctly, "I like the big ones." Another girl explained, "Well my favorites are the big ones because I feel like I won bigger and better on those."

With the trophies' size and shiny details, kids vastly prefer trophies to medals and ribbons. A dancer explained, "I like the trophies because they're bigger and they have more design to them. The ribbons are just a ribbon that says something on it."

Even if the awards are "only" ribbons, the children like to display the spoils of their victories. Ribbons are most common in dance because each member of the group gets a ribbon for each routine at each competition. Trophies are awarded, but often only for overall awards, and Let's Dance and Elite keep the winning trophy and put it on display. Most girls are in multiple routines and compete at several competitions a year, so the ribbons quickly pile up. The ribbons themselves are of different colors, depending on the judges' evaluations, and they are imprinted with the words *First, Second, Third* or *High Gold, Gold,* or *Silver.*

The common way that competition dancers keep all their ribbons to-gether is by getting a stuffed animal—one girl told me she has seen "a giraffe, a bear, and any animal you can think of"—and hanging the rib-bons around the neck or arms of the stuffed animal. The girls carry their stuffed animals on stage during award ceremonies and bring them to competitions for good luck. A competitor from Let's Dance explained, "At competitions I have a good luck charm named Lucky and it's a bear and I have all my ribbons and stuff on it. It's just like a real teddy bear and I put everything on it. I wish I could add more to it so that I know that I'm improving. Everybody has their ribbons on their bears!"

Bears and stuffed animals covered in ribbons are in fact ubiquitous at competitions, and the desire for ever more ribbons is evident. But with so many ribbons collected, most of the girls could not tell me where each one was won or for what routine. A few moms I met will label each one so their daughters do not forget where it came from, but that is far from the norm. As the Let's Dance dancer's comment suggests, the ribbons also function as a way for children to gauge how much they are improving in their activity.

Soccer kids have a similar system, though instead of ribbons they get patches, which sometimes are also called badges. The patches are placed, either with safety pins or by adhering them with glue, on the backpacks kids use to hold their gear at practices and tournaments. However, these patches often only signal attendance, not a specific placement in an event, as the dance ribbons do. For example, when I attended a state soccer expo, players who attended received a patch for their attendance, even though no games were played.

The soccer kids are aware of this distinction. A girl from Westfield Soccer Club said, "It's not like Boy Scout badges,[8] which say you did great. It's just like for being there. Like I have the badge from the NCAA tournament where University of Connecticut played, [but] I didn't play. But the badges help me remember tournaments and stuff that I went to."

In addition to the patches, soccer kids are passionate about trophies, which they win by doing well in a tournament. One boy explained the hierarchy of soccer rewards: "Patches is when you trade with the team that you had a game against, which is only in tournaments really. Then medals—most of them are for participation, like everyone gets one for participation. But I think the winning team and the second-place team *only* get a trophy." He had not yet been on a team that won a trophy at a tournament. Trophies are a highly valued form of currency and clearly at the top of the award hierarchy in soccer. Because most soccer kids attend only one or two tournaments a year there are fewer opportunities to acquire this hardware.

In contrast, chess kids have many more opportunities to collect trophies annually. Elementary school–age chess kids who play in scholastic events often get a trophy, a medal, or a similar reward at every tournament. Given that the chess kids I interviewed played in an average of six or seven tournaments per year, they have a lot of award hardware. In this case it is the size of the trophy that ends up mattering most.

When a child wins a trophy his or her parents usually put it on display somewhere at home. When I visited kids in their homes the trophies were usually in their bedroom. John, a fourth-grader who lives in Metro, exhibited great pride as he showed me all of his trophies, which were lined up in his bedroom. John had two shelves on his wall, opposite his bed, built specially by his dad to hold his trophies from sports and chess. He told me, "Well, I only keep the main ones here. The others are in the basement. [Starts pointing to particular trophies.] This is my first first-place trophy. Fox and University are some of my favorites, but PS 725 has good ones too. At least they are the tallest. I also like the ones that have the nice design on top [such as a castle or king]."

One of John's most insightful observations about trophies was this: "Some of my friends just like to have a lot of trophies. You can have a million last-place trophies, but that's not as important as having one first-place trophy." Not surprisingly, John values his chess trophies, especially the ones that signify he received a high placement, more than his sports participation trophies.

John and many of the other chess children I met are quite knowledgeable about the meaning of their awards. Another boy, gesturing to some trophies in his collection that he had received for participating in tennis and hockey seasons, explained, "Those aren't really *place* trophies, they are just *participation* trophies. When I count my trophies I only count the ones I won." Such statements contradict media reports and educational philosophies that claim every child needs to be a winner so participation trophies should be the norm.[9]

An exception is kids who participate in a competitive event for the first time. The first trophy appears to hold special significance. The children I met could easily recall the first trophy they received and the first trophy they won—an important distinction—so we might think of these first awards as similar to the practice of framing the first dollar earned, which indicates its important symbolic value. While John's first participation trophy was packed away in the basement (but recall that he keeps his first first-place trophy on display), he easily remembered the tournament he played in when he won it: "Well, the first trophy I ever got was at a tournament that my chess teacher organized. I got two and a half points out of four."

From my observations at scholastic chess tournaments, those in kindergarten and first grade tend to remain extremely excited about any trophy, whether earned or awarded for mere participation. This is consistent with psychological research, which finds that it is not until age nine that children begin to fully understand that effort is necessary for success.[10]

However, when I spoke to some of these kids they demonstrated a more complex understanding, similar to older elementary school–age kids. One first-grader, Daisuke, whom I discuss more below, told me, "My first tournament was a long time ago [in kindergarten]. . . . Everybody had the same trophy. I got the same as everyone." Perhaps because he went on to win a first-place trophy while in first grade, that first participation trophy has decreased in value.

As kids become exposed to more hierarchical competition at younger ages through these activities, some of the existing literature on kids and competition may need to be revisited, as Daisuke's experiences show. Overall for the vast majority of the competitive kids I interviewed, the first participation trophy (whether for chess, dance, soccer, skiing, basketball, cheer, softball, or other sport) and the first first-place trophy in a specific activity hold special significance for kids. They remember both but can distinguish the importance between them as well.

One other trophy exception to note is that in dance, trophies can be purchased. Recall from chapter 2 that dance parents have the option of buying a trophy for their child at most competitions (in theory, even for a place they did not win) for $40 and more (despite the fact that the trophies often do not cost more than $5 to make). Two of the dance moms had done so for their daughters, even though the women felt it was a little ridiculous. I spoke to one of the girls from Let's Dance whose mother bought her a trophy, and she did not see the bought trophy as less worthy, since she had won the placement—the trophy was just on top of the ribbon. The other girl, a fourth-grader with Elite, did say she had more pride in "the ones [she] got from dancing, not the ones [her] mom buys [her]."

Other dancers, when asked about buying trophies, agreed with this Elite dancer. They told me that they thought a bought trophy was not the same thing as a trophy awarded. A few of the dance girls told me that they wished they had more trophies to go with their ribbons, but they understand why their studios keep them and only one is awarded per routine, since it is a group effort. As a consequence, though, they frequently don't know which trophy they helped win. The same Elite dancer whose mom bought her a dance trophy of her own explained, "Our dance school is so full of trophies I don't really know [which ones are hers]."

For many kids, a trophy is great, but it is not the ultimate reward. On top of the awards competitions give out, some parents give their children their own rewards for doing well. Many kids get rewarded by their families for doing well at the end of a school year; kids specifically mentioned money, such as $20 for a good report card, or larger rewards like a trip to the American Girl store. The rewards I discuss below refer only to performance in competitive after-school activities.

The children openly speak about these material rewards, though they never refer to them as bribes.[11] Kids know that they must win or do very well, achieving some personal victory in a competition, to get these parental "trophies." One soccer boy explained what will happen when he reaches a particular soccer-related goal: "Right now I'm working towards 80 juggles with a soccer ball. I just passed 40, which was very good for me, so I just got a trip to the ice cream store and next time I do that I get an ice cream sundae. When I get 80 I get an ice cream sundae." A chess boy similarly reports his parents offering food as a reward for winning: "They took me out to dinner because I beat some 1,100 [rated player] when I was 900." Food, along with other treats, is offered to dance girls as well. Here is an excerpt from my conversation with a dancer about this:

NATALIA: Every time I go to a competition or I do a show, there's always something waiting for me.

HILARY: Like what?

NATALIA: Flowers, candy or going out to eat.

As Natalia mentioned, some kids get other small rewards, such as flowers. Other kids told me about more age-specific rewards they get from their parents for winning or attaining a personal goal at an event. John, the proud chess player with many trophies, explained to me what happened after he did well in a chess tournament:

JOHN: We kind of get to do something that, well, just something really special. Like get a pack of cards or get something, just really special, like watch TV all night.

HILARY: Did you get something special a couple of weeks ago?

JOHN: Yes.

HILARY: What did you get?

JOHN: I got a couple of Pokemon cards.

Games were popular rewards, and video games were one of the more desirable rewards. Another chess boy reported, "My dad said that after the city tournament I can buy a new video game." Even better than a video game is a personal video game player, such as a Game Boy. Recall that when Lottie, described at the beginning of chapter 4, earns enough points she can earn video games and even a video gaming system.

A different chess player told me that after he broke 1,000 in rating points he is supposed to get a big reward. He usually got video games for chess accomplishments, but for breaking 1,000 he was getting an even bigger parental prize:

HILARY: When you got over a 1,000, did you get a new game?

WAYNE: My dad didn't buy a Game Boy DS for me yet.

HILARY: But you're going to get it?

WAYNE: Yeah.

Dance girls also get many parental rewards, some of which can be pricey. Lauren, an Elite dancer, explained the three types of rewards she typically gets from her mom at each competition and at the end of a competitive season:

HILARY: What about with dance? If you guys get platinum or overall?

LAUREN: My mom gets me teddy bears or stuff [at the competition] if I do well.

HILARY: Do you guys usually get the program?[12]

LAUREN: I keep all the different programs from all the different
competitions. I got them in my room. So yes, I get a lot of
those.

HILARY: Do you circle your name?

LAUREN: Yes. I highlight it with a little highlighter.

As kids get older they expect more than an ice cream or video games
from their parents and more than a simple trophy from competition organizers. In chess and dance this means monetary prizes. Some scholastic chess tournaments award other prizes, including chess software or
wooden sets, even iPods, to older, advanced children instead of trophies.[13]
Chess player John told me he would rather win an iPod than a trophy,
and he thinks he can if he works hard enough for three or four more
years. Once money is involved, kids start to become motivated by real
scrip, as opposed to what was once a simple (fake) gold, shiny trophy.

With so many types of awards available, it is easy to understand how
kids can become extrinsically motivated and focused on rewards rather
then on the intrinsic process of learning and competing to improve oneself.[14] Children who are solely extrinsically motivated by prizes may drop
out of their activity if they do not continue to get trophies and other types
of rewards. In their classic work on middle-class preschool children, mentioned in the preface, Lepper and Greene find that those who expect to get
a reward from doing a particular activity, and who perform under adult
surveillance, are less interested in that activity in the future.[15] Notably, the
reward they used in the experiment was a certificate with a gold seal and
ribbon, awarded to children for drawing pictures. Lepper and Greene explain that the introduction of a reward can turn play into work.[16]

Perhaps unaware of the consequences of too many awards—or, more
simply, with an eye to keeping competitors and their families happy and
coming back—many competitions have created various categories to
help ensure that every child "wins" a prize, which results in the carving
up of honor described in chapter 5. It is no longer enough to be awarded a
trophy or ribbon, even with their shared symbolic property of being "tangible proof of victory."[17] Just any trophy will no longer do, particularly

when so many are offered. Like Veruca Salt in Roald Dahl's *Charlie and the Chocolate Factory*,[18] many want the biggest reward possible. Since children are smart enough to know when they did not truly win, the trophy can eventually become a reminder of a failure or disappointment instead of an accomplishment. So in addition to learning about the value of an earned reward, kids also learn how to interpret the carving up of honor, and they are not always happy with the system.

By learning this skill, another skill that parents really want their kids to learn is put into potential jeopardy: learning how to lose but to come back and win. If children see that they are not getting many awards, especially the biggest trophies and prizes, they can get so discouraged that they drop out. This is evident in Max's concerns about what a "real" win means.

As children become more experienced competitors, they become savvier as well. They learn how to read a competitive situation. Kids also know when they could have competed against a more difficult opponent, as Max pointed out, so they know when they just went for an easy victory and trophy. As a consequence, that trophy, or even video game, means less to them. On the whole, though, all of these rewards are teaching children that winning is the most important thing.

FACING THE JUDGES AND BEING RATED: NERVES AND LUCKY CHARMS

In order to get their various prizes these competitive kids have to face judges and evaluators. Being evaluated is part of the everyday lives of child competitors, and they frequently talk about feeling nervous when they have to perform or be judged. If trophies, ribbons, and patches are the end goal, dealing with nerves and performing under pressure are the means to this end as children build up their Competitive Kid Capital. Kids' thoughts on how to deal with their nerves shows that they understand and process three of the elements of Competitive Kid Capital: dealing with time pressure, coping with stressful situations, and performing under the gaze of others.

This is especially true in competitive dance. Competitive dancers are not just formally judged at three to five competitions a year; they also perform at recitals at least once a year and go through a selection process for competition groups. These kids, regularly faced with assessments by adults, have developed different ways to view their evaluations and steady their nerves.

In general, Elite dancers are far more concerned with what their teachers think of their performances than about the evaluations of judges at formal competitions. The teachers at Elite Dance Academy do not explicitly share the judges' comments with their students. Because of this, their students care more about a "good performance" than the results of any particular competition (so long as they keep accumulating ribbons).

Elite dancers told me they wanted to please their teachers and perform better at each competition (note that unlike on *Dance Moms,* both dance studios compete the same routines at each competition, not different ones each time). Their teachers are often more critical than the judges. Destiny told me, "We did horrible at one competition but the judges thought we did good so we still had platinum. But our teacher didn't. The next day she said she didn't know what was bringing us down." According to social psychologists, this focus on process more than winning is the right strategy for long-term growth and achievement.[19]

Students from Westbrook's Let's Dance Studio, on the other hand, are primarily worried about the judges' assessments. Their teacher actually reads the comments from judges' sheets or plays the tapes the judges made commenting on the routine. Nine-year-old Jennie explained how this works: "When we're dancing they'll have microphones and speak into the microphone and we'll get a tape. They'll say what they thought, 'Point your toe,' or something like that. They're [the tapes] funny because some judge will hum to the music." Jennie told me that she does not hear what the judges say when she is on stage, but she can see them talking into the microphone. She does find their comments—to point toes, straighten arms, or other similar details—helpful, and she thinks the group does get better after hearing an evaluation. But unlike Destiny's concern about her teachers, the primary focus for Jennie and her friends at Let's Dance is on what color ribbon the judges award them.

Whether being evaluated by teachers or judges, all the dancers I talked to have to learn how to deal with nerves. Veronica is nine and had just finished her third year with the company at Elite Dance Academy when we spoke at a bookstore near her home. She informed me that to combat her nerves at competitions she usually "looks over the judges out into the audience," meaning she pays them hardly any attention. Peering at me through her wire-rimmed glasses, Veronica went on to say that she does not get nervous before every competition; she only gets nervous, she says, "When it's the first time doing a routine and then [I] get used to it. It's always like that, I don't know why, every year." When it is the first time for a routine Veronica reports that she "has one of my friends tickle me and then I'm not nervous anymore!"

Other techniques dancers use to combat the occasional bout of nerves, which most agree occurs only before they premiere a new routine, are extra practice and prayer. Christina of Elite Dance Academy told me about a good luck charm she uses, tied to her religious beliefs: "When I was little I always said I wanted to be like St. Lucy, so my principal gave me this little necklace for my birthday with a cross on it. I always carry it around with me and I pray before my competitions and the night before with it." Another dancer from Elite described the ritual she goes through prior to a competition: "I have a four-leaf clover up in my room and every time before a competition I go pick it up and say, 'I hope I do good.' I kiss it and put it back."

Just like the dancers, chess and soccer kids get nervous before games. Also like the dance girls, they told me about getting nervous when in a new competitive situation, like playing in a section or soccer flight for the first time.[20] They mentioned similar tactics for coping with nerves, such as good luck charms (though none of them mentioned prayer), along with some other ways they deal with the stress of competition. One eight-year-old boy who plays soccer for Westfield Soccer Club and participates in West County Chess told me quite honestly that when he gets nervous, he "sweat[s] a lot." When he gets nervous during chess tournaments he "gets up to go to the bathroom and then puts some water on [his] face."

Tristan, who is eight years old and also plays with West County Chess, uses a different strategy to calm his nerves. He tries to convince his opponent that he is a better player than he is, especially if his opponent has a higher rating. Tristan said, "I try to go like this," and he showed me how he uses his hands to shield his eyes from his opponent, holding his head down in his hands. This is a technique used by professional players so opponents cannot see where their eyes are looking on the chess board. Tristan likes using this technique as a sign to his opponents that they need to "stretch their minds" to play him because he "is not easy" to play against.

Just as Tristan shields his eyes, Veronica mentioned that dancers deliberately disregard the judges' gaze by looking over them at dance competitions. One girl told me how she copes when she is nervous at a competition: "I just try to smile and not look at anyone, I just look straight." Another explained, "Well when I got onstage [the first time at a competition], the thing I didn't expect was the lights coming down on you. You couldn't see the people, so I just pictured it as nobody was there and I was just dancing. That's what I do now."

Though judges have the most power in dance because it is the most subjective of the activities, kids involved with soccer and chess still deal with evaluations by adults acting as referees and coaches. Westfield Soccer Club kids, like those from Elite Dance Academy, are more concerned with what their coach thinks of the team's performance than the calls or interventions of the referee. (None of the soccer competitors I interviewed complained about referees, though their parents certainly did.) One boy, Ben, who plays on a very competitive team, told me that his coach got mad at the team once even after they had won a game. He explained that the coach thought they "took it easy" after building up a lead, and that they should never stop fighting. As Ben relayed this story to me in his family's kitchen, his voice took on a serious tone.

Like soccer referees, adults who run chess tournaments sometimes have to make subjective decisions at tournaments, despite the objective nature of the game. Cassandra, a third-grader, told me about her experience playing in her first chess tournament, when she was in first grade. She was in the beginners' section, where none of the competitors were playing with chess clocks. In the last round the tournament director decided the game she was playing had gone on for too long, so the director said whoever had the most points on the board was the winner. Cassandra explained, "I had the Queen and the Rooks and a Knight and Bishop. He had nothing else. He had a few pawns on there and maybe a Knight or something. So [the tournament director] declared that I won the game." Because of her declared victory she finished, as she said, "in the trophies."

Chess kids are also monitored and evaluated by the chess rating system, and they are often *obsessed* with their rating. They check it online after each tournament and tell others what their rating number currently is. One first-grade boy I met, Sameer, asked everyone he met in a chess-related setting, including me, "What's your rating?" Sameer made me laugh when I heard a girl tell him, "My rating is 750," and he quickly replied, "Well, my rating is 751." Not only was this a lie, as his rating was in the low 500s, but it showed his desperation to have a high rating, be perceived as a strong player, and be better than everyone he met.

Psychologists find that children (especially starting in primary school), far more than adults, are concerned with their performance relative to peers and not in relation to an absolute standard.[21] Sameer is a good example of this, as he cared about his rating only in relation to those he met, not in terms of his performance compared to all first-graders, a group in which he was slightly better than average.

Unlike Sameer, a few of the chess children I met prefer not to know an opponent's rating. This seems to be a good strategy as psychologists find that in a competitive setting, knowing an opponent's skill level leads individuals to form expectations about their winning chances, both positive and negative.[22] As one boy told me, "You're pressured a lot when you know the rating because if it is higher [than yours] then you think you will lose."

Of course, other children see playing a higher rated opponent as a challenge; plus, winning against a higher rated opponent means earning even more rating points, and perhaps an extra parental reward as well. A highly ranked fifth-grader explained to me how he felt about this: "If there are weak people there [at the tournaments], I like to play more of the high-rated people usually, because if I lose [to the weak players], then

I lose a lot of ratings. But if I lose inside the high-rated section, then I don't lose as many points."

Soccer kids also know their relative ranking as players by their team's standing. Clubs have A and B teams, and even though they may have names such as Chargers or Crush, kids know whether or not they are on the "top" team. One girl explained, "I am on a B team in our area. It's like we know that there are better teams than us out there, who are the A teams."

On top of rankings within clubs, leagues place teams in flights based on their records and abilities. Again, the players know when they are a top team in their league, mainly because these flights are often explicitly labeled A, B, or C. For truly high-performing teams, soccer message boards nationally rank the top one hundred teams in each age group for boys and girls. But the kids know about these sites only if adults or older friends and siblings tell them. Given the age of the children I met, it's not surprising that only two boys mentioned these sites to me in passing during our conversations. They are far less central to soccer kids' lives than ratings are to chess kids.

The final evaluator in these competitive activities is the most objective: time. Time makes children feel pressured and evaluated. In most chess tournaments each player has thirty minutes to complete a game, though this varies. Most children do not like playing "with time." One West County Chess boy explained, "When you play with time, I don't really like that because it's frustrating and pressuring." An Uptown-Metro Chess girl told me, "Well there is something that I don't like about chess. If there is a clock on your side you have to move fast and you might not do a right move and you might lose."

Given the pressures of time and being evaluated, it's not surprising that tears make an appearance at various competitive events. One dancer from Westbrook's Let's Dance Studio summed up what happens when children cry at competitions: "Well, there was this girl, like when she made a mistake [on stage at a competition] she would cry. She knew she made a mistake and she just like bawled. This year, she didn't come back." Her comment jibes with my observations, especially at chess tournaments: children who cried multiple times after a loss or mistake were no longer participating by the next year.[23]

Of course, losing is never pleasant, but this is especially true in competitive children's activities because of the immediacy and public element of the loss. Children know very soon after performing and being evaluated how they did, and those results are then publicly announced at awards ceremonies (and they also are usually available on the Internet). When the results are announced they are sometimes met with pleasant surprise. Elite dancer and soloist Destiny explained her reaction at an awards ceremony when it was announced she had placed well:

DESTINY: When they announced my name I was real surprised
          because there are a lot of dancers who are higher than me
          and I beat them.

HILARY: What do you mean they're higher than you?

DESTINY: My dances are maybe like in the middle and they're more
          advanced than me in what they can do. They have more
          flexibility.

Unlike performance results in school, which are often private, known only to teachers and family members, everyone who attends a competition knows how others have performed in the competitive environment and then how they were assessed. When things don't go as well as they did for Destiny, this can make coping with a loss even more difficult for kids.

Not surprisingly children who compete in multiple activities see losses in different activities in different ways. Take this exchange I had with James, a fourth-grader who competes in West County Chess and on the A team with Westfield Soccer Club:

HILARY: Is there anything else you don't like about competing?

JAMES: Yeah! Losing.

HILARY: In general?

JAMES: Yes.

HILARY: How do you deal with it when you lose?

JAMES: I shake hands, finish it, but I'm a little frustrated and mad.

HILARY: Do you get most frustrated when you lose at a soccer game, or is it worse with chess?

JAMES: It's worse with chess because you kind of have to think a lot more, but in soccer you play a game, you actually move around instead of chess where you move only your hands. In soccer you get to use your athletic abilities instead of your logic.

James distinguishes between competing using his mind and competing using his body. Many children mentioned that chess is about using their brains and that is why it is sometimes harder to lose in chess; according to one child, it may mean you are "not smart enough." This is consistent with some of Carol Dweck's work, in which she finds that when students see their performance in an activity as a measure of their intelligence they feel stigmatized when they perform poorly.[24]

But if they stick with chess, most of the children understand that they will often lose, en route to future wins. Max, who has been playing competitive chess for about five years, spoke from experience when he told me, "You go through the losing times and it's very sad. But you can't lose everything and you can't win everything." Max also told me that during his losing times his chess friends helped support him and made him feel better. I now turn to these friendships, which are a highlight of the competitive experience for many kids and a way for them to cope with the stress of competition as they develop Competitive Kid Capital.

FRIENDSHIP AND A COMPETITIVE TEAM SPIRIT

Being part of a team and developing friendships is one aspect of the competitive experience often discussed by children. The development of friendships on teams and across competitive boundaries is a strategy that children have developed not only to cope with losing but also to cope with the reality of competing at a young age. Their peers understand what a competitive life is like, which helps them to develop strong bonds of friendship.

Unlike their parents and other adults who rank them against one another, children usually appreciate the talent of a friend or teammate. All of the kids I met were quite realistic about their abilities in relation to their peers. For many of them, just being on a winning team is enough. They do not want the additional pressure of competing as an individual. The problem of being around high-achieving teammates seems to be more of an issue for adults than for these kids—though this could change as the children age and more acutely feel the need to be the best.

Chess kids often talk about a schoolmate or peer by commenting, "He's really good. I hope I don't have to play him!" The soccer and dance kids are even more appreciative of peers' talents, given the team element in most of their interactions. This is especially true in soccer. While some parents openly complained to me about "ball hogs," the kids themselves seemed pleased with the high performance of teammates, especially if it helped the team to win.

A twelve-year-old boy on a Westfield Soccer Club A team said his coach told them they had to learn to juggle the ball, or keep it in the air using only their legs and chest, one hundred times. This boy, Dave, expressed awe and pride that two of his friends could do this easily, while he had to work much harder to reach the goal. Dave feels lucky to be on a team with talented peers. He didn't get upset that he could not be the best at everything, although perhaps this would not be true if he were not the best goalie on his team.

The dance girls are also proud of one another's abilities. I had expected to see some jealousy between the girls at Elite Dance Academy, where only a select number of girls are invited to do competition solos. One girl confessed that she has mixed feelings about not being asked to do a solo: "When you're up there by yourself the judges are staring you down, so it's hard. They're looking at your point and your arms. You have to be like literally perfect. I guess it would be really hard for me to do it. I am and I'm not jealous of soloists."

The girls who had friends in their age group doing solos went to cheer them on at both regional and national competitions. They spoke quite openly about the reasons they themselves were not solo dancers. One girl, Samantha, told me, "My flexibility and turns just aren't as good as Alice's."

The year I was doing fieldwork with Elite was ten-year-old Alice's first year doing a solo, and it was a major celebratory event for the family. I interviewed her mom, Tina, before Alice's first competition, and she told me how nervous the entire family was for Alice's first solo performance. Tina said she was probably more nervous for Alice to be "up there by herself" than Alice was.

I interviewed Alice after she had done her solo routine four times in competition. She told me she had never been as nervous as she was for her first solo; the night before she did it "a million times" to make sure she would not forget. Alice's main concern was forgetting her routine, along with generally worrying about "messing up," though she never specified what messing up might entail.[25] She explained that it could only be her fault if she did mess up, since she would not have any company members or friends on stage competing with her.

Some of the other dance girls told me that they would not want a solo because they would not want to be on stage by themselves in front of others and the judges. One girl's sentiment was similar to Alice's: "I'd be a lot more nervous if I had a solo because all the eyes are on you and if you make one mistake everybody can see it!"

Soccer children also highlighted the positive aspects of being part of a team instead of being on their own. One boy said, "I like being on a team, because if somebody is on you and you don't know what to do, you can always pass. And it's a way to make new friends." Kids liked the team aspect because when they won they had one another to celebrate with, and when they lost they could all be upset together. Other dance and soccer kids often mentioned how nice it was to be part of a team. This is consistent with previous findings by sports psychologists that children exhibit higher anxiety levels when they compete in individual sports than in team sports.[26]

Wanting to be part of a group can encourage some kids to shy away from learning to compete on their own and to be comfortable being individually evaluated and assessed. While teamwork is important, kids can learn that skill from participating recreationally in activities, so it would worry some of the parents to know that their kids are using teamwork as a crutch to prevent individual excellence.

Until an Uptown-Metro Chess girl mentioned it to me a few months into my fieldwork, I had not thought about friendship being part of the competitive experience. Parents I met emphasized learning about teamwork, but friendship is more of a personal experience than being part of a team. Eventually many children from all three activities told me that they liked participating because they made friends with children who went to schools other than their own, a point that no parent ever made.

One soccer boy explained, "If you're seeing someone every day and after school, ugh, it's a lot of them. . . . I think it's a good thing I don't go to school with all the kids [on my team] because then I'd just be so bored with them." Children from different backgrounds and schools (both public and private) frequently attended one another's birthday parties. One Metro Soccer Co-op player told me, "I have friends on my team [who come to my parties] but they're not from my school. I just know them because I played with them on the Stars [the name of his team]."

I witnessed a great example of diverse friendship with a group of girls from Westbrook's Let's Dance Studio. One girl explained, "We have a club after every dance class called DDGT, or Dunkin' Donuts Get Together. A group of girls, we all go to the Dunkin' Donuts after class, and we'll have donuts or ice cream or something like that." The DDGT group is made up of girls of different grade levels and from different schools. Competing and spending time together outside of classes and rehearsals brought them together as friends.

The friendships formed during competitive activities are a blessing for many children, who may not have close friends at school partly because they are so involved in outside activities. One girl told me why she loved going to rehearsals: "I want to see my good friends from dance, that's why I'm excited to go to dance class, so I can see them again. I feel more comfortable with them because they're nicer to me than the kids at school." Another dancer told me she doesn't like cheering at her school because that is the only time she experiences jealousy. At school her cheer teammates complain about her jumps, which are better than theirs.

At a national dance competition I noticed a T-shirt for sale that said, "I Can't, I Have Dance." One Elite dancer told me she owns the shirt and that one time it came in handy: "I was taking summer dance classes and a friend from school asked me for a play date. I told her to read the shirt!"

Of course, there is also a downside to this sociability: when one or more friends leave a particular activity, others often follow suit. For example, I met two brothers, Steven and Sam, only a year apart in age, one in second and one in third grade, who participated in competitive chess and travel soccer. Both told me separately that they loved "doing soccer" because all of their friends "do soccer." Sam even said that he played soccer only because of his friends and that he would be just as happy playing basketball instead.

When we spoke Steven and Sam were lukewarm about chess, even though they liked playing in tournaments with their friends. Sam explained, "They sometimes cheer me up if I lose a game." Two of their friends, Jordan and James, were planning on quitting chess, which was clearly affecting Steven and Sam. By the following school year all four boys had stopped playing chess. Sam and Steven continued to play travel soccer the following year, but Sam ended up playing basketball as well. Two years later they were done with both chess and soccer. For these boys, the desire to be competitive and participate at a higher level was largely determined by where they could be with their friends.

While close friendships can be a positive aspect for kids participating in competitive activities, they may also undermine some aspects of the lessons and skills parents want their kids to learn from participation. That so many children see themselves as being with *friends* and not with *competitors* may decrease their desire to be the best. In some cases, they may not try to win. None of the kids themselves told me this, but from what I saw at some events, and what parents told me, this is a possibility—a possibility that seems to matter more to girls than to boys. (Recall from chapter 5 Lois explaining that Lottie's girlfriend always tries to arrange a draw when she plays a friend so she doesn't have to beat her.)

BALL GIRLS AND PINK BOYS?

While these competitive activities are social and can transcend boundaries of age and the schools children attend, sex is one boundary that remains rigid. The children I met have very strong ideas about what is "right" for a boy and "right" for a girl, though they often cannot articulate why some activities are "best" for girls and others for boys. This was true even when they had a sibling of the opposite sex involved in an activity. The children's views of each activity's gender orientation are very similar to those of their parents, suggesting that by elementary school these gender roles are already powerful and pervasive.

I asked all the children what they thought about a member of the opposite sex competing in their activity. These questions often produced giggles and strong but short statements, especially from the chess and dance kids, who accurately observed that their activities mainly had boys and girls, respectively, and that the dominant sex was better in that activity. The soccer kids were more egalitarian, even though they did not often interact with the opposite sex on soccer fields, at either practices or games. The preponderance of a single sex in certain activities and the formal separation of boys and girls in certain sports shape children's thoughts about gender, even as they try to form their own opinions.[27]

Chess boys were quite blunt in their assessments of girls playing chess. Here is one exchange I had with six-year-old William, who plays West County Chess:

HILARY: Do you think that girls can play chess?

WILLIAM: Yeah.

HILARY: As good as boys?

WILLIAM: No.

When I asked another chess boy if girls can play chess as well as boys, he said, "No. They just don't want to play because maybe it's a boy sport."

Many of the kids had very strong opinions about the kinds of sports that are "boy sports" and the kinds that are "girl sports." Here is an excerpt from an interview with Sam, who competes in both chess and soccer in West County:

HILARY: If you had a little girl, would you put her in soccer?

SAM: (Shakes head no).

HILARY: Why not?

SAM: Because then she would get more hurt. She probably wouldn't like doing soccer. . . . It's a boy sport.

HILARY: What do you think are boy sports?

SAM: Soccer, basketball, baseball. Tennis is for girls and boys. Those are the three main sports that boys mostly do.

HILARY: Are there any other things that are just mainly for boys?

SAM: Yes.

HILARY: Like what?

SAM: Cars and video games.

HILARY: What about what's good for girls?

SAM: Barbie and dolls and stuff.

One soccer girl, Charlotte, told me about her experiences playing soccer and being perceived as a tomboy: "At recess I'm like the only girl playing soccer. Everyone else is doing something else. So usually they call me a tomboy because I'm playing with the boys. But I'm not a tomboy. A tomboy is somebody who like wants to be a boy and is like always being with the boys and stuff. I have dolls and I like pink. I really like girl things, like I painted my nails [shows me her nails]." When I asked Charlotte what she thinks only girly girls do, she answered, "Well, just like sitting around talking, wearing like the highest fashions, and just saying stuff like, 'Oh, my gosh!'"

To Charlotte being a tomboy is a negative and not a label to which she aspires. This is in contrast to C. J. Pascoe's conclusion, "Identifying as a tomboy aligns a girl with a romanticized history of masculine identification before she encountered a more restricting femininity."[28] Charlotte seems eager to identify with her femininity; she paints her nails and wears pink. But she still wants to be a strong, aggressive soccer player and not a girly girl. She said, "We [her team] play soccer against boys sometimes because it's better for the girls to learn to be more aggressive." While Charlotte thinks girls can be just as good as boys at soccer, she feels they do need to be more aggressive, like the boys. Notwithstanding Charlotte's views, the vast majority of both soccer boys and girls I spoke with told me that girls *can* play soccer well—though not as well as boys.

The aggressiveness in boys that Charlotte mentions is not only physical. Boys can also be more aggressive in chess, according to some of the kids. Though in this case the aggression is seen as a negative. Here is an excerpt from my field notes taken during a summer chess camp which speaks directly to how girls and boys handle aggression and winning and losing in different ways and how adults shape and reinforce children's thoughts about gender:

> Hannah was playing a game with a seven-year-old boy, Tal. He beat her for the second day in a row and when he won he loudly said "Checkmate!"—so loud in fact that I looked over to their spot at the table. He then got up and started getting a snack. Hannah sat in front of the board pushing her hands into her eyes. I knew she was upset since she had argued over a move in a game with Tal yesterday. I walked over to her to talk and as soon as I saw her face I knew she wouldn't be able to talk. I started comforting her and then the teacher saw her crying and came over. I stepped away to let him handle the conflict. The teacher started saying that boys aren't as mature as girls, so she shouldn't get upset. Hannah complained that Tal "shouted and told everyone that he beat her" [which wasn't true]. The teacher again said that boys and girls handle winning in different ways. Another teacher then came over. He told her that she shouldn't get so upset because Tal is "just a little kid." [I couldn't help but think this probably didn't make eleven-year-old Hannah feel better, to know that a kindergartener beat her.] Hannah keeps crying and I eventually bring her a tissue, since neither of the men offered her one. She quiets down

and they drift away. Hannah comes over to me and I give her a hug. . . . She told me that her mom says boys are different from girls and she shouldn't get upset when boys win and brag, because that is just the way they are. She tells me she agrees and that she has never known any girls who would shout "I won!" Hannah, in a whispered tone, tells me that she thinks girls are more mature and nicer when they win.

Hannah's and Charlotte's words and actions illustrate that girls want to win, and be aggressive, but they still want to be thought of as feminine in terms of either appearance or disposition. Neither of these girls wants to be thought of as a boy. In fact, none of the chess, dance, and soccer girls I met wanted to be boys; likewise, none of the boys wanted to be girls. "Playing like a girl" was an insult I sometimes heard.

That soccer is seen as "okay" for girls, even with this aggressive and masculine element, is partly because the boys and girls are so segregated. Dance is different because one or two boys often dance with girls. The dance girls did not see this mingling of boys and girls as problematic.

In fact, the girls often remarked that these boys are very good dancers. They say that they wish they could jump as high or spin as fast as some of their male teammates and competitors. Yet they can understand why more boys do not dance. One girl dancer explained, "Because when you think of dance, you think of your hair perfect, in a bun or in a ponytail, makeup, leotards, tights. The boys would think that would be too girly for them and people would make fun of them. I don't know why people think about it that way, but they do."

Another girl identified a different way in which activities can be identified as masculine or feminine: "Soccer is more like you're trying to achieve, like getting goals and everything. I think people think it's more boyish than dancing in some way because we don't score." Kids see dance as more feminine, with scoring as a proxy for masculinity, which is consistent with the majority of adults I met as well.

All of the children I interviewed had very strong notions about gender and their activities, notions that were sometimes more rigid than those of their parents. The children see girls and boys as separate categories, often with distinct activities and distinct behaviors within those activities. At this age they have difficulty seeing how a girl can be feminine but also aggressive, without being negatively labeled a tomboy. Not yet on their radar is the idea of being a pink warrior girl, as they are most concerned with simply being clearly identified as a boy or a girl—though Charlotte does seem to be moving in that direction with her aggressive soccer play and her pink nails. Their competitive activities create and reinforce their gender identities, which will surely impact their future identity.

FUN AND THE FUTURE

Despite the tears, the pressures, and the judges, girls and boys do find participation in their competitive activities fun. They enjoy being with their friends, and it is fun to win, fun to be at many events, fun to win trophies, and fun to participate in the activities themselves. Sports psychologists find that it is important for children in sports to have fun, especially because having fun can decrease postgame stress, particularly after a loss.[29] Other recent work by sociologists finds that participating in organized activities is not associated with greater stress for kids.[30] In fact, those kids who are the least involved have more stress-related symptoms, though it's unclear what role competition plays for them in their organized activities.

Of course, there are times when going to practice or to an event is not fun, and some of the children complained about not having enough time to relax. For the most part, kids' negative comments are about practices and not games, competitions, and tournaments. Soccer kids voiced the least number of complaints about practices, and the complaints they did have primarily focused on the weather. One boy told me, "If it's really hot, then like I'd rather be sitting in the shade with a water bottle and a book."

Chess children definitely complained the most about the time commitment, saying that they sometimes miss friends' birthday parties to play in tournaments. A few children also said that sometimes they would prefer to "play with [a] friend, or do video games, or watch TV." Two of the children added that sometimes they would prefer to read.

Dance girls never complained about going to competitions, but they did say that sometimes they are tired after school and wish they did not have to go to class or rehearsal so often. One of the Let's Dance girls also told me, "Sometimes if there's like a show premiere or a movie premiere on TV, I will be a little upset that I'm going to miss that. But other than that, no, I like to go to dance." And one of the Elite dancers said that she regretted her tight schedule: "When I was little, I used to think about swimming. But now, yeah, not going to happen. I don't want to do swimming instead of dance. Dance is my life now."

Overall kids in these activities learn to deal with their busy lives and schedules. They also know that they are expected to win and that adults rank them, and they need to figure out which adult's opinion matters most to them. By getting ratings and placement trophies the competitive children I met are learning the subtleties of distinction and judgment at a young age. They can distinguish between true achievement and the ersatz versions. For instance, they can judge a participation trophy, along with an award based on limited criteria, as less meaningful than a true first-place finish. The children also realize that their parents usually give them extra prizes only when they win, not just when they finish. Clearly the biggest rewards come with the biggest victories.

At the same time, the children learn that their rewards carry status; the prizes act as symbols that convey information about the kids themselves. Trophies, patches, and ribbons announce to others that you are a winner. But such status symbols carry responsibility: if you fail to perform well when you are sending the signal that you are a winner, this may be discrediting or embarrassing.[31] So part of the process of competition is learning how to present oneself as a winner and perform like a winner. Competitions, and all of their preparations, become a performance much of the time for kids, not just when they are on stage.

I have tried to emphasize the complexity with which children think about their participation in these competitive activities. However, adults in their lives, especially parents, do influence them. For example, after interviewing Daisuke, a first-grader who started playing competitive chess in kindergarten, we stood in the hallway of his parents' law office talking with his mom and dad. As I prepared to leave, Daisuke told me that he actually does not like competition much and that it "hurts his stomach." His parents both jumped in, saying that the more experience he gets, the less his stomach will hurt. Obviously children sometimes tell adults about their stresses, but the adults often try to dismiss or rationalize them.[32]

Parents also pass down their orientation toward the future, particularly with respect to college attendance and future professions. Children named the following schools as colleges they would like to attend: Harvard, Princeton, Yale, Duke, MIT, Syracuse, Howard, Rutgers, and the University of Florida. That children name schools that are geographically close indicates just how much these competitive young children pay attention to the idea of college. One dance and soccer girl in fifth grade told me how some people think of one of her relatively noncompetitive activities: "A lot of the girls in my Girl Scout troop are thinking about quitting because like they want to do sports. But their parents want to keep them in because it looks good on their college resume."

Like many children, kids who compete have ideas about what they would like to be when they grow up. Many gave expected answers— being a movie star, teacher, or sports star—while others were a bit more creative, such as being a hat maker. The majority of professions named were quite achievement-oriented and will require years of credentials acquisition in competitive environments. These include doctor, lawyer, astronaut, engineer,[33] banker, and politician.

Surprisingly few of the kids aspire to be the professional version of the competitive activity in which they participate; it seems that these kids are more practical than other kids who may dream big, likely because, as mentioned in the introduction, none of the parents wants his or her children to be professional chess players, dancers, or soccer players. Even at this age, the children seem to understand that their participation is a means to an end—or a line on their resume. Of course, they are still kids and not quite ready to focus on just one dream yet. One Elite Dance Academy dancer who is nine told me, "In the night I'm going to be a dance teacher, and in the morning I'm going to be a lawyer, and my husband's going to take care of the children."

Most of the kids knew that there must be a reason their parents thought they should participate in their respective activities. Often they were not sure of the precise reason—which is not surprising, given that some parents admitted they didn't have detailed conversations with their kids about what they want them to learn, although the kids had some sense of how their goals might link up at some point. This statement reflects the general consensus: "Well, I know that I do [learn something], but I just don't know how it helps me yet. I know that it helps me with other things, but I'm not sure what it helps me in now."

One chess player was on the right track, at least according to his parents' ideas, when he observed, "I keep doing tests and in chess you have a clock and it is timing you and giving you time to calculate. Tests are timed also so you have to calculate at that right time so I think chess increases the time speed of how you think so on timed tests, math and reading, it helps you calculate faster." Other kids simply knew that their participation was supposed to make them "smarter."

Recall the quote from a soccer boy I discussed in the introduction. In his unintentionally funny and prescient comment about how busy his young life is and how busy his schedule will likely be as an adult, he told me that he thinks soccer helps him learn about "dodging everything": "Like when we have to catch a train, and there are only a few more minutes, we have to run and dodge everyone. So, soccer teaches that."

For the most part, we do not have a good understanding of the long-term effects of competition on children. Will these children, exposed to rankings and performance pressures from a young age, end up surviving the psychological rigors of the college admissions process better, performing better academically and in their extracurricular activities? Or will they burn out? There is some evidence that children lose creativity when constantly exposed to competition and extrinsic rewards, so we should be on the lookout for signs of burnout.[34] Others argue that given the right combination of personality traits, competition can help foster more intrinsic motivation and creativity.[35] We need more research in this area by talking to kids, especially in collaboration with psychologists, who have developed such questionnaires as the sixteen-point Achievement Orientation scale of the Personality Research Form.[36]

By talking with children you hear their own views, which are basically complementary to their parents' but also give a special perspective as to how competition impacts them at this young age. Because the children I spoke with are in elementary school they are likely processing competitive pressures differently from high school age students. Recently stories of pressured high schoolers have been a media focus in documentaries like *Race to Nowhere* and in the books of Madeline Levine.[37] In these works academically enriched and successful adolescents are said to be more likely to be depressed, to be dependent on various drugs, to inflict self-harm, and even to commit suicide. My conversations with these kids suggest that they are coping better than we might think based on such reports. Perhaps developing these competitive coping skills at younger ages will help them manage increased pressure as they age.

That said, there are clearly some costs to kids who participate in these competitive activities, from stomach aches to concerns about self-worth and limited time with school friends. In most families the benefits of participation outweigh these downsides, even for the kids. When they don't, as in Daisuke's case, those kids do drop out.

For the most part the children I spoke with are doing well and seem well-adjusted in their competitive activities. It's possible that participation has much more harmful effects on kids I did not meet or speak with. But the children were very honest with me—in many ways more honest than their parents—and they talked about when kids cry and when they themselves get upset. It is not always smooth sailing, but they cope with lucky charms, friendships, and the like, and trophies and other rewards keep them motivated at this age.

It is not new that children love to receive public recognition and totems for their achievements, even in settings surrounded by friends. When the Boy Scouts started awarding badges around the turn of the twentieth century, many became "badge prodigies," racing to acquire the most in their troop.[38] But much has changed since those early, relaxed days of organized competition. Today boys and girls treat their "second shift" of organized, competitive activities as a job. Even as they have fun, these kids are clearly operating in a world where they are treated as mini professionals, concerned with acquiring Competitive Kid Capital to help them succeed throughout adolescence and into adulthood.

Conclusion

THE ROAD AHEAD FOR MY COMPETITIVE KIDS

When people find out that I study competitive after-school activities, they want to know what my own children do. I have always been able to dodge the question, replying that I don't have children. But I can't avoid an answer any longer. As I was finishing *Playing to Win* I had a baby boy. Will I teach him chess in the hopes that he'll compete at the 2018 National Championships? Get him on a travel soccer team by age eight? Enroll him in dance classes so he can appear on a series like *Dance Moms*? Or decide to forgo all activities that involve trophies?

It might seem that many parents are making the last choice and forgoing trophy-giving activities. There has been a popular backlash against competitive childhood and competitive parenting. A smattering of new books are illustrative of this trend: *Not Everyone Gets a Trophy, The Trophy Kids Grow Up, Free-Range Kids: How to Raise Safe, Self-Reliant Chil-*

dren, The Idle Parent: Why Laid-Back Parents Raise Happier and Healthier Kids, and *The Blessing of a B Minus.*[1] Theories abound that overscheduled, too competitive kids actually grow up to be lazy because over involved helicopter parents are ultimately creating neurotic slackers rather than go-getters with a solid supply of Competitive Kid Capital.[2] Despite these theories we have little evidence that participation in these activities is harmful—or that parents are pulling back when it comes to exposing their elementary school–age kids to competitions run by adults.

When I started this research I planned to interview parents whose children did *not* participate in competitive after-school activities. I identified a local business in West County, part of a nationwide franchise, that promotes itself as pro-play and anticompetition. But it turned out that the children who attended were either too young to participate in competitive activities or participated in some other competitive activity in addition to getting physical exercise in this noncompetitive setting. Because I had such a hard time finding any noncompetitive elementary school–age kids living in West County and Metro, I stopped actively looking for them.[3]

OPTING OUT AND DROPPING OUT

Of course there are families in both communities and across the United States who cannot afford to cultivate Competitive Kid Capital in their children. There are even families who purposively shun participation in organized activities in general, favoring a free-range or idle parenting approach. Some academic sociologists (who should know better than to do social science by personal anecdote) often seemed to chastise me: "But *I* don't do that with my kids—I'm not a part of that world."

Such vociferous denials are evidence of how powerful competition is for young children today. Parents often make choices deliberately in opposition to what is now regarded as the standard model. When pressed, many of these protesting parents concede that while they do not push their elementary school–age children, they do understand that as their children get older they must specialize and find a "passion" at which they excel in order to stand out during the looming college admissions process, and beyond.

Of course, professors have the luxury of some insider knowledge with respect to how colleges and universities work, which may allow their children to enjoy a slightly more relaxed childhood. Still, they admit to being pressured by the prevailing culture of competitive childhood; they see what other parents do and hear what the competitive childhood industry tells parents. The sociologist Dalton Conley, dean of social sciences at New York University, wrote a column in the *Chronicle of Higher Education*, "Harvard by Lottery," detailing research that suggests it does not matter whether or not you attend Harvard or schools like it when it comes to future earnings. Yet Conley writes, "Such evidence aside, however, when I take off my social-scientist hat and put on my parental cap, I can't imagine not taking my kids on a coast-to-coast college tour. . . . I couldn't live with myself if I didn't pay for an SAT prep class. And damned if I let them just hang out . . . after school rather than pursue serious internships and other extracurriculars."[4]

Competitive pressures clearly impact a variety of families, which increasingly includes families with young children. A recent article on the rise of test preparation courses for kindergarten could just as easily describe parents' descent into competitive after-school activities: "There was a time, not that long ago, when few parents attempted to prep their 4-year-olds for kindergarten-admissions exams. But then a few more began to do it, and then a few more after that, and then suddenly, normal-seeming people with normal-seeming values began doing it, too, and an arms-race mentality kicked in."[5] In this context it's understandable that I had a hard time identifying any families with elementary school–age kids who did not participate in a single competitive after-school activity.

While it was hard to locate noncompetitive families, I did interview nineteen parents whose children had been competitive participants in chess, dance, or soccer at one time but had since stopped competing in those activities. Coaches and current competitive parents connected me with these families—nine from soccer, eight from chess, and two from dance. Did this dropout occur because of competitive pressures, costs, time limitations, lack of talent, or some other reason?

Few elementary school–age girls drop out of competitive dance. According to the dance teachers I interviewed, dropout is most likely to occur during high school, when academic and social pressures increase. The two families I met with daughters who dropped out offered different explanations. One of the mothers pulled her daughter out of Let's Dance to focus more on Indian dance. The other mom was concerned about her eldest daughter's academic performance. Instead of withdrawing her completely from Elite Dance Academy, she let her continue taking dance classes but pulled her from the competition team. Her younger daughter remained a part of Elite's competition team, though. It is important to note that while dance is the most expensive of the three activities, no one reported dropping out because of cost.

Similarly, none of the eight chess families left due to cost. Instead they complained about the increasing time commitment required to compete at a high level, particularly beginning around third grade. Some of these children were clearly not top competitors, so their departures were part of the problem of the high-achieving child phenomenon, and their parents chose to invest resources in other activities, such as music and sports. Other kids dropped out mainly because their friends stopped playing, so it was no longer fun for them. Unlike dance, competitive chess dropouts skew much younger, and dropping out during elementary school is not unusual; in fact it is almost expected.

Travel soccer had the most dropouts, and the reason was mainly time constraints. None of the kids in the families I met told me that he or she left travel soccer due to cost, ability, or even injuries (which could have been a contributing factor given the physical nature of the game). Instead parents said that most kids left because they had to choose between soccer and another sport. The majority of the time, especially in West County, this sport was lacrosse. It is nearly impossible for kids to participate in two travel sports given time constraints and coaching demands. Lacrosse and soccer have a lot of overlap in terms of physical skills and the timing of their seasons. Because of the high-level commitment expected of these young kids, they were forced to specialize in a particular sport, often by fourth grade.

Soccer parents were insistent that their kids could not just drop out of physical activity—they had to participate in some other physical activity.

This was a common refrain among the parents I met: children could not stop participating in organized competitive activities altogether. They had to be involved in "something," usually a different sport, music lessons, or some other after-school endeavor.

While kids who dropped out of the three activities I focused on generally had a different set of reasons across the activities, what stands out is that none of their parents really complained about the effects of competitiveness on the kids. Of course I was not able to observe these families in action, so I had to accept their dropout narratives at face value. But given the similarities within activities and differences across them, I think there is truth in the narratives told to me.

At the same time I also think each family's story is more complicated. Recall Daisuke from chapter 6, who complained of stomach aches when he participated in chess tournaments. By the time my fieldwork ended he had dropped out of scholastic chess. His reason was that he could not handle the competitive environment, but I suspect if I had met his parents a year later they would have simply cited the time commitment required rather than their son's limitations.

Also somewhat surprising is that no one cited the cost of participation as a limiting factor, perhaps out of embarrassment or a combination of other, more primary factors. However, I finished doing formal fieldwork before the economic collapse that occurred in the fall of 2008. What happened to competitive participation as a result of the financial crisis?

I envisioned two scenarios about how competitive parents would react to the financial crisis: either parents would take the opportunity to pull back from their children's intense participation in competitive after-school activities, citing financial concerns, or they would intensify their children's participation, being even more concerned about downward mobility and investing even more in the college admissions process starting at younger ages. In the fall of 2009 I emailed all the parents I had interviewed and asked them to complete a survey. About three-fourths of the parents responded, and of those 64 percent had children still involved in competitive chess, dance, and soccer nearly two years later. It appears that participation in competitive after-school activities is fairly recession-proof.

Chess had the most attrition, not surprising given the dropouts I interviewed earlier; the reason most commonly provided, again, was time. Soccer was in the middle, with the majority of these children leaving to pursue other athletic opportunities. And, once more, dance had the fewest dropouts, with only three (one girl had been cut from the team, and the parents of two others marked "child's choice to leave" on the survey).

While most of the families said that the economic crisis had not affected their children's participation in their particular activity, parents did report that it had affected their families overall. Dance moms were the group most likely to report that the economy made them consider their participation more, but it did not produce dropouts. (That dance moms thought about the economy more than chess and soccer families is not surprising, given that in comparison to families in the other two activities their family income in general is lower and the costs often higher for competitive participation.) It would seem that instead of taking the opportunity to pull back from competitive involvement, parents see the acquisition of Competitive Kid Capital as more important than ever and worth the investment of family money and time.

WHAT (PARENTS THINK) CHILDREN NEED
TO SUCCEED

This Competitive Kid Capital—internalizing the importance of winning, learning how to recover from a loss to win in the future, managing time pressure, performing in stressful environments, and feeling comfortable being judged by others in public—is seen as important in uncertain times partly because it is during times of uncertainty that schooling becomes even more important. Parents hope that credentials will serve as a cushion, helping their children retain their relative position in society or gain an advantage. While many parents listen when the dean of admissions at Harvard, William Fitzsimmons, says, "Even fifth-graders in Wellesley, Newton, and Brookline [affluent Boston suburbs], who as adults will face international competition for jobs, should begin beefing up their academic resumes if they want a shot at an Ivy League education," these parents *really* listen during times of uncertainty.[6]

Admissions offices like the one that Fitzsimmons runs read applications from thousands of specialist "national champions" and generalist "top" students each year. The carving up of honor that now begins in childhood continues through the teenage years and into young adulthood. An article published in 2010 titled "As Honor Students Multiply, Who Really Is One?" again quotes Harvard's Fitzsimmons about scholastic honor societies: "Many college admissions offices, which inadvertently inspired the growth of such societies, find them confusing. 'It's very difficult to know with so many different honor societies and so many different criteria, what exactly we have in front of us,' said [Fitzsimmons]."[7] Membership in multiple honor societies become like hollow participation trophies. As one educational expert said, "Once everyone's wearing rhinestones, you might not notice someone wearing diamonds."[8]

Without doubt there is a correlation between the lessons, like those associated with Competitive Kid Capital, that parents push onto their children and with what parents believe elite institutions like Harvard prefer. But we don't know conclusively that the activities that fill the leisure time of affluent American children are central to maintaining an advantage for these kids into adulthood. It could be that the "diamonds" would succeed even without participation in competitive after-school activities because of material advantages or innate abilities.

What we do know is that parents are acting to prepare their children to best succeed in the future, as they understand it. Whether or not this is ultimately dysfunctional class frenzy, *Playing to Win* has shown how that frenzy developed over time and how an infrastructure has developed to support it. A growing bureaucracy exists to translate the suggestions of the dean of Harvard admissions into childhood institutions that have slowly taken over much of American middle-class family life.

By giving a context to competitive children's after-school activities through the three case studies of chess, dance, and soccer, I have explored why parents are not willing to risk *not* encouraging their children to participate and succeed in competitive after-school activities. Chapter 1 described the historical evolution of these activities, showing how a variety of changes in the American educational system (from the rise of compulsory education to increased competition for college admissions) have led to the current system, in which middle- and upper-middle-class kids are the dominant presence in competitive after-school activities.

Drawing on extensive fieldwork and triangulating between observations and interviews with adults and children, as described in chapter 2, I then detailed how parental decisions are embedded in those childhood institutions. Placing parental decisions in this context helps us to understand that some questionable parental decisions are not just related to apparently deviant individual psychologies. The similarities across activities, presented in chapter 5, show that an institutionalized world exists around competitive childhoods, convincing parents that they are necessary. Other parallels across activities, such as the use of fallback ages and the problem of the high-achieving child, are further evidence of how this version of contemporary American childhood is structured around competition.

Of course there are also differences across activities, especially when it comes to gender, as chapter 4 explained. There I described the important finding that upper-middle-class girls appear to be more strategically prepared to enter hegemonic male culture than middle- and lower-middle-class girls through their parents' choice of after-school activities for them. Based on conversations with some of those girls, along with boys, it is clear that they are aware of the strategic lessons their parents want them to learn even if they aren't quite sure why. Chapter 6 showed that competitive kids have learned to cope with the pressures of competition by forging friendships within their activities, activities they generally regard as fun.

Whether or not Competitive Kid Capital successfully works to help children gain admission to elite colleges, it is shaping their relationships with family and friends. There may be reason to worry that children are focusing too much on winning, according to a variety of psychologists who study children's self-esteem and assessment of self-worth, but the other elements of Competitive Kid Capital certainly are not bad skills to learn at an early age. It is important to learn about time and stress management, and it is essential to learn how to bounce back from a failure. While some might not like it that competitive kids are learning how to perform in front of others, it is a reality of modern life that we are assessed every day in jobs and in other ways, like on social media.

Whether or not we need to be imparting this lesson to kids at such young ages is an open question. As these elementary school–age children get older we will be able to better assess the long-term consequences—both positive and negative—of participating in competitive activities during childhood. I met the *Playing to Win* kids at a particular moment in time, when they were not close to actually applying to college or even high school. Some of them participated in these competitive activities only for a few years, so it would be difficult to determine exactly how much impact—again, positive or negative—these specific activities have on their lives.

These are not the only problems with *Playing to Win*, of course. In focusing predominantly on middle-class American families other perspectives are lost. The same can be said for focusing only on those who are engaged in competitive activities. Also, because of the qualitative nature of this work, the ninety-five families I met are in no way statistically representative of all American middle-class families. One strength of this type of work, though, is that I will be able to follow some of these kids through college and beyond, and through conversations I will be able to continue to get nuanced reflections from both children and their parents—replies that would not easily be captured by simply responding to multiple-choice questions.

For instance, in interviews parents were able to convey their mixed emotions about both the "need" to keep up and their exhaustion from trying to keep up. Even parents of kids who usually get first place expressed ambivalence about having their children focus on winning trophies at such a young age. One father of a Top Five chess player in his age division said, "The hardest part of playing chess is being a six-year-old and winning and losing. I mean, when we were six, did our parents ever put us in competition where you win and lose? And get trophies if you win, but if you lose, you don't get a trophy? I mean that to me is the most difficult part of chess for a child."

The deep ambivalence about the best way to raise children captured in this quote and in others throughout *Playing to Win* is not unique to the families I met. In a recent book on why French parenting is more effective and easier than the current American style—work that the author refers to as the backlash to the backlash—Druckerman writes, "Nobody seems to like the relentless, unhappy pace of [middle-class] American parenting, least of all parents themselves."[9] She correctly points out that stories of extreme parenting are not just the province of New Yorkers.[10]

Despite their unhappiness and ambivalence, parents continue to sign their children up for these activities. And many parents often find that once you get started in a competitive activity, it can be difficult to stop. Industry people target you to stay involved, extolling the potential benefits of participation, to help prevent dropouts. If your kids are having fun and seem to be learning, that promotes continued involvement as well.

But more than anything, the winning can be addictive. Seeing your child win can be thrilling, and even when he or she does not land the top spot, that loss can add fuel to the competitive fire. In general, competitive activities are quite successful at drawing people in and keeping them, a similarity across competitive worlds that are targeted at both children and adults. In a book on competitive dog shows, a top judge explained, "Like everybody else in the world, I got started by buying a dog and getting talked into going to a dog show and winning a ribbon and getting hooked for life."[11] While few children get "hooked for life" in their specific activities of chess, dance, and soccer, their parents' hope is that they do become hooked on competing and winning throughout life by learning how the process works while still young.

CHILDHOOD IS A BUFFET

By giving a historical and contemporary context to children's competitive activities and analyzing the reasons parents get their children involved in these activities, *Playing to Win* can help parents make sense of their decisions. One of the most gratifying moments I had while doing research for this book occurred when a mother told me that our interview helped her make sense of the everyday decisions she makes for her sons. This West County mom of two soccer- and chess-playing boys met me in a coffee shop, where we had a lively and freewheeling conversation that lasted over two and a half hours. We discussed various childhoods (hers, her sons', and even mine), views on American society, and poetry. The next day I sent her an email to thank her for being so generous with her thoughts and time. In her reply she wrote, "At the risk of totally abusing poetic imagery, if our thoughts are sometimes like a pasture of lone horses, each munching his own spot of grass, then yesterday all of mine came together, galloping in step to let me know what I really thought, so that was fun. Really, it was very interesting."

At the risk of abusing clichés, I want my son to be successful and happy—what this poetic mom wants for her kids, as do all of the parents I met. Like Dalton Conley, though, I understand the research and the numbers that say it might not matter where you go to college. I also know that what happens on a soccer field at age eight won't determine my son's future.

But like the *Playing to Win* parents, I construct my actions based on my beliefs about how the world works, whether or not those beliefs are right or wrong. For that reason it is a good bet that my son will be involved in at least one competitive after-school activity while he is still in elementary school. Though he is just one, we show him the family's chess set and have tried baby music classes run by the Boston Ballet School. I have seen the ads for Super Soccer Stars at our local Jewish Community Center, when we head in for his infant swim class. You get the idea . . .

Right after my son was born I read a book about boys' development. I was struck by this quote, so relevant to both my professional and personal lives:

> So much of life in our competitive culture is required to be strategic and performance- or outcome-based, it is tempting to apply the same approach to parenting. With hopes of producing the best boy ever, we might set out to cultivate the best of traditional male attributes (smart, strong, steady, and uncomplaining), but then perfect him by adding the quality of emotional literacy and subtracting violence and excessive aggression so he can be successful in life. Many parents speak about

parenting as if it were a giant school project: if you just start soon enough, read the right research, and do the right things, you can get the particular end product you have in mind.[12]

By doing this research I have been fortunate to be able to think deeply about my own parenting philosophy and gather all my own lone horses together in a pasture while my son is still young. But instead of thinking of boyhood, and childhood in general, as a project, I prefer to think of it as a buffet. At a buffet you can sample lots of dishes, and then go back to get a larger serving of your favorites. I plan to approach my children's after-school hours in the same way that I approach a buffet: children should sample a lot of different things so that they can figure out their favorites.

What parents choose to expose their kids to is ultimately shaped by a variety of individual and societal factors. To continue the buffet metaphor, not everyone will have grits or lox on their Sunday buffet, but most people will have eggs and bacon. (Some will have the free-range and organic choices, and others will not.) For example, in certain parts of the country ice hockey is popular, and in others Pop Warner football dominates. On top of regional preferences, parental background matters. More educated parents may shy away from activities they consider dangerous, like boxing, and instead push weekend math classes. And, as I have shown, parents of boys and girls tend to favor different sorts of activities, even within the same family.

In some families mom played the violin, so she wants her daughter to as well. Or perhaps she never played a musical instrument and that is the reason she is so adamant that her kids learn to play music. Other parents might emphasize physical fitness, so participation on an athletic team will be very important. Within those categories of music and sports there are more choices. A child can play a string instrument, the piano, drums, recorder, or clarinet, and the list goes on. Athletics is even more complex: Will a child play a team sport or an individual one? Will it be a popular sport, like soccer or tennis, or a more rarefied one, like lacrosse or squash?

Of course, this isn't an either/or enterprise. Many kids play sports *and* a musical instrument *and* do something else (drawing, Mandarin lessons, theater, or chess, and again the list goes on). Recall the mom in chapter 3 who evocatively described her parenting strategy by saying she is striving to raise "little Renaissance men."

But not all boys will grow up to be Renaissance men, and not all kids are destined to be "well-rounded." While these are worthwhile goals, parents must also listen to their children. Based on my interactions with the *Playing to Win* kids, I know that children are an integral part of the process of choosing an activity. In some cases, kids will approach their parents with an activity that they would like to try out. Perhaps a friend at school is a skateboarder, or a girl saw the U.S. gymnasts win the gold in the Olympics and she wants to try gymnastics. If a child expresses interest in a particular activity it is a good idea to explore a class in that, or something very similar—perhaps biking if you do not like skateboarding, or dance or cheerleading if you do not think gymnastics is safe.

At other times, such as when an activity is parent-driven and a child wants out (or even when a child requests more of a particular activity), parents should listen to their child's desires, especially before investments of time and money get too high. What is important is that kids are exposed to a wide range of options when they are young so they can explore, be creative, and start to gain mastery. This helps ensure that kids will be intrinsically motivated and hopefully develop a genuine interest and passion in a given area.

One area in which parents actually should step in is when they worry about the qualifications of those they are paying to teach their children. As I wrote in chapter 5, the coaches and teachers who work with children in these activities do not have to be formally credentialed or trained. In some cases they are not even vetted for basic safety, like making sure they have never sexually molested a child.[13] Anyone can open a dance studio or charge for chess lessons or start a soccer club. Parents must exercise caution when selecting programs for their children, and lawmakers, or even insurers, should step in to better protect children who increasingly spend many hours neither at home nor in school. This new childhood space must be better regulated to protect children.

In general, though, there is no right or wrong way to raise your children, so long as you listen to your child and to your own common sense.

No magic number of activities or number of hours of participation exist that will ensure your little one gets into an Ivy League school. No equation can tell us whether or not our children will rebel later in life if they go to ballet instead of karate. But there is a way to keep childhood fun and full of creativity and exploration while still training kids for the next steps in their lives. By allowing kids to explore within a structured set of choices, they will be able to know what they really love as they move into middle school and high school, where those specific choices start to matter more.

It is a long march to get through all of today's credentials checkpoints. There is not just college anymore. In our household there were master's programs, PhD programs, and postdoctoral programs. My friends went to law school and then clerked, and others went to medical school and then went through residencies and specialty fellowships. Our son will surely start preparing for similar credentials checkpoints at a young age, with doses of competition, to build up his Competitive Kid Capital—and he will likely sample chess, dance, and soccer at the buffet spread we lay out for him. Because the reality is that as long as winning remains important in American culture, playing to win will remain a central focus in many American childhoods.

APPENDIX **Questioning Kids**

EXPERIENCES FROM FIELDWORK
AND INTERVIEWS

In the tradition of both classic and contemporary ethnographers,[1] I present this appendix to detail how personal experiences in the field impacted my research. The appendix reviews three aspects of my fieldwork: first, how I went about identifying field sites and research subjects; second, my personal strategies for managing the researcher role; and third, special features and challenges posed by child respondents. I also discuss some practical strategies I learned for researchers who are involved with questioning kids and families in the city and the suburbs.

SELECTING FIELD SITES AND INTERVIEWEES:
MEETING FAMILIES IN THE CONTEXT
OF DROP AND RUN

I selected Metro and West County as my urban and suburban locations partially due to geographic convenience and partially due to established programs in these areas. I then identified specific programs, clubs, and studios within these communities; I expanded to additional sites after gaining knowledge from these initial interviews. The purpose of having a multisite ethnography was twofold: first, to meet a range of people with varied experiences to ensure breadth within the sample; second, to test the validity of responses across sites.

I began my fieldwork studying scholastic chess, the activity I knew the least about when I began this research, and ended with dance, the activity I previously knew the most about. Before starting this project my chess knowledge was minimal; I did not even know the names of the chess pieces or how they moved, let alone how to play. I got started by reading about the history of chess and discovered that one of the oldest American chess clubs was located in Metro. When I went on the club's website I discovered that they offered chess instruction for children, so I contacted the instructor and asked for recommendations for scholastic chess programs. This led to my connection with Uptown-Metro Chess. After a month and a half of fieldwork with them, I met one of the teachers involved with Charter-Metro Chess at a tournament, and he invited me to visit its summer camp and classes.

It was easy to meet parents involved with Uptown-Metro Chess. They were usually around during tournaments, summer camps, and classes. At tournaments, and with all of the activities, I began by identifying those families who were most involved, and then I met many other parents and families simply by being present. The only group of parents I needed a snowball sample to find was those with children who had dropped out of competitive chess.

With all three activities, I set out to learn about a range of family experiences. I often targeted families with girls and boys, high-performers or average-performers, and minorities. Across all the field sites I employed Glaser and Strauss's principles of grounded theory,[2] collecting, coding, and analyzing data until reaching theoretical saturation, which took at least six months for each activity.

I always tried to interview the parent who made most of the decisions about the child's participation by asking which parent it would be best to interview. Three families requested I interview both parents separately, but most deferred to the more knowledgeable parent. This is consistent with previous work, especially Annette Lareau's aptly titled article, "My Wife Can Tell Me Who I Know."[3] For six families, I interviewed both parents at the same time, at their suggestion. I found those interviews among the most difficult to conduct, as parents often looked to one another before answering questions, and their responses were less detailed and open. In later phases of my fieldwork, I tried to interview parents separately if both wanted to be interviewed.

All interviews were transcribed and coded using the qualitative data software AtlasTI.[4] Table 4 summarizes parent, teacher/coach, and kid interviews by length, number, and activity.

Table 4.   Number of Interviews and Their Length

	N	Average Length (in minutes)
Parents* (average length: 91 minutes)		
Chess	29	130
Dance	35	85
Soccer	32	83
Teachers/Coaches (average length: 83 minutes)		
Chess	13	76
Dance	8	65
Soccer	21	93
Children (average length: 41 minutes)		
Chess	15	45
Dance	11	38
Soccer	17	41

* I also interviewed 19 "dropout" families (8 from chess, 9 from soccer, and 2 from dance).

It was far more difficult to connect with the Charter-Metro Chess parents than the Uptown-Metro Chess parents. While I easily connected with the children (one of my favorite fieldwork memories is sitting for two hours as a group of girls braided my hair—until I thought they might pull it all out), I never really met, and scarcely saw, their parents. The Charter-Metro coaches took responsibility for getting children home from events. I eventually asked the coaches to introduce me to some parents, but they told me that as a white woman asking questions—and asking parents to sign a confidentiality form for human subjects reasons—most of the parents would not feel comfortable talking to me, possibly seeing me as a government representative. In her study of children's consumption, Alison Pugh worked for years to gain access to a similar group of low-income parents.[5] So, while frustrating, my problem was not unique.

Somewhat surprisingly I also had trouble meeting soccer parents, but for a different reason. Parents almost always attended games, and they usually dropped their children off at practices. However, in what I call the problem of "drop and run," the parents would simply pull up to the field, drop their kids off, and run off to do errands. The process occurred in reverse at pick-up time. It was also hard to speak with parents at games because they were focused on the game itself—because unlike chess, soccer parents can watch their children compete—and they then quickly left after the game ended. This was a problem for both soccer field sites, but it was heightened with Metro Soccer because of carpools to and from practices and games. (Carpools were used in Metro more than in West County given the distance to practice fields and games, and the fact that some families did not have cars.)

Having families at both soccer field sites who participated with West County and Metro Chess is what really helped me gain access and standing with other families, which was a happy coincidence at the start of field work. While doing fieldwork with Uptown-Metro Chess at a tournament, some parents heard there was a West County family there. I was introduced to the mother of two West County kids who had decided to try a more difficult chess tournament in Metro. She was also very active in leading West County Chess, so she was able to connect me to classes there, coaches, and other families. It turned out that these two boys also happened to play Westfield Soccer, the most visible program in West County. I first learned about Westfield Soccer because of road advertisements, and after investigating various clubs I decided it was the best fit for my research. I had already been working with Westfield Soccer's leadership to begin field-work with them, so it was an especially advantageous coincidence to meet this mother at a chess tournament. As a result of this encounter, I met a Westfield soccer family before starting my formal fieldwork with Westfield Soccer Club and made an early personal connection within West County Chess.

I learned about Metro Soccer Co-op from the many Uptown-Metro Chess families who had children or friends whose kids were involved. They vouched for me when I contacted the Co-op's leadership about gaining access and attending events. Many parents, both in this instance and at other times, were enormously helpful and generous in sharing their own experiences, giving me suggestions about other interviewees, and helping to connect me with specific people or organizations.

With no overlap between chess/soccer and dance, connections to dance field sites were made through other connections. I initially started fieldwork with Metroville Elite Dance Academy because I had known of their reputation for many years, having attended dance competitions as a child. While I myself never competed, my mother was a judge at competitions and had judged Elite students, so I referenced her during my initial contact with Metroville Elite Dance Academy, a strategy that helped me gain entry at this top dance studio.

Unlike chess, where I could independently hang out at tournaments and events and easily meet parents, the Elite Dance Academy teachers initially asked me to sit with them during competitions. Though this was helpful, since I heard their perspectives on the competition, dancers, and families (and it was often enjoyable, as we talked about dance in general and our lives), it initially limited my ability to meet a lot of families. I first interviewed those recommended by the teachers—which slightly concerned me, as I assumed they would give only a specific type of feedback. I then asked these parents to recommend other parents. By the third competition, I felt comfortable approaching parents myself, as I was then recognized by the group.

Like Westfield Soccer, I found out about Westbrook Let's Dance because of their presence in the community. While none of my Westbrook dancers participated in Westfield soccer (the two Westbrook dancers who played travel soccer did so with other clubs), my knowledge of the community enabled me to quickly gain rapport with the Westbrook families and teachers. Again, as at Elite, Let's Dance teachers helped connect me with families. Thanks to one of the mothers, I was eventually able to get many Westbrook dance families' email addresses through a dance company list, which helped move the interview process along without a focus on teacher-approved families.

Overall, two problems I encountered really surprised me. The first was how difficult it was to interview both parents at the same time. In these conversations there were lots of pauses, and I often felt uneasy about responses as parents looked to one another, which I felt sometimes led to censoring. Interviewing both parents separately was more helpful, and I encourage other researchers to conduct separate interviews, even though it can be more time-consuming.

The other problem that surprised me speaks to difficulties in conducting suburban ethnography: the aforementioned issue with "drop and run." Their having cars meant parents were simply less visible. They rarely hung out in waiting rooms at dance studios or on the sidelines at soccer practice, instead dashing off to grocery shop or run other errands. Even chess parents in West County were less likely to enter the class to pick up their kids, instead having the kids walk out to the car. Even though some soccer families in Metro had cars, they stuck around during practices because parking spaces were scarce and it wasn't as easy to run errands during practice as it was in West County. I certainly felt it was easier to conduct an urban ethnography by virtue of more people being physically present. Though the specific problem of drop and run likely only applies to fieldwork with parents and children, those thinking about conducting fieldwork in suburban areas must address the issue of cars, which means less hanging-out space and time.

"WHICH ONE IS YOURS?" IDENTITY IN THE FIELD

I was always careful about how I presented myself to those in the field and was not shy to admit lack of knowledge, such as not knowing how to play chess or soccer. I took special care about how I presented myself physically, and I thought deeply about how parents perceived me, both as a model student and as a potential parent.

While I gave little thought to how I dressed when I was doing chess fieldwork, as there was an "anything goes" attitude, I was more careful when it came to soccer and dance. When I went to soccer practices and games, I tried to dress in a sporty manner, mainly wearing shorts or jeans and sneakers so I would blend in with the participants. With dance, I often wore skirts and dresses and more feminine colors, like pink and purple. My outfits were frequently complimented while at dance competitions, and it was basically the only time when my appearance was noted, though if I was dressed up when doing chess fieldwork, parents sometimes asked me what I was doing later based on my more formal and unexpected attire.

Whenever I conducted parent interviews I was careful to look more professional than a typical graduate student, which meant avoiding jeans. This was especially true when I interviewed parents at their offices. I paid even more attention to my appearance after I realized that I was often perceived as a parent.

Often parents did not know how to make sense of my presence at practices and events. For example, early in my fieldwork I was asked, "Which one is yours?" When this occurred the first time, I was surprised. As a young woman in her mid-twenties it *was* biologically possible for me to have children who were old enough to be attending this summer camp, but it would have been socially unexpected given my educational background. I wrote up this exchange in my field notes as it made an impression on me in terms of the ways I was perceived by others in the field.

A few weeks later I was asked the same question, and I responded the same way, talking about my research. The woman who questioned me, needlessly embarrassed for what she perceived as a social gaffe, was interested in my research and said she would be willing to sit down over coffee and share her family's experiences. At this point I began thinking about the ways in which having or not having my own children may have helped or hurt me in the ethnographic process.

By the third time I was asked this question, this time on a soccer field, I knew it was a question worth considering more thoroughly. What does it mean that when a young white woman is around children the automatic assumption is that she is a mother; and how different would the reaction have been had I not been white or been a male?[6] Based on the seemingly innocuous question, I began thinking about the ways in which fieldwork with and around children presents particular challenges for an ethnographer.[7]

As I did not have children of my own at the time, the children I met during fieldwork helped build relationships for me in two ways. First, they helped me establish relationships with teachers, who often acted as gatekeepers, controlling access to families and various sites. For example, after spending two days as an observer at an Uptown-Metro Chess camp, I found myself pitching in to tie shoelaces, comforting a crying child who lost a chess game, and putting on a Band-aid. At the end of the week the head teacher informed me, "The children like you and children can really see [the inside of] people." Because the children trusted me, the teachers trusted me as well and allowed me to continue to attend the camp to meet families.

Second, some children told their parents about me, which prompted the parents to ask to meet me. One exchange particularly stands out because a mother came to camp at the end of the day asking to meet "the new girl teacher."[8] Because almost all of the adults involved with scholastic chess are male, her son went home all excited to have a "girl teacher," so the mom wanted to meet me. When I explained that I was actually there doing research, she quickly handed me a business card (not her own, but that of her six year-old son) and said she was happy to help me, especially because her son liked me so much.[9]

Other parents I met through their children were equally willing to help me with my research. It is interesting that several parents remarked that they liked the fact that I did not have children of my own (at the time). One father explained in an interview, after the microphone had been turned off, that he would not have been as open with me if I had children, because he would have thought I was implicitly comparing his son to my child—showing that not only are kids competitive in these activities, but some parents can be as well.

Many parents viewed me as an expert on achievement and competition by virtue of my academic credentials, including my status as a graduate student at Princeton. After learning that I had been an undergraduate at Harvard, parents also often asked me, "What does my child have to do to get into Harvard?" My scholastic affiliations gave me instant credibility with some parents, and I took advantage of that. I was always careful to use my academic email address and have business cards printed with my office mailing address displayed. I did sometimes worry that some parents might be trying to impress me (Michael Messner reported having a similar concern when he was studying youth sports)[10] or were more likely to highlight their interest in elite universities. In the end, I felt that my scholastic affiliations gave parents a natural entrée to discuss selective colleges and universities. Other parents did not seem to care or be impressed with my status as a Princeton student; their only concern related to my schooling was when I would finish "my paper" and when they could receive a copy.

QUESTIONING KIDS

I interviewed children only after I had met and interviewed their parents. Initially I broached the subject of interviewing their children only to parents with whom I felt I had particularly good rapport. As time went on, a few parents individually volunteered that I should interview their children. Given the positive response, by the halfway point in my fieldwork I felt comfortable asking those I did not know well if I could separately interview their kids.

I would explain to the children that they were helping me with my homework, which was to write a "really big paper." Parents signed a consent form, and the children signed an assent form. The assent form was simplified. It said that the child was willing to talk to me about his or her participation in chess, dance, or soccer. It then specifically said, "I have been told what the research is about. I know that it is not a test and my teachers and parents won't know exactly what I tell you. I also know that I can stop whenever I want." Children then wrote their name, the date, and their birthday in the spaces provided. The only question kids ever asked about the form was about the date. A few wrote their birthday in the spot for the current date but drew an arrow to correct their mistake.

Prior to starting interviews with children I had some methodological questions—such as how to build rapport and explain my research—so I turned to the literature for guidance. I discovered that not nearly as much has been written on conducting interviews with children as I expected. One article I located sums up the situation:

> Given the existence of power and conceptual differences between interviewing adolescents and adults, social scientists' frequent use of the interview in the study of adolescents would suggest the existence of a plethora of practical information on the conduct of and the creation of the adolescent social research interview. A review of the literature, however, reveals a paucity of such information, with the exception of information on conducting the child clinical interview.[11]

There are some sociological texts that focus on methodologies for doing research with children. The most notable is *Knowing Children*, by Gary Alan Fine and Kent Sandstrom.[12] More recently William Corsaro has written about conducting fieldwork with children in a collected volume on various types of research with children, including in the for-profit research sector and psychology.[13] Amy L. Best's edited volume, *Representing Youth*, addresses how to study and frame youth, and Sheila Greene and Diane Hogan's edited collection *Researching Children's Experiences: Methods and Approaches* focuses mostly on ethical issues and the use of interviews, observations, and focus groups.[14]

Other disciplines have also weighed in. Anthropologists offer more specific insight into understanding children and ethnography by way of four edited collections.[15] The authors focus on the experiences of ethnographers taking their own children into the field and the ways in which the children affected the research. European scholars, medical researchers, social workers, education researchers, and geographers have published more extensively on interviewing children as part of the research process than have their North American counterparts.[16]

These works were helpful when I entered the field. Nonetheless, during my fieldwork with kids I encountered two issues I did not find covered by the literature: children's behavior as I directly questioned them, and questions children had for me.

Distracted and Hijacked Interviews

There was a clear difference in how most children and adults comported themselves during their interviews. Parents presented more carefully crafted responses and presentations of self. As others have stated, adults tend to provide longer answers, sometimes as a monologue, and have an agenda for what they want to say or discuss in an interview.[17] Children often did not have knowledge of social norms or (learned) inhibitions about how to act in an interview, so there was very little self-censorship of actions or words.

Children's behavior during interviews was uninhibited, and, in general, the kids were less singularly focused than their adult counterparts, frequently doing other things while we spoke. One soccer girl jumped on her bed and tried to do flips as we talked. A chess girl drew a picture of me as we sat and talked at her dining room table, presenting it to me at the end of our conversation when she asked how to spell my name. (I was honored and still have the drawing.) One chess boy played a game against himself, with both the white and the black pieces, as we spoke. I tried to incorporate his game into our conversation, commenting on the white queen's position. His play did not distract him from answering my questions, but his lack of eye contact and apparent indifference to the experience differed drastically from my experiences with adults. I found these behaviors to be unsettling at first, as I worried that I was simply boring the children or making them uncomfortable. But over time I began to realize that these behaviors were normal, and while they might seem distracted the kids were paying attention; they were simply multitasking.

To place these distracted children in context, some adults were distracted by BlackBerrys or phones. Being prone to distraction was not necessarily unique to the children. However, the adults did do a better job of appearing solely focused on and interested in our conversation, even if they were not. I never had a parent stop the interview, even if we had been speaking for some time, which is similar to other researchers' experiences.[18] If a parent had to attend to another matter, he or she asked to be excused to take a phone call, but then returned to our conversation. I never had a parent handle a work-related matter during an interview, but parents always took phone calls from their children, recognizing the number that appeared when the call came in.

During one interview with a seven-year-old soccer player, the boy surprised me by attending to other needs without excusing himself. He abruptly stood up in the middle of our interview and wordlessly walked out of the living room in his house, where we were talking. I heard a door close nearby, and I was at first worried I had upset him. After about a minute I wondered if I should find his mother. But then I heard a toilet flush and a door reopen. I realized he had needed to use the restroom. He returned to the living room and starting talking right where we left off, without a word being said about his absence. I was so caught off guard that I did not mention the interruption to him, or his mother, after we had finished our conversation.

Though this was the only unacknowledged absence I experienced, I did have other interactions with children that were definitely unexpected for me—when children hijacked the interview process. One boy asked me to tell him specifically how many more questions I would ask him. When I told him there were about five questions left, he kept track and would not let me ask any follow-up or clarifying questions after I reached five. A few other children tried to read the questions from my interview schedule sheet, often upside-down, trying to do so discreetly, even though I could not help but notice.

Then there was Archibald, a chess player in first grade. Archibald actually took the paper out of my hand and began reading it aloud. He wanted to hurry through the interview to watch afternoon cartoons, so he said, "How many questions are you asking me?" We then had the following exchange:

ARCHIBALD: Did you ask all of them yet?
    HILARY: No, almost.
ARCHIBALD: How many? What are you up to?
    HILARY: I think we're up to here (indicates on sheet). Should we keep going?
ARCHIBALD: You asked me bunches of questions already.

It was difficult when Archibald asked me what question we were "up to" since the interview was semistructured, with questions listed as topics to cover and not in a rigid, set order. We continued to talk, with Archibald consulting the sheet when I asked him a question. At one point he told me I couldn't ask him a particular question because it was above the point I said I was at on the sheet, and he refused to answer. A few minutes later he unilaterally and emphatically declared:

ARCHIBALD: One more question.

HILARY: One more question, okay. Are you going to ask it or should I?

ARCHIBALD: (Thinks for a moment) You ask me.

Our interview concluded with that final question and a short answer from Archibald.

Did You Do This?

While not all of the kids were as direct as Archibald, when given the opportunity many of them did ask me direct questions. Other researchers have written about children asking questions about the interviewer's age, where he or she has come from, and why.[19] All of the children I interviewed wanted to know even more about my life, beyond where I went to school—another difference from most of their parents' behavior during interviews.

In particular, the kids wanted to know if I had participated in their activity when I was a child. More than half asked if I was a chess player, dancer, or soccer player. They would ask this question in slightly different ways. One child asked, "What do you play?" Another, "Did you do any of those activities when you were younger?" Others, "Did you use to dance?" and "Do you dance?" Finally, one child pointedly asked about my participation in dance as a child: "Did you want to do it or did your mom want you to do it?"

At the conclusion of one interview a dance girl asked me a completely unrelated question: "Do you have a pet?" I said that I did not. She responded, "Okay," and when I asked if she had any other questions for me she replied that she did not. I am still not sure what made her ask this particular question, as she had not spoken about animals or pets during our conversation. I admit I felt I had failed some test when I replied negatively to her question.

One other topic many children asked me about was my education and the purpose of my "homework." Kids often wondered, "Where do you go to school?" Another asked, "Is college hard?" And one boy (sweetly) wondered, "Are you in high school?" I thanked him for thinking I looked so young and then explained that I had actually already gone to high school and college and was now doing even more school.

Many of the children were shocked by my answer when they asked how long my "paper" would be (answer: Nearly three hundred pages). They wanted to know when they could read it (answer: Not for a few years). One girl asked, "So what page will I be on?" (answer: I don't know yet, but I will change your name so your parents and teachers do not know exactly what you said).

I did use pseudonyms for all participants, with the exception of three adults who are public figures in chess. Some qualitative researchers argue that the use of pseudonyms should be abandoned,[20] but I felt some parents and their children would be recognizable in a way that could be embarrassing or uncomfortable in their communities (though of course those who are part of a specific club, team, or studio might recognize some families despite name changes and other modifications to identifying characteristics). Some researchers allow the participants to select their own pseudonym to be used in published texts;[21] among child researchers, Marjorie Orellana and Virginia Morrow have allowed children to pick their own pseudonyms.[22] However, like Debbie Epstein,[23] I decided against the children selecting their own pseudonym because I wanted to maintain similarities to the actual name in terms of ethnicity and gender. Epstein found that children often selected names that were entirely different from their own, or they decided to use the name of their best friend.[24]

I had a special experience with a few chess children who were able to teach me how to play chess. As I said, when I started this research I did not even know how the chess pieces move. After a girl asked me to play a game with her at a chess camp, I had to tell her I did not know how to play. She immediately offered to teach me, and soon another girl joined us. Eventually other children would help me play games, telling me the names of certain opening sequences, such as the Italian, and special rules, such as castling. When this occurred I was immediately reminded of William Corsaro's work with children in Italy and how his lack of Italian fluency helped him bond with the kids because they loved "teaching the teacher."[25] My lack of experience ultimately helped me build rapport. As I learned the game better (though I certainly did not become a particularly strong player) I often was careful not to beat the children so that they could continue to feel they were teaching me—which, honestly, they almost always were.

LESSONS LEARNED: PRACTICAL ADVICE IN CONDUCTING QUALITATIVE RESEARCH WITH KIDS

During the course of my sixteen-month-long fieldwork with kids in chess, dance, and soccer I learned how to be a better qualitative researcher, especially one who works with children. On a practical level there are three important lessons I want to emphasize: setting up interviews with kids, the way children differentially respond to questions, and managing rapport with children.

When I set up interviews with parents I could tell them about my research directly, invite their participation, and set up a convenient time to meet. With the kid interviews their parents became a third party, and all of my initial interactions related to the interview itself had to go through the parent, even when I knew the child well from fieldwork. I was looking for children's own thoughts on their lives, but I simply do not know if their parents shaped their attitude toward the interview, and hence their responses, in positive or negative ways. Luckily only one parent blocked access, but it can be a problem if parents block access when their child really wants to be interviewed and share his or her thoughts.

Given that Institutional Review Boards (IRBs) expect adult consent before a child can formally participate in research, there is little to do about this other than to be aware of its possible effects. I found it interesting that for this project the IRB did not comment at all on the substance of the questions I would be asking of kids or adults. They instead focused on the assent and consent forms, both their content and how they were formatted.

One other issue I faced in gaining access to the children was timing. My fieldwork spanned two summers, though during the first summer I did not interview any children as I was just starting in the field. The following summer I was interviewing dance and soccer kids (I had completed all of the chess research at that point), but I encountered serious difficulties with the soccer children. This was because of summer camp. Many of these children went away for weeks or months at a time so it was difficult to schedule time to meet with them. After nine failed attempts, I stopped trying to interview soccer kids and waited until school started again to interview them. I had fewer problems with dance since the girls had studio and competition obligations during the summer, at least through July, so they were around in the early summer. This is an important practical point for those who want to study children during the summertime— particularly children from upper-middle-class families. I have not come across any researchers describing this sleep-away summer camp problem, but it can be an impediment to research with kids and should be taken into account if a researcher is on a strict timeline.

When I was able to find the right time to formally sit down and interview children I learned another practical lesson. The youngest child I interviewed was seven, and most of the children were between nine and eleven, with a few twelve-year-olds included. Consistent with other research in this area, the younger children had less elaborate answers. They frequently provided only yes or no responses but did elaborate slightly more when prompted. In general I received less descriptive responses from the youngest kids, and they rarely offered additional information or stories without being asked direct questions. Researchers conducting interviews with younger children should not be alarmed if this happens, thinking it means children cannot provide a lot of information about their lives.

Giving brief answers does not at all mean that the information kids do provide is incomplete or inaccurate, as funding agencies and other researchers sometimes think.[26] One group of researchers wrote that "children's responses are frequently compared with adults' reports of events for validation, and adult reports are upheld as the 'gold standard' or benchmark against which the reliability of children's contributions are assessed."[27] My research calls this common wisdom into question. I found that children often knew their activity schedule and history of participation better than their parents. When I asked parents what other activities their children participate in during a given week, they often forgot to mention an activity, but the children never forgot. Parents also admitted to not remembering what events their child competed in or how a child did at a particular event. The kids did not have any difficulties remembering or recounting their past experiences with a high level of specificity, as they show in their own words in chapter 6.

My own knowledge of their tournament schedules, their performance in games, and the content of their routines helped me achieve rapport with the kids. I also made sure I knew about youth trends, like *High School Musical* and the new Game Boy, so that I could draw on a variety of topics relevant to their lives. To many kids I seemed "cool," and a few parents even told me that they needed me to fill them in on youth pop culture.

I was aware of building good rapport with the kids throughout the research process. I initially was concerned that some children would be reluctant to talk to me, especially because of "stranger danger" issues that adults impress upon children.[28] For that reason I initially interviewed only children who had seen me at several events or practices and who knew I knew their parents. That also raised some concerns, as I worried that these kids might be more reluctant to share negative accounts of their competitive experiences—making mistakes, being nervous, or feeling pressured by adults—for fear I would tell their teachers, parents, or friends. While I provided an assent form saying I would not do that, confidentiality is a difficult idea for children to grasp.[29] In the end I need not have worried as all the children were quite open; many told me about some of the unpleasant consequences of competition they experienced, such as stomach problems and excess sweat, from the stress of competing.

One difference that surprised me was that some of the most focused interviews were with children I knew less well. The children who knew me well felt more comfortable to misbehave or act silly (for example, doing flips on the bed) during the interview. Researchers should not feel they must know a child well before an interview, though in many cases it can help. Other ways to build rapport exist, such as talking about a popular song, television show, or sporting match.

Overall I found the interviews I conducted with children to be enormously important and interesting. While other researchers have decided against interviewing children, believing it is "a method better suited to adults,"[30] I believe that by taking seriously children's statements, behaviors, and questions during interviews we are deepening our understandings of childhood and research methods. Not only that—I had a lot of fun talking with kids and receiving hugs, drawings, and other tokens from them. It was a definite highlight of my field-work experience.

Notes

PREFACE

1. I think one of the best examples of this type of work is Jay MacLeod's *Ain't No Makin' It* (1995), which I first gulped down in 1999 during a required sociology course. MacLeod began his work examining the aspirational pathways of black and white teenage boys in a Boston-area housing project as a Harvard undergraduate, and though he is not an academic sociologist, it has gone through several reprints and is still a model of how to do important and effective sociological research.

2. Brooks 2012.

3. Spence 1985: 1285.

4. Tocqueville 2003.

5. Orenstein 2009.

6. Duina 2011: 60.

7. D'Esto 1995: 602.

8. I recommend a variety of books, documentaries, and television shows on these topics: TLC's series *Toddlers & Tiaras* that began in 2009; the 2009

documentary *Bigger Stronger Faster;* the 2002 documentary *Spellbound;* and the 2007 documentary *King of Kong.* And yes, rollersoccer is an actual sport (http://rollersoccer.com/).

9. Fagone 2006: 16.
10. Lamont 1992: 41.
11. Schumpeter 2010: 70.
12. For example, see Brewer et al. 1999; Dale and Krueger 2002.
13. Rivera 2011.
14. Dominus 2009.
15. Otterman 2009.
16. Best 2011.
17. Hibbard and Buhrmester 2010.
18. Lepper and Greene 1973.
19. Chua 2011: 5.
20. Chua 2011: 97.
21. For example, Stabiner 2010.
22. Conley 2008: 369.

INTRODUCTION

1. Bughouse, also known as tandem or exchange chess, usually has four players in teams of two playing with rapid time controls. Normal rules of chess apply, except that captured pieces join the opponent's side of the board.

2. All names are pseudonyms, along with the names of locations. Major identifying characteristics (e.g., occupation) have also been changed, but the changes have all been comparable shifts.

3. For example, see Foderaro 2006; Miranda 2006; Winerip 2008.

4. Hochschild and Matchung 1989.

5. Darrah et al. 2007. It is worth considering that since children seem not to be "bowling alone," their parents aren't either (Putnam 2001). Perhaps parents no longer have time to participate in their own activities and organizations amid the busyness of family and work obligations, which include taking their children to practices, but the settings of children's activities provide the space to make community connections among adults now—as Josh's comment about starting a parent book club at chess tournaments suggests. Josh also volunteers as an assistant soccer coach, a new form of volunteerism rarely acknowledged or studied by academics.

6. Bianchi et al. 2006.

7. Hofferth et al. 2009.

8. Wrigley 1995: 126.

9. Goodwin 2006: 93.

10. Lareau 2003.

11. Additionally, most of Lareau's observations, and those of others who study socialization, are grounded in the home and the residential neighborhoods of her target families, whereas I take my fieldwork beyond these two settings into the competitive venues themselves.

12. "Competitive dance" refers to for-profit dance competitions that organize regional and national competitions for all forms of dance.

13. Kinetz 2004.

14. Heisman 2002: 4. It has been reported that about thirty thousand of those members are under the age of fifteen (Mitchell 2006: 69). USCF officials confirmed via personal correspondence with the author in August 2008 that at that time there were approximately 28,800 members under twelve.

15. Travel can also be referred to as "elite" or "club" soccer, depending on region of the country.

16. McClelland 1967.

17. Collins 1979; English 2005.

18. Weber 1978: 999–1000.

19. Macleod 1983: 25.

20. Saulny 2006.

21. Paul 2008: 150.

22. Martinez 2011.

23. For example, see Armour 2007; Carroll 2005; Fortin 2008.

24. For example, see Boncompagni 2006; Hu 2008.

25. Easterlin 1987: 30.

26. Newman 1994.

27. Druckerman 2012: 4.

28. Ellis 2012; Gilmore 2012.

29. Ferguson 2011; Rothman 2012.

30. Lareau 2008: 7.

31. For example, see Warren and Warren Tyagi 2003.

32. Lamont 1992: 71.

33. Ramey and Ramey 2010.

34. Shulman and Bowen 2001.

35. For example, see Dunn 1995; Onishi 2008.

36. Levey 2009a.

37. Golden 2006; Kaufman and Gabler 2004.

38. Sullivan Moore 2005.

39. Some parents push their children athletically in the hopes that their success on the field will translate into scholarship money. But the odds of winning an NCAA scholarship, particularly in a Division I program, are quite low. For

example, in the 2003–4 academic year, only about 2 percent of the 6.4 million collegiate athletes received scholarship monies from NCAA institutions (Pennington 2008). You stand a better chance of getting into Harvard than getting athletic money to attend any college, provided you are even good enough to play in college.

40. Shulman and Bowen 2001: xxxvi.
41. Karabel 2006.
42. Karabel 2006: 3.
43. Golden 2006: chapter 4.
44. Rivera 2011.
45. Stevens 2007: 15.
46. Elkind 2007.
47. Levey 2009a.
48. Bourdieu 2007; Bourdieu and Passeron 1973.
49. Attewell 2001; Frank and Cook 1995.
50. Kindlon 2006.

CHAPTER ONE

1. A version of this chapter previously appeared as Levey 2010a.
2. Lareau 2003.
3. Applebome 2004; Tugend 2005. The term "overscheduled child" is from Rosenfeld and Wise 2001.
4. Belluck 2005; Gupta 2005; Hack 2005.
5. Nir 2001.
6. Kleiber and Powell 2005: 23.
7. It's worth observing that growth in competitive after-school activities appears to occur after the United States participates in major wars: after World War II, after Vietnam, and after the first Iraq war.
8. For a full discussion of child-saving practices during this time, see Katz, 1986: chapter 5.
9. The last better baby contests were held in 1952.
10. Dorey 1999.
11. We can think of these contests as early versions of child beauty pageants.
12. Zelizer 1994.
13. Halpern 2002: 180.
14. Paris 2008: 53.
15. Spears and Swanson 1988: 179.
16. MacLeod 1983: 32. This is also the time when the Boy Scouts, Campfire Girls, Girl Scouts, Woodcraft Folk, and the like were founded. With their focus

on patches and achievement hierarchies, some could define these activities as competitive, though they are not explicitly so. Note too that these activities were not consciously part of the larger child-saving movement of the Progressive Era, even though they were founded at the same time. As historian Stacy Cordery notes, writing about the Girl Scouts, "Daisy Low and her organization were not consciously part of this larger movement. She neither knew the reformers nor took much notice of their work, beyond initiating Girl Scout patrols at Hull House" (2012: xi). It's interesting to note that summer camps, with competitive events like Color War, also developed during this time (Paris 2008).

17. Halpern 2002: 181
18. Cited in Jable 1984: 222.
19. Jable 1984: 232.
20. Maguire 2006: 56.
21. Clement 1997: 89.
22. Maguire 2006: 68.
23. DiMaggio and Mullen 2000: 137.
24. Horowitz 1990: 68.
25. Graff 1995: 271.
26. Clement 1997: 162.
27. Miller 2007: 203.
28. Berryman 1988: 5.
29. Margolin 1994; Stone 1992.
30. Passer 1988: 203.
31. Fine 1987: 4.
32. Stearns 2003.
33. Chudacoff 2007: 133.
34. Farrey 2008: 19.
35. This statement is based on the assessment of an industry insider (Stanley 1989: 265) rather than numbers, since there are not hard facts on events such as this collected over time, or even in the present.
36. Gallagher 1977.
37. Chudacoff 2007: 165.
38. Seefeldt 1998: 337.
39. Kleiber and Powell 2005: 28.
40. Chudacoff 2007: 165–66.
41. As Grasmuck (2005) shows for youth baseball.
42. Hofferth and Sandberg 2001.
43. Sternheimer 2006.
44. For example, see Adler and Adler 1998; Fine 1987; Levey 2009a.
45. Brower 1979.
46. Engh 2002.

47. Averbuch and Hammond 1999.
48. Matchan 2012.
49. Farrey 2008: 159.
50. For example, see Saint Louis 2007; Sheff 2006.
51. Bick 2007.
52. Pennington 2003.
53. Ryan 2000: 142.
54. Talbot 2003.
55. Sand 2000: 157.
56. Feldman 1991: 4.
57. Quart 2006.
58. Adams and Bettis 2003.
59. Torgovnick 2008: xvii.
60. *The Insider* 2005.
61. Yalom 2004.
62. Ashley 2005: 48.
63. Shenk 2006.
64. Waitzkin 1984.
65. Weinreb 2007: 93.
66. Heisman 2002: 4.
67. Ashley 2005: 53
68. Ashley 2005: 54.
69. Fortanasce et al. 2001: 15.
70. Ever wonder why it is called soccer? According to Hendrik Hertzberg, it is "not some Yankee neologism but a word of impeccably British origin. . . . 'Soccer' is rugger's equivalent in Oxbridge-speak. The 'soc' part is short for 'assoc,' which is short for 'association,' as in 'association football'" (2010: 29–30).
71. McShane 2002: 10.
72. Markovits and Hellerman 2001: 123.
73. While it is difficult to prove this, several soccer writers make this claim, such as Averbuch and Hammond (1999: 4) and Haner (2006: 48).
74. Haner 2006: 48.
75. A "trainer" runs a practice, while a "coach" may lead the team at a game. Most coaches act as both trainers and coaches.
76. Haner 2006: 29.
77. Applebome 2004; Foer 2004: 235.
78. O'Neill 1948.
79. McMains 2006: 72.
80. Kendall 1984: 7.
81. Hall 2008; Masten 2009.
82. Chancey 2004: 6.

83. Roberts 1999: 129.

84. McMains 2006: 89.

85. Picart 2006: 70.

86. Tu and Anderson 2007: 70.

87. Kinetz 2004.

88. Darrah et al. 2007: 49.

89. Stearns 2003.

90. For a discussion on the significance of cohort sizes for life experiences, see Easterlin 1987.

91. Stearns 2003: 100.

92. Shulman and Bowen 2001: 21.

93. Stevens 2007.

94. Stearns 2003: 104.

95. Faust et al. 1999.

96. For example, see Jih 2009.

97. For example, see Willen 2003.

98. For example, see Williams 2007.

99. Collins 1979: 94.

100. Zelizer 1994.

101. Dean 2012: 74–75.

102. Scott 2007: 9.

103. Bean 2005: 1.

104. Markovits and Hellerman 2001: 50.

105. English 2005: 72.

106. Horowitz 1990: 14.

107. Fagone 2006.

108. Anand and Watson 2004: 60.

109. *Brooklyn Castle* 2012.

CHAPTER TWO

1. The Northeast is known as a particularly competitive area. However, local and regional newspapers around the country, along with writers and social commentators, have written about the increased competition in children's lives and their participation in competitive, organized activities. Recent works by the psychologists Hinshaw and Kranz (2009), Levine (2006), and Luthar (2003) illustrate the types of pressure affecting affluent children nationwide. I have also had conversations with parents in various parts of America, and they all talk about the pressures on their children and that the level of competition with which the children need to contend is more than they themselves had to

deal with. While competition may be heightened in the Northeast for a variety of reasons, the larger issues seem to be affecting elementary school–age children across the United States.

2. In addition to scholastic tournaments there are also "open" tournaments, which are open to everyone but usually are dominated by adult players. Some talented children do play in open tournaments, but most focus on scholastic tournaments, so they are my focus.

3. For example, see Redman 2007: 69. Note that the rest of the eighty-five thousand members are predominantly male, and the adult members are generally college-educated and affluent, according to the USCF website (http://main.uschess.org/content/view/7850/385/, accessed May 5, 2008).

4. The USCF also puts out a monthly publication, *Chess Life*, which has some articles on scholastics but is meant to be read by the general USCF membership.

5. For a more complete discussion, see Glickman and Doan 2008; Goldowsky 2006.

6. Heisman 2002: 71.

7. Almost all scholastic chess tournaments use the Swiss system, a non-elimination round-robin format that aims to match strong players against strong players and weak against weak. In the first round, the top players are paired against the weaker players, based on ratings. In the next round, winners play winners and losers play losers. Pairings are again based on ratings, with stronger playing weaker. Throughout the following rounds—there are usually four rounds during a local, one-day tournament, and seven at state- or national-level tournaments—players are matched based on their performance in that tournament, and then on their rating.

8. A bye is awarded to a player when the number of players in his or her section is uneven and he or she does not have an opponent to play in that round.

9. The most prestigious chess titles, Grandmaster and International Master, are awarded by the World Chess Organization (Fédération internationale des échecs, FIDE). FIDE uses a rating system similar to the one used by the USCF, and top players have to earn a FIDE rating and play in FIDE tournaments to be recognized. The vast majority of scholastic players in the United States will never play in a FIDE tournament.

10. Chabris and Glickman 2006.

11. The system for recording the moves of a chess game is known as algebraic notation. Algebraic notation uses symbols for pieces and specific moves, such as check or castling. This is important for two reasons: to be able to study a game after the tournament to analyze what occurred for instructional purposes and to have a record of the game in case there are any disputes. The most common dispute in scholastic chess revolves around a rule called "touch-move": if

you touch a piece, you have to move it. Children frequently argue about what piece was where and who touched what piece.

12. Of course, the shortest chess games are those called speed chess, or more commonly "blitz." Blitz games can take place in minute increments and usually last no longer than five minutes. Blitz tournaments sometimes take place at large scholastic tournaments, as a fun side event, but they are not the main focus, because blitz is seen as a fun trick or skill.

13. The Internet Chess Club is one of the most popular providers of this service.

14. It is important to note that other chess organizations call some of their tournaments "Nationals," but they do not carry the same prestige as the USCF Nationals.

15. The USCF reports (personal communication, May 11, 2009) that Burt Lerner is a longtime supporter of scholastic chess whose son donated money to sponsor the National Elementary Championship, with the proviso that his father's name be used in the title.

16. Waitzkin 1984.

17. Other hotspots for scholastic chess are Texas, California, and Florida.

18. Curriculum chess refers to classes taught as part of the normal school day. These typically occur once a week, like a gym, art, or music class that is supplemental to the traditional curriculum.

19. Different parts of the country use different terms for competitive soccer, but in the Northeast *travel* predominates, so that is the term I use most often.

20. Farrey 2008: 183.

21. U.S. Youth Soccer. The total number of children who play recreational soccer through AYSO or AAU or even the local YMCA is even higher.

22. Glamser and Vincent 2004.

23. Both of the soccer clubs I worked with offered scholarships for those in need, which require an application and a copy of the family's 1040 tax form. None of the families I met, with children in elementary school, asked for or were awarded these funds. I did hear that some high school players received them, or the families of their team members covered their fees (especially if a player was talented and could help the team achieve on a national level).

24. Another goal of many travel soccer kids is to make their state's Olympic Development Program (ODP) team or pool. I do not discuss ODP further, as the children I focused on are too young to participate in this program.

25. Black 2008; *Kicking and Screaming* 2005; Star 2008.

26. While Metro in particular has many Latino immigrants interested in soccer, at the elementary school–level they did not play on Co-op teams, though that picture changes at the high school level.

27. *First Position* 2012.

28. *Mad Hot Ballroom* 2005.

29. It is important to note that anyone can become a dance teacher or dance studio owner as well. There is no regulation, apart from insurance companies that offer studio insurance, about who can or cannot have this job and the type of training required to do it well.

30. Surprisingly, even large national organizations, such as Little League Baseball, do not keep track of the characteristics of their competitors, such as sex (Messner 2009: 17).

31. Showstopper.

32. I looked on multiple dance competition system websites and could often not find any advertised standards, but I never once heard teachers or parents complain about this lack of information.

33. Pictures and personal video cameras are not allowed in the competition room, both to prevent choreography theft, which has happened in the past, and to enable organizers to make more money by charging a high price for these visual memories.

34. Ryan 2000.

35. Of all the organizations I worked with, Elite Dance Academy is the oldest and most established. The other organizations have been around in their current form, with current leaders and owners, about five to fifteen years.

CHAPTER THREE

1. Blair-Loy 2003.
2. Frank 2007: 65.
3. Bearman 2005.
4. Hofferth et al. 2009.
5. Chess kids also quit playing earlier.
6. While a little less than half of the kids in the families I studied attend private school, this is significantly higher than the overall number of American children who attend private schools. (In 2008 around 24 percent of U.S. kids attended private elementary and secondary schools.) The chess group had the most kids in private school (nearly half), while dance had the fewest (less than a fifth), and all of those girls attended a parochial school. This is another indicator of some of the class differences across activities.

7. Levey 2009a.
8. Lareau 2003.
9. Messner 2009: 13.
10. Blair-Loy 2003; Hays 1998.
11. Lareau 2003.

12. Bourdieu and Passeron 1973.

13. For example, see Dumais 2006.

14. Bourdieu 2007.

15. Bourdieu 2007.

16. Rohde 2001.

17. Kusserow 2004.

18. Parents did sometimes say that there is a trade-off between school and these activities, in terms of both school performance and finances. Because these children are young, there is less academic pressure than there is in high school. Parents often remarked that if their older children were to experience an academic decline, then they would have to drop some of their out-of-school activities. But I never heard this talked about before high school.

19. For example, see Jarovsky 1995.

20. Lever 1978: 472.

CHAPTER FOUR

1. Lareau 2003.

2. West and Zimmerman 1987.

3. Bettie 2003: 33; Pascoe 2007: 12.

4. Fine 1987; Grasmuck 2005.

5. Thorne 1993.

6. Adler and Adler 1998; Eder et al. 1995.

7. Eder et al. 1995, see chapter 7 in particular, "Learning to Smile through the Pain."

8. The family is also largely absent in studies of masculine socialization. For example, in a recent *Annual Review* piece on masculinity, only the media and schools are discussed (Schrock and Schwalbe 2009).

9. Lever 1978: 480.

10. Ring 2009: 35.

11. Jable 1984: 232.

12. DeBare 2005: 98.

13. Lamont 1992: 121.

14. Ostrander 1984.

15. Friedman 2010; Goudreau 2011; Jones 2002.

16. Stevenson 2010.

17. For example, see Erickson 1996.

18. Hibbard and Buhrmester 2010: 413.

19. McGuffey and Rich 1999.

20. One exception is Ferguson 2001.

21. Bettie 2003; Lareau 2008: 7.

22. Lacy 2007.

23. A working-class family is defined as those who fall below the specifications of the lower-middle class, but who do not fall below the poverty line.

24. A *battement* is a ballet/dance term that refers to kicks, or extensions of the legs.

25. Adler et al. 1992: 170.

26. Connell 1995.

27. Connell 1995: 67.

28. Britton 2000.

29. Pascoe 2007: 133.

30. Kane 2006: 149; McGuffey and Rich 1999: 621.

31. Graff 1995.

32. For example, see Best 2000; Pascoe 2007: 41–42, 69.

33. Shahade 2005.

34. Polgar and Truong 2005.

35. Goffman 1959.

36. Collins 1993.

37. Aranda-Alvarado 2012.

38. Grainey 2012: 6.

39. Rudd et al. 2008.

40. Daniels and Leaper 2006: 876.

41. Pierce 1995: 24.

42. Hinshaw and Kranz 2009.

43. Pascoe (2007) discusses the hierarchy of jocks, nerds, and "fags."

44. Messner 2009: 160.

45. I interviewed the mothers of three of these four boys, but all three boys were out of elementary school; two were in middle school and one was in high school. The parents of the fourth boy ignored repeated requests for an interview.

46. Adler and Adler 1998; Pascoe 2007.

47. Theberge 2000: 1.

48. Newman et al. 2004: 29.

49. Pascoe: 63.

50. Recall the song "I Can Do That" from *A Chorus Line,* when the character tells about stuffing his older sister's dance shoes with socks so he could dance when she was sick.

51. Chafetz and Kotarba 1995.

52. Thompson 1999.

53. Recall the comment made by the dance teacher earlier in this chapter, which is true based on my fieldwork, that it is always the mom involved with

dance. Since the vast majority of dancers are girls, this is pretty exclusively a mother-daughter activity.

CHAPTER FIVE

1. Note that this is not true only for the children's versions of some of these competitive activities. Competitive ballroom dancing for adults, or DanceSport, for example, has many businesses surrounding the competitive endeavor: competition owners, studios, dressmakers, shoe manufacturers, magazine publishers, and music distributors (McMains 2006: 1).

2. Becker 1984.

3. Note that "there is virtually no serious scholarship on dance competitions. Nor has there been a significant critical inquiry into the institutional and economic structures of dance as an industry" (McMains 2006: 199). This book, and this chapter specifically, work to fill this gap in the growing dance literature.

4. Tanier 2012.

5. Note that both Westfield Soccer Club and Metro Soccer Co-op are registered nonprofits dedicated solely to providing soccer instruction to children (though they are commercial nonprofits, since they charge a fee). Charter-Metro Chess is affiliated with a nonprofit, but that nonprofit is not focused only on chess. It is not clear why the soccer clubs have this status and dance studios do not. The major difference is that the dance studio owners pocket all profits, while the soccer clubs place profits into a bank account to be used by the club at a later date, due to the nondistribution constraint for all nonprofits (for a discussion, see Hansmann 1996). But both are about producing winners, and profits. In their article on not-for-profit entrepreneurs, specifically examining why some businesses go the not-for-profit route, economists Glaeser and Schliefer (1998) lay out four reasons for the choice, but soccer clubs do not easily fit into any of these. Hansmann explains that some daycare centers choose to be nonprofit in order to attract customers and get taxation and regulation breaks, which may be the case with soccer clubs. But this still does not explain why dance studios are for-profit, especially when arts organizations in general tend toward nonprofit status. Historically arts organizations have been nonprofits and sports activities for-profit, so this is quite a reversal in contemporary competitive children's activities.

6. This is not surprising, given traditional ways of thinking about childhood, particularly its status as sacred and a time of innocence. Additionally, many parents' assumption, and preference, is that these teachers care about their children enough to go out of their way to help them without financial incentives being a consideration. This is similar to many parents' concerns about

child care, since this market is so "thickly social and relational" (Zelizer 2005: 300), and other forms of care work in general.

7.   Ericksen 2011: 11.

8.   The one teacher who refused, a dance teacher, has a business partner whose husband is an accountant and said that it is not a legitimate tax deduction. I spoke with a tax consultant who confirmed this. According to the tax code, parents are able to deduct the cost of classes only if the child is thirteen or younger (after this age children can legally be left alone). Additionally, it only counts as a deduction if no adult needs to transport the child to an activity. (Thus dance and soccer would not count since they are at locations other than the school, but some chess classes count.)

9.   Grainey 2012: 6.

10.   This is yet another time during my fieldwork where someone assumed I was a mother, which I discuss more fully in the appendix.

11.   I also wrote about this experience in Levey Friedman 2011c.

12.   Rosenbury 2007. Another example of this is a now common practice: high school students attending conferences, such as the National Young Leaders Conference. Essentially these conferences are for-profit events disguised to look like honors for students (see Schemo 2009). The not-for-profit aspect of these activities no longer exists, even though the company tries to portray themselves as a nonprofit. In 2009 the Better Business Bureau (BBB) downgraded this organization to an "F" rating, but unfortunately, most children's activities and competitions are not part of the BBB, so they cannot even be downgraded or reprimanded.

13.   Farrey 2008: 165.

14.   Harrington 2007.

15.   Some children are homeschooled, though traditionally only at the elite levels. That is changing, though, as younger and younger pre-elites now go the homeschool route to give them an extra edge (for example, see Bernstein 2011).

16.   Sokolove 2010.

17.   DuBois 2007.

18.   Farrey 2008: 160.

19.   This is often less of a problem in elite competitive kids' activities, like gymnastics, tennis, golf, and figure skating (for example, see Jordan 2008), because top-performing children attend a training academy, such as IMG in Florida, or are homeschooled and can spend more time each day devoted to practice. This is sometimes also true for chess, but only for children who are already on the path to being Grandmasters and not for any of the families I met.

20.   Chaves 2004.

21.   Goode 1978: 166.

22. This is very common in child beauty pageants as well, as I have written about elsewhere (Levey 2007). The system in pageants actually awards each winner a "title," some of which sound nonsensical, like the "Ultimate Grand Supreme" or the "4–12 Mini-Beauty Supreme."

23. Stearns 2003: 116.

24. English 2005.

25. McMains 2006: 77.

26. Sauder and Espeland 2009: 63.

27. Sauder and Espeland 2009: 73.

28. Note that basketball does this even more intensely. Individual players, starting at age nine, are ranked on sites like Hoop Scoop (Himmelsbach 2009).

29. Dean 2012: 123.

30. For example, see Grasmuck 2005; Messner 2009: 137.

31. Lareau and Weininger 2008: 447.

32. Elite used to have an observation window, but they took it out after it created too many issues between mothers, mothers and dance teachers, and mothers and their children.

33. Hall 2008: 50.

34. This idea is attributed to a conversation with Gary Alan Fine in Fagone's book on competitive eating (2006: 21).

35. Competitive Irish dancing also has a "transfer rule" during the competitive season, as talent is seen as a limited resource (Hall 2008: 55).

36. This happens in international soccer as well; Grainey (2012: 130–31) describes cases in Nigeria and Azerbaijan.

37. Associated Press 2001.

38. Ring 2009: 3.

39. Deming and Dynarski 2008; Musch and Grondin 2001.

40. Buchmann et al. 2008.

41. Graue and DiPerna 2000: 513.

42. Levey Friedman 2010, 2011a.

43. Gerson 1985: 44–45.

44. It is fascinating that conflicts do not arise more often in dance, which has the least amount of organization and regulation and is subsequently difficult for parents to understand. How does a hierarchy within dance emerge, and how do participants map it? For parents, understanding usually comes from their own evaluative skills in terms of judging the types of skills their children can perform and how good they look while doing so compared to children from other dance studios or on TV. But since this relies on parental knowledge, it is easy to exploit those without knowledge. Knowing what and who is legitimate helps to limit anarchy within the dance world, and parents can help one another judge quality. Teachers apply the same rubric to dance competitions.

45. Messner 2009: 96.

46. Hunt 1973; *Racing Dreams* 2010; Thomas 2010.

47. Hall 2008; Levey 2009a; *Mad Hot Ballroom* 2005; *Pursuit of Excellence: Synchronized Swimming* 2007; Ruh 2011; Ryan 2000; *Sync or Swim* 2011.

48. Araton 2011; Grasmuck 2005; Jordan 2008; Nir 2011; Powell 2003; Ring 2009.

49. Fatsis 2002; Hu 2011; *Spellbound* 2004; Wolitzer 2011; *Word Wars* 2005.

50. Dean 2012; Fagone 2006; *Pursuit of Excellence: Ferrets* 2007; *Pursuit of Excellence: Lords of the Gourd* 2007; Scott 2011.

51. Levey Friedman 2011b.

52. Paris 2008: 81.

CHAPTER SIX

1. A version of this chapter previously appeared as "Trophies, Triumphs, and Tears: Children's Experiences with Competitive Activities," in Heather Beth Johnson, ed., *Sociological Studies of Children and Youth* (Bingley, UK: Emerald Group, 2010), 319–49.

2. Christenson and James 2000. Despite this shift, we still do not know a lot about how children themselves understand the purpose of their daily after-school organized activities. Adler and Adler (1998) do devote a chapter of *Peer Power* to after-school activities, but they never ask the children what they think about them, instead focusing on classifying these activities. Gary Alan Fine (1987) and Sherri Grasmuck (2005) have both studied youth baseball and spent countless hours around the young athletes. While they devote entire chapters to adult conceptions of the sport, the children themselves make only brief appearances, so their actions are portrayed in relation to adult conceptions and interpretations. Furthermore neither Fine nor Grasmuck tells us a lot about conversations they had with the kids, like asking them explicitly what they think about various aspects of youth baseball.

3. For example, see Dweck 1999.

4. The appendix has more details on how I conducted interviews with kids and specific issues that arose during the course of the fieldwork related to children.

5. His reason was that he worried his son would analyze the questions too much and possibly think there was something wrong with him, which suggested to me that either his son had previously complained about competition and his father didn't want his son to tell me about this, or that the father had not done much in terms of discussing the purpose of competition with his son and perhaps thought he should have so did not want me to know he had not.

6. Despite being disappointed at not interviewing these children, I felt reassured that they felt able to withhold their consent when their parents, teachers, and some friends had consented. Gallagher et al. (2010) argue that children are sometimes influenced by the social nature of consent giving, but I know not every child was influenced in this way during my fieldwork.

7. Harden et al. 2000: 11.

8. Scouting patches (for boys and girls) were designed to so that children "literally wore their competence on their sleeves" (Cordery 2012: 238).

9. For example, see Tierney 2004.

10. Roberts 1980.

11. For a discussion of tangible reinforcers as bonuses and bribes, see O'Leary et al. 1972.

12. Programs cost money, so not everyone always get them at each dance competition.

13. Tournament organizers told me that they award these types of prizes to get older children to continue to play in scholastic tournaments rather than shift to open events, which award money to the top finishers (who are often adults).

14. Ablard and Parker 1997.

15. See Greene and Lepper 1974; Lepper and Greene 1973, 1975.

16. They also found that those children who expect to get this reward worked quicker but at lower quality, and this pattern persisted over time.

17. Goode 1978: 167.

18. Dahl 2011.

19. Elite Dance Academy has very few dropouts, and it is rare for anyone to leave the company before middle school, suggesting that this strategy may help keep kids involved longer as well.

20. This is also a major source of stress and anxiety cited by former elite figures in Scanlan et al. 1991: 107.

21. Roberts 1980.

22. Epstein and Harackiewicz 1992: 129.

23. Crying at chess tournaments is actually so common that a chapter in a recent volume on chess and education is devoted to crying (Root 2006a). Elsewhere Root argues that tears in chess may sometimes "be an expression of a competitive desire to excel" (2006b: 16), and this may be true. But the tears I saw and talked about with kids were more about disappointment and feelings of inadequacy or loss; private tears may of course be about missed opportunities and the desire to do better, but I did not witness this.

24. Dweck 1999: 3.

25. It became clear how a dancer might "mess up" when Alice's friend, also competing in a solo for the first time, fell on stage after doing a leap at a regional

competitions. Thankfully she was not hurt, and she still ended up with a high score because of the difficulty of her routine.

26. Simon and Martens 1979.

27. Thorne 1993.

28. Pascoe 2007: 117.

29. Scanlan and Passer 1979: 151.

30. Hofferth et al. 2009: 198.

31. Goffman 2007: 260.

32. A few months after our interview, Daisuke stopped playing tournament chess, though he still took chess classes as school.

33. One boy told me he wants to be an engineer specifically to "make a lot of money."

34. For example, see Amabile 1982.

35. Reeve and Deci 1996.

36. As used in Epstein and Harackiewicz 1992: 132.

37. Levine 2006, 2012; *Race to Nowhere* 2009.

38. Macleod 1983.

CONCLUSION

1. Alsop 2008; Hodgkinson 2010; Mogel 2010; Skenazy 2010; Tulgan 2009.

2. Kimmel 2008: 27.

3. Note that I did not contact local schools in either West County or Metro because I was most interested in the activities themselves and in competition. An alternative research design could have been to target second-, third-, or fourth-graders at a particular school, as opposed to finding families through the activities themselves. Doing so may have gotten me access to families whose kids did not do any competitive, or even organized, after-school activities, but I would have lost the depth I got by spending time with particular clubs and studios.

4. Conley 2012.

5. Senior 2010.

6. Quoted in Jan 2008.

7. Hu 2010.

8. Hu 2010.

9. Druckerman 2012: 4.

10. Druckerman 2012: 140.

11. Dean 2012: xi.

12. Thompson and Barker 2009: 25.

13. Levey Friedman 2011b.

QUESTIONING KIDS: EXPERIENCES FROM
FIELDWORK AND INTERVIEWS

1. For example, see Lareau 2000; Whyte 1993.

2. Glaser and Strauss 1967.

3. Lareau 2000.

4. The numbers in Table 4 total 181, not 172, because some families had children who competed in two activities, or one child in one activity and another in a different activity.

5. Pugh 2009: 31.

6. Robert Petrone's (2007) experiences as a white male studying adolescent boys who skateboard in a midwestern city provide a clue: when parents found out he did not "have one" of the boys at the skateboard park and that he was "hanging out" around them, they often asked him point-blank, "Are you a pedophile?"

7. Parts of this section are adapted from the article I wrote, which appeared in *Qualitative Sociology* titled " 'Which One is Yours?' Children and Ethnography" (Levey 2009b). A more complete discussion of these issues occurs there.

8. I never taught chess at all, especially given my lack of knowledge, but the children often referred to me as a teacher, not knowing how else to refer to me. This is similar to Debbie Epstein's (1998) experiences with children; they frequently referred to her as a teacher as they did not have another frame of reference for understanding her presence.

9. This was Daisuke, described in chapter 6 and the conclusion.

10. Messner 2009: 18.

11. Weber et al. 1994: 42.

12. Fine and Sandstrom 1988.

13. Corsaro and Molinari 2000.

14. Best 2007; Greene and Hogan 2005.

15. Butler and Turner 1987; Cassell 1987; Flinn et al. 1998; Sutton and Fernandez 1998.

16. For example, see Cree et al. 2002; Hart 1997; Irwin and Johnson 2005; Morrow 2008.

17. Harden et al. 2000: 11.

18. Lareau 1996: 212.

19. Gallagher et al. 2010: 476.

20. For example, see Duneier 2000.

21. For example, see Liebow 1995.

22. Morrow 2006; Orellana et al. 2003.

23. Epstein 1998.

24. Epstein 1998: 35.

25. Corsaro and Molinari 2000.

26. As discussed in Boocock and Scott 2005: x.
27. Hogan et al. 1999: 94.
28. Irwin and Johnson 2005: 823.
29. Gallagher et al. 2010.
30. Pugh 2009: 39.

Works Cited

Ablard, Karen E., and Wayne D. Parker. 1997. "Parents' Achievement Goals and Perfectionism in Their Academically Talented Children." *Journal of Youth and Adolescence* 26(6): 651–67.

Adams, Natalie Guice, and Pamela J. Bettis. 2003. *Cheerleader! An American Icon.* New York: Palgrave Macmillan.

Adler, Patricia A., and Peter Adler. 1998. *Peer Power: Preadolescent Culture and Identity.* New Brunswick, NJ: Rutgers University Press.

Adler, Patricia A., Steven J. Kless, and Peter Adler. 1992. "Socialization to Gender Roles: Popularity among Elementary School Boys and Girls." *Sociology of Education* 65 (July): 169–87.

Alsop, Ron. 2008. *The Trophy Kids Grow Up.* New York: Jossey-Bass.

Amabile, Teresa M. 1982. "Children's Artistic Creativity: Detrimental Effects of Competition in a Field Setting." *Personality and Social Psychology Bulletin* 8: 573–78.

Anand, N., and Mary R. Watson. 2004. "Tournament Rituals in the Evolution of Fields: The Case of the Grammy Awards." *Academy of Management Journal* 27(1): 59–80.

Applebome, Peter. 2004. "Remember, Soccer Fans, Children Start Kicking in the Womb." *New York Times*, October 17.

Aranda-Alvarado, Belen. 2012. "Give a Girl a 'Hook,' Get Her into College." *New York Times*, May 29.

Araton, Harvey. 2011. "12-Year-Old Girl May Embody McEnroe's Vision." *New York Times*, March 7.

Armour, Stephanie. 2007. "'Helicopter' Parents Hover When Kids Job Hunt." *USA Today*, April 23.

Ashley, Maurice. 2005. *Chess for Success: Using an Old Game to Build New Strengths in Children and Teens.* New York: Broadway.

Associated Press. 2001. "He's 14: Almonte's Team Forfeits LLWS Victories." September 1. http://sportsillustrated.cnn.com/more/news/2001/08/31/almonte_14_ap/.

Attewell, Paul. 2001. "The Winner-Take-All High School: Organizational Adaptations to Educational Stratification." *Sociology of Education* 74(4): 267–95.

Averbuch, Gloria, and Ashley Michael Hammond. 1999. *Goal! The Ultimate Guide for Soccer Moms and Dads.* Emmaus, PA: Rodale Press.

Bean, Dawn Pawson. 2005. *Synchronized Swimming: An American History.* Jefferson, NC: McFarland.

Bearman, Peter. 2005. *Doormen.* Chicago: University of Chicago Press.

Becker, Howard S. 1984. *Art Worlds.* Berkeley: University of California Press.

Belluck, Pam. 2005. "Girls and Boys, Meet Nature: Bring Your Gun." *New York Times*, September 18.

Bernstein, Basil. 2003. *Class, Codes, and Control.* New York: Routledge.

Bernstein, Lenny. 2011. "Home Schooling for Child Athletes Raises Questions Large and Small." *Washington Post*, August 9.

Berryman, Jack W. 1988. "The Rise of Highly Organized Sports for Preadolescent Boys." In Frank L. Smoll, Richard A. Magill, and Michael J. Ash, eds., *Children in Sport.* 3rd ed. Champaign, IL: Human Kinetics Books. 3–16.

Best, Amy L. 2000. *Prom Night: Youth, Schools, and Popular Culture.* New York: Routledge.

———, ed. 2007. *Representing Youth: Methodological Issues in Critical Youth Studies.* New York: New York University Press.

Best, Joel. 2011. *Everyone's a Winner: Life in Our Congratulatory Culture.* Berkeley: University of California Press.

Bettie, Julie. 2003. *Women without Class: Girls, Race, and Identity.* Berkeley: University of California Press.

Bianchi, Suzanne M., John P. Robinson, and Melissa A. Milkie. 2006. *Changing Rhythms of American Family Life.* New York: Russell Sage Foundation.

Bick, Julie. 2007. "Looking for an Edge? Private Coaching, by the Hour." *New York Times*, February 25.

Black, Alan. 2008. *Kick the Balls: An Offensive Suburban Odyssey*. New York: Hudson Street Press.

Blair-Loy, Mary. 2003. *Competing Devotions: Career and Family among Women Executives*. Cambridge, MA: Harvard University Press.

Boncompagni, Tatiana. 2006. "Baby Shall Enroll: Mommy Knows." *New York Times*, May 11.

Boocock, Sarane, and Kimberly Scott. 2005. *Kids in Context: The Sociological Study of Children and Childhoods*. New York: Rowman and Littlefield.

Bourdieu, Pierre. 2007. *Distinction: A Social Critique of the Judgment of Taste*. Cambridge, MA: Harvard University Press.

Bourdieu, Pierre, and Jean-Claude Passeron. 1973. "Cultural Reproduction and Social Reproduction." In Richard K. Brown, ed., *Knowledge, Education, and Cultural Change*. London: Tavistock. 71–112.

Brewer, Dominic J., Eric R. Eide, and Ronald G. Ehrenberg. 1999. "Does It Pay to Attend an Elite Private College? Cross-Cohort Evidence on the Effects of College Type on Earnings." *Journal of Human Resources* 34(1): 104–23.

Britton, Dana M. 2000. "The Epistemology of the Gendered Organization." *Gender & Society* 14(3): 418–34.

Brooklyn Castle. 2012. Dir. Kate Dellamaggiore. DVD. Producers Distribution Agency.

Brooks, David. 2012. "The Opportunity Gap." *New York Times*, July 9.

Brower, Jonathan J. 1979. "The Professionalization of Organized Youth Sport: Social Psychological Impacts and Outcomes." *Annals of the American Academy of Political and Social Sciences* 445: 39–46.

Buchmann, Claudia, Thomas A. DiPrete, and Anne McDaniel. 2008. "Gender Inequalities in Education." *Annual Review of Sociology* 34: 319–37.

Butler, B., and D. M. Turner, eds. 1987. *Children and Anthropological Research*. New York: Plenum Press.

Carroll, Felix. 2005. "No Escape from 'Helicopter Parents': Constant Hovering Can Kick Up a Cloud of Troubles." *Albany Times Union*, January 27.

Cassell, Joan, ed. 1987. *Children in the Field: Anthropological Experiences*. Philadelphia: Temple University Press.

Chabris, Christopher, and Mark E. Glickman. 2006. "Sex Differences in Intellectual Performance: Analysis of a Large Cohort of Competitive Chess Players." *Psychological Science* 17(12): 1040–46.

Chafetz, Janet Saltzman, and Joseph A. Kotarba. 1995. "Son Worshippers: The Role of Little League Mothers in Recreating Gender." *Studies in Symbolic Interaction* 18: 217–41.

Chancey, Pam. 2004. *The Right Moves: Preparing for Dance Competitions*. New York: Rosen Group.

Chaves, Mark. 2004. *Congregations in America*. Cambridge, MA: Harvard University Press.

Christenson, Pia, and Allison James. 2000. "Introduction: Researching Children and Childhood: Cultures of Communication." In Pia Christenson and Allison James, eds., *Research with Children: Perspectives and Practices*. London: Routledge/Falmer. 1–9.

Chua, Amy. 2011. *Battle Hymn of the Tiger Mother*. New York: Penguin Press.

Chudacoff, Howard P. 2007. *Children at Play: An American History*. New York: New York University Press.

Clement, Priscilla Ferguson. 1997. *Growing Pains: Children in the Industrial Age, 1850–1950*. New York: Twayne.

Collins, Randall. 1979. *The Credential Society*. New York: Elsevier.

———. 1993. "Women and the Production of Status Cultures." In Michele Lamont and Marcel Fournier, eds., *Cultivating Differences: Symbolic Boundaries and the Making of Inequality*. Chicago: University of Chicago Press. 213–31.

Conley, Dalton. 2008. "Reading Class between the Lines (of This Volume): A Reflection on Why We Should Stick to Folk Concepts of Social Class." In Annette Lareau and Dalton Conley, eds., *Social Class: How Does It Work?* New York: Sage. 366–73.

———. 2012. "Harvard by Lottery." *Chronicle of Higher Education*, April 1.

Connell, R. W. 1995. *Masculinities*. Berkeley: University of California Press.

Cookson, Peter W., Jr., and Caroline Hodges Persell. 1985. *Preparing for Power: America's Elite Boarding Schools*. New York: Basic Books.

Cordery, Stacy A. 2012. *Juliette Gordon Low: The Remarkable Founder of the Girl Scouts*. New York: Viking.

Corsaro, William A., and Luisa Molinari. 2000. "Entering and Observing in Children's Worlds: A Reflection on a Longitudinal Ethnography of Early Education in Italy." In Pia Christenson and Allison James, eds., *Research with Children: Perspectives and Practices*. London: Routledge/Falmer. 179–200.

Cree, Viviene E., Helen Kay, and Kay Tisdall. 2002. "Research with Children: Sharing the Dilemmas." *Child and Family Social Work* 7: 47–56.

Dahl, Roald. 2011. *Charlie and the Chocolate Factory*. New York: Puffin.

Dale, Stacy Berg, and Alan B. Krueger. 2002. "Estimating the Payoff to Attending a More Selective College: An Application of Selection on Observables and Unobservables." *Quarterly Journal of Economics* 117(4): 1491–527.

Daniels, Elizabeth, and Campbell Leaper. 2006. "A Longitudinal Investigation of Sport Participation, Peer Acceptance, and Self-esteem among Adolescent Girls and Boys." *Sex Roles* 55: 875–80.

Darrah, Charles N., James M. Freeman, and J. A. English-Lueck. 2007. *Busier Than Ever! Why American Families Can't Slow Down.* Stanford, CA: Stanford University Press.

Dean, Josh. 2012. *Show Dog: The Charmed Life and Trying Times of a Near-Perfect Purebred.* New York: HarperCollins.

DeBare, Ilana. 2005. *Where Girls Come First: The Rise, Fall, and Surprising Revival of Girls' Schools.* New York: Tarcher Penguin.

Deming, David, and Susan Dynarski. 2008. "The Lengthening of Childhood." *Journal of Economic Perspectives* 22(3): 71–92.

D'Esto, Carlo. 1995. *Patton: A Genius for War.* New York: Harper.

DiMaggio, Paul, and Ann L. Mullen. 2000. "Enacting Community in Progressive America: Civic Rituals in National Music Week, 1924." *Poetics* 27: 135–62.

Dominus, Susan. 2009. "Connecting Anxious Parents and Educators, at $450 an Hour." *New York Times,* August 18.

Dorey, Annette K. Vance. 1999. *Better Baby Contests: The Scientific Quest for Perfect Childhood Health.* Jefferson, NC: McFarland.

Druckerman, Pamela. 2012. *Bringing Up Bebe: One America Mother Discovers the Wisdom of French Parenting.* New York: Penguin.

DuBois, Joan. 2007. "National Burt Lerner Elementary Chess Championship Attracts 2,100+ Young Competitors to Music City." USCF Press Release, June 22. http://main.uschess.org/content/view/7684/319/.

Duina, Francesco. 2011. *Winning: Reflections on an American Obsession.* Princeton, NJ: Princeton University Press.

Dumais, Susan. 2006. "Early Childhood Cultural Capital, Parental Habitus, and Teachers' Perceptions." *Poetics* 34: 83–107.

Duneier, Mitchell. 2000. *Sidewalk.* New York: Farrar, Straus and Giroux.

Dunn, Ashley. 1995. "Cram Schools: Immigrants' Tools for Success." *New York Times,* January 28.

Dweck, Carol S. 1999. "Caution: Praise Can Be Dangerous." *American Educator* 23(1): 4–9.

Easterlin, Richard A. 1987. *Birth and Fortune: The Impact of Numbers on Personal Welfare.* Chicago: University of Chicago Press.

Eder, Donna, Catherine Colleen Evans, and Stephen Parker. 1995. *School Talk: Gender and Adolescent Culture.* New Brunswick, NJ: Rutgers University Press.

Elkind, David. 2007. *The Power of Play: How Spontaneous, Imaginative Activities Lead to Happier, Healthier Children.* Cambridge, MA: Da Capo.

Ellis, Blake. 2012. "Harvard, Princeton Post Record Low Acceptance Rates." *CNN Money,* March 30.

Engh, Fred. 2002. *Why Johnny Hates Sports: Why Organized Youth Sports Are Failing Our Children and What We Can Do About It.* Garden City Park, NY: Square One.

English, James F. 2005. *The Economy of Prestige.* Cambridge, MA: Harvard University Press.

Epstein, Debbie. 1998. "'Are You a Girl or Are You a Teacher?' The 'Least Adult' Role in Research about Gender and Sexuality in a Primary School." In G. Walford, ed., *Doing Research in Education.* London: Falmer Press. 27–41.

Epstein, Jennifer A., and Judith M. Harackiewicz. 1992. "Winning Is Not Enough: The Effects of Competition and Achievement Orientation on Intrinsic Interest." *Personality and Social Psychology Bulletin* 18: 128–38.

Ericksen, Julia. 2011. *Dance with Me: Ballroom Dancing and the Promise of Instant Intimacy.* New York: New York University Press.

Erickson, Bonnie. 1996. "Culture, Class, and Connections." *American Journal of Sociology* 102: 217–51.

Fagone, Jason. 2006. *Horsemen of the Esophagus: Competitive Eating and the Big Fat American Dream.* New York: Crown.

Farrey, Tom. 2008. *Game On: The All-American Race to Make Champions of Our Children.* New York: ESPN Books.

Fatsis, Stefan. 2002. *Word Freak: Heartbreak, Triumph, Genius, and Obsession in the World of Competitive Scrabble Players.* New York: Penguin.

Faust, Kimberley, Michael Gann, and Jerome Mckibben. 1999. "The Boomlet Goes to College." *American Demographics* 21(6): 44.

Feldman, David Henry. 1991. *Nature's Gambit: Child Prodigies and the Development of Human Potential.* New York: Teachers College Press.

Ferguson, Andrew. 2011. *Crazy U: One Dad's Crash Course in Getting His Kid into College.* New York: Simon & Schuster.

Ferguson, Ann. 2001. *Bad Boys: Public Schools in the Making of Black Masculinity.* Ann Arbor: University of Michigan Press.

Fine, Gary Alan. 1987. *With the Boys: Little League Baseball and Preadolescent Culture.* Chicago: University of Chicago Press.

Fine, Gary Alan, and K. L. Sandstrom. 1988. *Knowing Children: Participant Observation with Minors.* New York: Sage.

First Position. 2012. Dir. Bess Kargman. DVD. MPI Home Video.

Flinn, J., L. Marshall, and J. Armstrong, eds. 1998. *Fieldwork and Families: Constructing New Models for Ethnographic Research.* Honolulu: University of Hawaii Press.

Foderaro, Lisa W. 2006. "Families with Full Plates, Sitting Down to Dinner." *New York Times,* April 5.

Foer, Franklin. 2004. *How Soccer Explains the World: An Unlikely Theory of Globalization.* New York: Harper Perennial.

Fortanasce, Vincent, Lawrence Robinson, and John Oullette. 2001. *The Official American Youth Soccer Organization Handbook.* New York: Fireside.

Fortin, Judy. 2008. "Hovering Parents Need to Step Back at College Time." CNN, February 4.

Frank, Robert H. 2007. *Falling Behind: How Rising Inequality Harms the Middle Class*. Berkeley: University of California Press.

Frank, Robert H., and Philip J. Cook. 1995. *The Winner-Take-All Society: Why the Few at the Top Get So Much More Than the Rest of Us*. New York: Penguin.

Friedman, Danielle. 2010. "Female Jocks Rule the World." *Daily Beast*, September 29.

Gallagher, Jim. 1977. "Pageants: Little Misses, Big Dreams (for Their Mommies)." *Chicago Tribune*, July 28.

Gallagher, Michael, Sarah L. Haywood, Manon W. Jones, and Sue Milne. 2010. "Negotiating Informed Consent with Children in School-Based Research: A Critical Review." *Children and Society* 24: 471–82.

Gerson, Kathleen. 1985. *Hard Choices: How Women Decide about Work, Career, and Motherhood*. Berkeley: University of California Press.

Gilmore, Janet. 2012. "Campus Releases 2012–3 Freshman Admissions Data." UC Berkeley News Center, April 17.

Glaeser, Edward L., and Andrei Schliefer. 1998. "Not-for-Profit Entrepreneurs." NBER Working Paper 6810.

Glamser, Francis D., and John Vincent. 2004. "The Relative Age Effect among Elite American Youth Soccer Players." *Journal of Sport Behavior* 27(1): 31–38.

Glaser, Barney G., and Anselm L. Strauss. 1967. *Discovery of Grounded Theory: Strategies for Qualitative Research*. New York: Aldine.

Glickman, Mark E., and Thomas Doan. August 21, 2012. "The USCF Rating System." January 29. http://www.glicko.net/ratings/rating.system.pdf.

Goffman, Erving. 1959. *The Presentation of Self in Everyday Life*. London: Penguin.

———. 2007. "Information Control and Personal Identity: The Discredited and the Discreditable." In Edward J. Clarke and Delos H. Kelly, eds., *Deviant Behavior*. New York: Macmillan. 259–63.

Golden, Daniel. 2006. *The Price of Admission: How America's Ruling Class Buys Its Way into Elite Colleges—and Who Gets Left Outside the Gates*. New York: Brown.

Goldowsky, Howard. 2006. "A Conversation with Mark Glickman." *Chess Life*, October: 29–33.

Goode, William J. 1978. *The Celebration of Heroes: Prestige as a Control System*. Berkeley: University of California Press.

Goodwin, Marjorie Harness. 2006. "Socialization for the Competitive Spirit and Excellence: A Case Study." Sloan Center on Everyday Lives of Families Working Paper.

Goudreau, Jenna. 2011. "The Secret to Being a Power Woman: Play Team Sports." *Forbes*, October 12.

Graff, Harvey J. 1995. *Conflicting Paths: Growing Up in America*. Cambridge, MA: Harvard University Press.

Grainey, Timothy F. 2012. *Beyond Bend It Like Beckham: The Global Phenomenon of Women's Soccer*. Lincoln: University of Nebraska Press.

Grasmuck, Sherri. 2005. *Protecting Home: Class, Race, and Masculinity in Boys' Baseball*. New Brunswick, NJ: Rutgers University Press.

Graue, M. Elizabeth, and James DiPerna. 2000. "Redshirting and Early Retention: Who Gets the 'Gift of Time' and What Are Its Outcomes?" *American Educational Research Journal* 37: 509–34.

Greene, David, and Mark. R. Lepper. 1974. "Effects of Extrinsic Rewards on Children's Subsequent Intrinsic Interest." *Child Development* 45(4): 1141–45.

Greene, Sheila, and Diane Hogan. 2005. *Researching Children's Experience: Methods and Approaches*. Thousand Oaks, CA: Sage.

Gupta, Sanjay. 2005. "NASCAR Ride 'More Than a Little Terrifying.'" CNN, October 13.

Hack, Damon. 2005. "Youth Is Served Earlier in LPGA." *New York Times*, July 3.

Hall, Frank. 2008. *Competitive Irish Dance: Art, Sport, Duty*. Madison, WI: Macater Press.

Halpern, Robert. 2002. "A Different Kind of Child Development Institution: The History of After-School Programs for Low-Income Children." *Teachers College Record* 104(2): 178–211.

Haner, Jim. 2006. *Soccerhead: An Accidental Journey into the Heart of the American Game*. New York: North Point Press.

Hansmann, Henry. 1996. "The Changing Roles of Public, Private, and Non-profit Enterprise in Education, Health Care, and Other Human Services." In Victor Fuchs, ed., *Individual and Social Responsibility: Child Care, Education, Medical Care, and Long-Term Care in America*. Chicago: University of Chicago Press. 245–76.

Harden, Jeni, Sue Scott, Kathryn Backett-Milburn, and Stevi Jackson. 2000. "Can't Talk, Won't Talk? Methodological Issues in Researching Children." *Sociological Research Online* 5(2).

Harrington, David E. 2007. "Markets: Preserving Funeral Markets with Ready-to-Embalm Laws." *Journal of Economic Perspectives* 21(4): 201–16.

Hart, Roger. 1997. *Children's Participation: The Theory and Practice of Involving Young Citizens in Community Development and Environmental Care*. New York: UNICEF.

Hays, Sharon. 1998. *The Cultural Contradictions of Motherhood*. New Haven, CT: Yale University Press.

Heisman, Dan. 2002. *A Parent's Guide to Chess*. Milford, CT: Russell Enterprises.

Hertzberg, Hendrik. 2010. "The Name of the Game." *New Yorker*, July 12 and 19: 29–30.

Hibbard, David R., and Duane Buhrmester. 2010. "Competitiveness, Gender, and Adjustment among Adolescents." *Sex Roles* 63(5–6): 412–24.

Himmelsbach, Adam. 2009. "First Impressions Can Create Unrealistic Expectations for Recruits." *New York Times*, March 10.

Hinshaw, Stephan, and Rachel Kranz. 2009. *The Triple Bind: Saving Our Teenagers from Today's Pressures*. New York: Ballantine Books.

Hochschild, Arlie, and Anne Matchung. 1989. *The Second Shift: Working Parents and the Revolution at Home*. New York: Avon.

Hodgkinson, Tom. 2010. *The Idle Parent: Why Laid-Back Parents Raise Happier and Healthier Kids*. New York: Tarcher.

Hofferth, Sandra L., Kinney, David A., and Janet S. Dunn. 2009. "The 'Hurried' Child: Myth vs. Reality." In Kathleen Matsuka and Charles Christiansen, eds., *Life Balance: Multidisciplinary Theories and Research*. Bethesda, MD: AOTA Press. 183–206.

Hofferth, Sandra L., and John F. Sandberg. 2001. "Changes in Children's Time with Parents: United States, 1981–1997." *Demography* 38(3): 423–36.

Hogan, Diane M., Kathleen E. Etz, and Jonathan R. H. Tudge. 1999. "Reconsidering the Role of Children in Family Research: Conceptual and Methodological Issues." *Contemporary Perspectives on Family Research* 1: 93–105.

Horowitz, Joseph. 1990. *The Ivory Trade: Music and the Business of Music at the Van Cliburn International Music Competition*. New York: Summit Books.

Hu, Winnie. 2008. "Where the Race Now Begins at Kindergarten." *New York Times*, August 6.

———. 2010. "As Honor Students Multiply, Who Really Is One?" *New York Times*, January 1.

———. 2011. "For Students Raised on iPods, Lessons in Bridge." *New York Times*, April 24.

Hunt, C. O. 1973. "Why Competitive Music Festivals: The Music Festival Provides a Check on the Competence of Teachers." *School Musician Director and Teacher*, December: 46–47.

The Insider. 2005. "Tiny Texas Cheerleaders."

Irwin, Lori G., and Joy Johnson. 2005. "Interviewing Young Children: Explicating Our Practices and Dilemmas." *Qualitative Health Research* 15: 821–31.

Jable, Thomas J. 1984. "The Public Schools Athletic League of New York City: Organized Athletics for City Schoolchildren, 1903–1914." In Steven A. Reiss, ed., *The American Sporting Experience: A Historical Anthology of Sport in America*. Champaign, IL: Kinetics Press. 219–38.

Jan, Tracy. 2008. "Colleges Scour China for Top Students: A Star Search That May Affect U.S. Applicants." *Boston Globe,* November 9.

Jarovsky, Ben. 1995. *Hoop Dreams.* New York: Turner.

Jih, Sophia. 2009. "Record Applicant Numbers for Class of 2013 Fall Short of Peers." *Daily Princetonian,* February 2.

Jones, Del. 2002. "Many Successful Women Also Athletic." *USA Today,* March 26.

Jordan, Pat. 2008. "Daddy's Little Phenoms." *New York Times,* March 2.

Kane, Emily W. 2006. " 'No Way My Boys Are Going to Be Like That!' Parents' Responses to Children's Gender Nonconformity." *Gender & Society* 20: 149–76.

Karabel, Jerome. 2006. *The Chosen: The Hidden History of Admission and Exclusion at Harvard, Princeton, and Yale.* New York: Mariner Books.

Katz, Michael B. 1986. *In the Shadow of the Poorhouse: A Social History of Welfare in America.* New York: Basic Books.

Kaufman, Jason, and Jay Gabler. 2004. "Cultural Capital and the Extracurricular Activities of Girls and Boys in the College Attainment Process." *Poetics* 32: 145–68.

Kendall, Elizabeth. 1984. *Where She Danced: The Birth of American Art-Dance.* Berkeley: University of California.

Kicking and Screaming. 2005. Dir. Jesse Dylan. DVD. Universal Pictures.

Kimmel, Michael. 2008. *Guyland: The Perilous World Where Boys Become Men.* New York: Harper.

Kindlon, Dan. 2006. *Alpha Girls: Understanding the New American Girl and How She Is Changing the World.* New York: Rodale.

Kinetz, Erika. 2004. "Budding Dancers Compete, Seriously." *New York Times,* July 7.

King of Kong. 2008. DVD. Dir. Seth Gordon. New Line Home Video.

Kleiber, Douglas, and Gwynn M. Powell. 2005. "Historical Change in Leisure Activities During After-School Hours." In Joseph L. Mahoney, Reed W. Larson, and Jacqeulynne S. Eccles, eds., *Organized Activities as Contexts of Development: Extracurricular Activities, After-School and Community Programs.* Mahwah, NJ: Lawrence Erlbaum. 23–44.

Kusserow, Adrie. 2004. *American Individualisms: Child Rearing and Social Class in Three Neighborhoods.* New York: Palgrave Macmillan.

Lacy, Karyn R. 2007. *Blue-Chip Black: Race, Class, and Status in the New Black Middle Class.* Berkeley: University of California Press.

Lamont, Michèle. 1992. *Money, Morals, and Manners: The Culture of the French and the American Upper-Middle Class.* Chicago: University of Chicago Press.

Lareau, Annette. 1996. "Common Problems in Field Work: A Personal Essay." In Annette Lareau and Jeffrey Shultz, eds., *Journeys through Ethnography.* New York: Westview. 196–236.

———. 2000. "My Wife Can Tell Me Who I Know: Methodological and Conceptual Problems in Studying Fathers." *Qualitative Sociology* 23(4): 407–33.

———. 2003. *Unequal Childhoods: Class, Race, and Family Life*. Berkeley: University of California Press.

———. 2008. "Introduction: Taking Stock of Class." In Annette Lareau and Dalton Conley, eds., *Social Class: How Does It Work?* New York: Russell Sage. 3–24.

Lareau, Annette, and Elliot B. Weininger. 2008. "Time, Work, and Family Life: Reconceptualizing Gendered Time Patterns through the Case of Children's Organized Activities." *Sociological Forum* 23(3): 419–54.

Lepper, Mark R., and David Greene. 1973. "Undermining Children's Intrinsic Interest with Extrinsic Reward: A Test of the 'Overjustification' Hypothesis." *Journal of Personality and Social Psychology* 28(1): 129–37.

———. 1975. "Turning Play into Work: Effects of Adult Surveillance and Extrinsic Rewards on Children's Intrinsic Motivation." *Journal of Personality and Social Psychology* 31(3): 479–86.

Lever, Janet. 1978. "Sex Differences in the Complexity of Children's Play and Games." *American Sociological Review* 43(4): 471–83.

Levey, Hilary. 2007. "Here She Is and There She Goes." *Contexts*, Summer: 70–72.

———. 2009a. "Pageants Princesses and Math Whizzes: Understanding Children's Activities as a Form of Children's Work." *Childhood* 16(2): 195–212.

———. 2009b. "Which One Is Yours? Children and Ethnography." *Qualitative Sociology* 32(3): 311–31.

———. 2010a. "Outside Class: A Historical Analysis of American Children's Competitive Activities." In Karen Sternheimer, ed., *Childhood in American Society*. Boston: Pearson Allyn & Bacon. 342–54.

———. 2010b. "Trophies, Triumphs, and Tears: Children's Experiences with Competitive Activities." In Heather Beth Johnson, ed., *Sociological Studies of Children and Youth*. Bingley, UK: Emerald Group. 319–49.

Levey Friedman, Hilary. 2010. "Capitalized Communism in U.S. Sports from Women's Gymnastics to IMG Academies." *Huffington Post*, November 10.

———. 2011a. "Age Cut-offs, Limits, and Manipulations in Sports." *BlogHer*, August 2.

———. 2011b. "In the Wake of the Sandusky Scandal, a Call for Youth Coaching Certifications." *Huffington Post*, November 14.

———. 2011c. "Why Summer Camp Isn't as Safe as You Think." *Huffington Post*, August 9.

Levine, Madeline. 2006. *The Price of Privilege: How Parental Pressure and Material Advantage Are Creating a Generation of Disconnected and Unhappy Kids*. New York: HarperCollins.

———. 2012. *Teach Your Children Well: Parenting for Authentic Success*. New York: Harper.

Liebow, Elliot. 1995. *Tell Them Who I Am: The Lives of Homeless Women.* New York: Penguin.

Luthar, Suniya S. 2003. "The Culture of Affluence: Psychological Costs of Material Wealth." *Child Development* 74(6): 1581–93.

Luthar, Suniya S., Karen A. Shoum, and Pamela J. Brown. 2006. "Extracurricular Involvement among Affluent Youth: A Scapegoat for 'Ubiquitous Achievement Pressures'?" *Developmental Psychology* 42(3): 583–97.

Macleod, David I. 1983. *Building Character in the American Boy: The Boy Scouts, YMCA, and Their Forerunners, 1870–1920.* Madison: University of Wisconsin Press.

MacLeod, Jay. 1995. *Ain't No Makin' It: Aspirations and Attainment in a Low-Income Neighborhood.* New York: Westview.

Mad Hot Ballroom. 2005. Dir. Marilyn Agrelo. DVD. Paramount.

Maguire, James. 2006. *American Bee: The National Spelling Bee and the Culture of Word Nerds. The Lives of Five Top Spellers as They Compete for Glory and Fame.* New York: Rodale.

Margolin, Leslie. 1994. *Goodness Personified: The Emergence of Gifted Children.* New York: Aldine.

Markovits, Andrei S., and Steven L. Hellerman. 2001. *Offside: Soccer and American Exceptionalism.* Princeton, NJ: Princeton University Press.

Martinez, Jose. 2011. "Manhattan Mom Sues $19k/yr. Preschool for Damaging 4-Year-Old Daughter's Ivy League Chances." *Daily News*, March 14.

Masten, April. 2009. "The Challenge Dance." Unpublished paper. Shelby Cullom Davis Center for Historical Studies, Princeton, NJ.

Matchan, Linda. 2012. "Defying Societal Habits, Spelling Regains Its Dignity." *Boston Globe*, January 9.

McClelland, David. 1967. *The Achieving Society.* Free Press: New York.

McGuffey, C. Shawn, and B. Lindsay Rich. 1999. "Playing in the Gender Transgression Zone: Race, Class, and Hegemonic Masculinity in Middle Childhood." *Gender & Society* 13: 608–27.

McMains, Juliet. 2006. *Glamour Addiction: Inside the American Ballroom Dance Industry.* Middletown, CT: Wesleyan University Press.

McShane, Kevin. 2002. *Coaching Youth Soccer: The European Model.* Jefferson, NC: McFarland.

Messner, Michael A. 2009. *It's All for the Kids: Gender, Families, and Youth Sports.* Berkeley: University of California Press.

Miller, Susan A. 2007. *Growing Girls: The Natural Origins of Girls' Organizations in America.* New Brunswick, NJ: Rutgers University Press.

Miranda, Carolina A. 2006. "The Magic of the Family Meal." *Time*, June 12: 50–54.

Mitchell, Deborah. 2006. "Chess Is Child's Play." *Mothering*, November/December: 68–71.

Mogel, Wendy. 2010. *The Blessing of a B Minus*. New York: Scribner.

Morrow, Virginia. 2006. "Conceptualizing Social Capital in Relation to Children and Young People: Is It Different for Girls?" In B. O'Neill and E. Gidengil, eds., *Social Capital and Gender*. London: Routledge. 127–50.

———. 2008. "Ethical Dilemmas in Research with Children and Young People about Their Social Environments." *Children's Geographies* 6(1): 49–61.

Musch, Jochen, and Simon Grondin. 2001. "Unequal Competition as an Impediment to Personal Development: A Review of the Relative Age Effect in Sport." *Developmental Review* 21: 147–67.

Newman, Katherine S. 1994. *Declining Fortunes*. New York: Basic Books.

Newman, Katherine, Cybelle Fox, David Harding, Jal Mehta, and Wendy Roth. 2004. *Rampage: The Social Roots of School Shootings*. New York: Basic Books.

Nir, Sarah Maslin. 2011. "Little Lambs, Not the Sheep, Get Early Lessons in Rodeo Life." *New York Times,* July 25.

O'Leary, K. Daniel, Rita W. Poulos, and Vernon T. Devine. 1972. "Tangible Reinforcers: Bonuses or Bribes?" *Journal of Consulting and Clinical Psychology* 38(1): 1–8.

O'Neill, Rosetta. 1948. "The Dodworth Family and Ballroom Dancing in New York." In Paul Magriel, ed., *Chronicles of the American Dance: From the Shakers to Martha Graham*. New York: Da Capo. 81–100.

Onishi, Norimitsu. 2008. "For English Studies, Koreans Say Goodbye to Dad." *New York Times,* June 8.

Orellana, Marjorie Faulstich, Lisa Dorner, and Lucila Pulido. 2003. "Accessing Assets, Immigrant Youth as Family Interpreters." *Social Problems* 50(5): 505–24.

Orenstein, Peggy. 2009. "Kindergarten Cram." *New York Times,* May 3.

Ostrander, Susan A. 1984. *Women of the Upper Class*. Philadelphia: Temple University Press.

Otterman, Sharon. 2009. "Tips for the Admissions Test . . . to Kindergarten." *New York Times,* November 21.

Paris, Leslie. 2008. *Children's Nature: The Rise of the American Summer Camp*. New York: New York University Press.

Pascoe, C. J. 2007. *Dude, You're a Fag: Masculinity and Sexuality in High School*. Berkeley: University of California Press.

Passer, Michael. 1988. "Determinants and Consequences of Children's Competitive Stress." In Frank L. Smoll, Richard A. Magill, and Michael J. Ash, eds., *Children in Sport*. 3rd ed. Champaign, IL: Human Kinetics Books. 203–27.

Paul, Pamela. 2008. *Parenting, Inc.: How We Are Sold on $800 Strollers, Fetal Education, Baby Sign Language, Sleeping Coaches, Toddler Couture, and Diaper Wipe Warmers—and What It Means for Our Children*. New York: Times Books.

Pennington, Bill. 2003. "As Team Sports Conflict, Some Parents Rebel." *New York Times*, November 12.

———. 2008. "Expectations Lose to Reality of Sports Scholarships." *New York Times*, March 10.

Petrone, Robert. 2007. "Facilitating Failure." Paper and discussions from the 2007 Spencer Foundation Fall Fellows' Workshop, Santa Monica, CA.

Picart, Caroline Jean S. 2006. *From Ballroom to DanceSport: Aesthetics, Athletics, and Body Culture.* Albany: State University of New York Press.

Pierce, Jennifer L. 1995. *Gender Trials: Emotional Lives in Contemporary Law Firms.* Berkeley: University of California Press.

Polgar, Susan, and Paul Truong. 2005. *Breaking Through: How the Polgar Sisters Changed the Game of Chess.* New York: Everyman Chess.

Powell, Robert Andrew. 2003. *We Own This Game: A Season in the Adult World of Youth Football.* New York: Grove Atlantic.

Pugh, Allison J. 2009. *Longing and Belonging: Parents, Children, and Consumer Culture.* Berkeley: University of California Press.

Pursuit of Excellence: Ferrets. 2007. Dir. Mark Lewis. DVD. PBS.

Pursuit of Excellence: Lords of the Gourd. 2007. Dir. Mark Lewis. DVD. PBS.

Pursuit of Excellence: Synchronized Swimming. 2007. Dir. Mark Lewis. DVD. PBS.

Putnam, Robert D. 2001. *Bowling Alone.* New York: Simon & Schuster.

Quart, Alissa. 2006. *Hothouse Kids: The Dilemma of the Gifted Child.* New York: Penguin Press.

Race to Nowhere. 2009. Dir. Vicki Abeles. Reel Link Films.

Racing Dreams. 2010. Dir. Marshall Curry. DVD. Hannover House.

Ramey, Garey, and Valerie A. Ramey. 2010. "The Rug Rat Race." *Brookings Papers on Economic Activity*, Spring: 129–76.

Redman, Tim. 2007. "A Second Scottish Enlightenment? CISCCON." *Chess Life*, December: 38–40.

Reeve, Johnmarshall, and Edward L. Deci. 1996. "Elements of the Competitive Situation That Affect Intrinsic Motivation." *Personality and Social Psychology Bulletin* 22: 24–33.

Ring, Jennifer. 2009. *Stolen Bases: Why American Girls Don't Play Baseball.* Urbana: University of Illinois Press.

Rivera, Lauren. 2011. "Ivies, Extracurriculars, and Exclusion: Elite Employers' Use of Educational Credentials." *Research in Social Stratification and Mobility* 29: 71–90.

Roberts, Debbie. 1999. *The Ultimate Guide to a Successful Dance Studio.* Louisville, KY: Chicago Spectrum Press.

Roberts, Glyn C. 1980. "Children in Competition: A Theoretical Perspective and Recommendations for Practice." *Motor Skills: Theory into Practice* 4(1): 37–50.

Rohde, David. 2001. "Refereeing Grown-ups Who Meddle in Child's Play." *New York Times*, September 6.

Root, Alexey. 2006a. "Chess Crying: Children's Preparation and Tournament Structure." In Tim Redman, ed., *Chess and Education: Selected Essays from the Koltanowski Conference*. Dallas: Studies on Chess in Education. 179–94.

———. 2006b. *Children and Chess: A Guide for Educators*. Westport, CT: Teacher Ideas Press.

Rosenbury, Laura. 2007. "Between Home and School." *University of Pennsylvania Law Review* 155: 833.

Rosenfeld, Alvin, and Nicole Wise. 2001. *The Over-Scheduled Child: Avoiding the Hyper-Parenting Trap*. New York: St. Martin's Press.

Rothman, J. D. 2012. *The Neurotic Parent's Guide to College Admissions*. Pasadena, CA: Prospect Park Media.

Rudd, Elizabeth, Emory Morrison, Renate Sadrozinski, Maresi Nerad, and Joseph Cerny. 2008. "Equality and Illusion: Gender and Tenure in Art History Careers." *Journal of Marriage and Family* 70 (February): 228–38.

Ruh, Lucina. 2011. *Frozen Teardrop: The Tragedy and Triumph of Figure Skating's "Queen of Spin."* New York: Select Books.

Ryan, Joan. 2000. *Little Girls in Pretty Boxes: The Making and Breaking of Elite Gymnastics and Figure Skaters*. New York: Warner Books.

Saint Louis, Catherine. 2007. "Train Like a Pro, Even If You're 12." *New York Times*, July 19.

Sand, Barbara Lourie. 2000. *Teaching Genius: Dorothy DeLay and the Making of a Musician*. Pompton Plains, NJ: Amadeus Press.

Sauder, Michael, and Wendy Nelson Espeland. 2009. "The Discipline of Rankings: Tight Coupling and Organizational Change." *American Sociological Review* 74 (February): 63–82.

Saulny, Susan. 2006. "In Baby Boomlet, Preschool Derby Is the Fiercest Yet." *New York Times*, March 3.

Scanlan, Tara, and Michael W. Passer. 1979. "Sources of Competitive Stress in Young Female Athletes." *Journal of Sport Psychology* 1: 151–59.

Scanlan, Tara K., Gary L. Stein, and Kenneth Ravizza. 1991. "An In-depth Study of Former Elite Figure Skaters: III. Sources of Stress." *Journal of Sport & Exercise Psychology* 13: 103–20.

Schemo, Diana Jean. 2009. "Congratulations! You Are Nominated. It's an Honor. (It's a Sale Pitch.)." *New York Times*, April 19.

Schrock, Douglas, and Michael Schwalbe. 2009. "Men, Masculinity, and Manhood Acts." *Annual Review of Sociology* 35: 277–95.

Schumpeter Column. 2010. "Too Many Chiefs: Inflation in Job Titles Is Approaching Weimar Levels." *Economist*, June 26: 70.

Scott, Aurelia C. 2007. *Otherwise Normal People: Inside the Thorny World of Competitive Rose Gardening*. Chapel Hill, NC: Algonquin Books.

Scott, Julia. 2011. "The Race to Grow the One-Ton Pumpkin." *New York Times*, October 5.

Seefeldt, Vern. 1998. "The Future of Youth Sport in America." In Frank L. Smoll, Richard A. Magill, and Michael J. Ash, eds., *Children in Sport*. 3rd ed. Champaign, IL: Human Kinetics Books. 335–48.

Senior, Jennifer. 2010. "The Junior Meritocracy." *New York Magazine*, January 31.

Shahade, Jennifer. 2005. *Chess Bitch: Women in the Ultimate Intellectual Sport*. Los Angeles: Siles Press.

Sheff, David. 2006. "For 7th Grade Jocks, Is There Ever an Off-Season?" *New York Times*, July 20.

Shenk, David. 2006. *The Immortal Game: A History of Chess*. New York: Doubleday.

Showstopper. "Welcome to Show Stopper." http://www.showstopperonline.com/aboutus/ (accessed April 30, 2009).

Shulman, James L., and William G. Bowen. 2001. *The Game of Life: College Sports and Educational Values*. Princeton, NJ: Princeton University Press.

Simon, Julie A., and Rainer Martens. 1979. "Children's Anxiety in Sport and Nonsport Evaluative Activities." *Journal of Sport Psychology* 1: 160–69.

Skenazy, Lenore. 2010. *Free-Range Kids: How to Raise Safe, Self-Reliant Children (Without Going Nuts with Worry)*. New York: Jossey-Bass.

Sokolove, Michael. 2010. "How a Soccer Star Is Made." *New York Times Magazine*, May 31.

Spears, Betty, and Richard Swanson. 1988. *History of Sport and Physical Education in the United States*. Dubuque, IA: Championship Books.

Spellbound. 2004. Dir. Jeffrey Blitz. DVD. Sony Pictures Home Entertainment.

Spence, Janet T. 1985. "Achievement American Style: The Rewards and Costs of Individualism." *American Psychologist* 40(12): 1285–95.

Stabiner, Karen. 2010. *Getting In*. New York: Voice.

Stanley, Anna. 1989. *Producing Beauty Pageants: A Director's Guide*. San Diego: Box of Ideas.

Star, Nancy. 2008. *Carpool Diem*. New York: 5 Spot.

Stearns, Peter N. 2003. *Anxious Parents: A History of Modern Childrearing in America*. New York: New York University Press.

Sternheimer, Karen. 2006. *Kids These Days: Facts and Fictions about Today's Youth*. Lanham, MD: Rowman & Littlefield.

Stevens, Mitchell. 2007. *Creating a Class*. Cambridge, MA: Harvard University Press.

Stevenson, Betsy. 2010. "Beyond the Classroom: Using Title IX to Measure the Return to High School Sports." *Review of Economics & Statistics* 92(2): 284–301.

Stone, Elizabeth. 1992. *The Hunter College Campus Schools for the Gifted: The Challenge of Equity and Excellence.* New York: Teachers College Press.

Sullivan Moore, Abigail. 2005. "The Lax Track." *New York Times,* November 6.

Sutton, David, and Renate Fernandez. 1998. Introduction to special issue of *Anthropology and Humanism,* 111–17.

Sync or Swim. 2011. Dir. Cheryl Furjanic. DVD. Garden Thieves Pictures.

Talbot, Margaret. 2003. "Why, Isn't He Just the Cutest Brand-Image Enhancer You've Ever Seen?" *New York Times Magazine,* September 21.

Tanier, Mike. 2012. "Big Price Tags Attached to Even the Littlest Leagues." *New York Times,* April 23.

Theberge, Nancy. 2000. *Higher Goals: Women's Ice Hockey and the Politics of Gender.* Albany: State University of New York Press.

Thomas, Kate. 2010. "Competitive Cheer Fans See Acceptance in Future." *New York Times,* July 22.

Thompson, Michael, and Teresa H. Barker. 2009. *It's a Boy! Your Son's Development from Birth to Age 18.* New York: Ballantine.

Thompson, Shona M. 1999. *Mother's Taxi: Sport and Women's Labor.* Albany: State University of New York Press.

Thorne, Barrie. 1993. *Gender Play: Girls and Boys in School.* New Brunswick, NJ: Rutgers University Press.

Tierney, John. 2004. "When Every Child Is Good Enough." *New York Times,* November 21.

Tocqueville, Alexis de. 2003. *Democracy in America.* New York: Penguin Classics.

Torgovnick, Kate. 2008. *Cheer! Three Teams on a Quest for College Cheerleading's Ultimate Prize.* New York: Touchstone.

Tu, Jeni, and Jennifer Anderson. 2007. "Past, Present, and Future." *Dance Teacher,* October: 70–72.

Tugend, Alina. 2005. "Pining for the Kick-Back Weekend." *New York Times,* April 15.

Tulgan, Bruce. 2009. *Not Everyone Gets a Trophy.* New York: Jossey-Bass.

U.S. Youth Soccer. "What Is Youth Soccer?" http://www.usyouthsoccer.org/aboutus/WhatIsYouthSoccer.asp (accessed April 15, 2009).

Waitzkin, Fred. 1984. *Searching for Bobby Fischer: The Father of a Prodigy Observes the World of Chess.* New York: Penguin.

Warren, Elizabeth, and Amelia Warren Tyagi. 2003. *The Two-Income Trap: Why Middle-Class Mothers and Fathers Are Going Broke.* New York: Basic Books.

Weber, Linda R., Andrew Miracle, and Tom Skehan. 1994. "Interviewing Early Adolescents: Some Methodological Considerations." *Human Organization* 53(1): 42–47.

Weber, Max. 1978. *Economy and Society.* Ed. Guenther Roth and Claus Wittich. Berkeley: University of California Press.

Weinreb, Michael. 2007. *The Kings of New York: A Year among the Geeks, Oddballs, and Geniuses Who Make Up America's Top High School Chess Team*. New York: Gotham.

West, Candace, and Don H. Zimmerman. 1987. "Doing Gender." *Gender & Society* 1(2): 125–51.

Whyte, William Foote. 1993. *Street Corner Society: The Social Structure of an Italian Slum*. Chicago: University of Chicago Press.

Willen, Liz. 2003. "New Yorkers Queue to Buy Their Kids a Future." Bloomberg, February 14.

Williams, Alex. 2007. "And for Sports, Kid, Put Down 'Squash.'" *New York Times*, December 9.

Winerip, Michael. 2008. "It's a Mad, Mad, Mad, Mad Dash." *New York Times*, September 24.

Wolitzer, Meg. 2011. *The Fingertips of Duncan Dorfman*. New York: Dutton Juvenile.

Word Wars—Tiles and Tribulations on the Scrabble Game Circuit. 2005. Dir. Eric Chaikin and Julian Petrillo. DVD. Starz Anchor Bay.

Wrigley, Julia. 1995. *Other People's Children*. New York: Basic Books.

Yalom, Marilyn. 2004. *Birth of the Chess Queen: A History*. New York: HarperCollins.

Zelizer, Viviana A. 1994. *Pricing the Priceless Child: The Changing Social Value of Children*. Princeton, NJ: Princeton University Press.

———. 2005. *The Purchase of Intimacy*. Princeton, NJ: Princeton University Press.

Index

after-school hours, utilizing, 25–26
aggressive gender script, 135–37
Almonte, Danny, 172
Amateur Athletic Union (AAU), 31, 34
Amateur Sports Act (1978), 31
American Youth Soccer Organization
  (AYSO), 39–40
Ashley, Maurice, 38

Baby Boomers, 12, 45
baby contests, 26
ballet, 69
ballroom dancing, 43, 164
beauty pageants, children's, 31, 89,
  243n22
biddy basketball, 30
bouncing back, from loss to win,
  97–100
boys: adherence to gender roles, 144; in
  dance, 149; fear of homosexuality,
  146–48; and hegemonic masculinity,
  129–30; labels applied to, 144–46;

masculine hierarchy for 145, 144; playing
  chess, 145–46. *See also* gender
Busier Than Ever! 7, 44

carving up of honor, 163–64, 191–92
challenge dancing, 42
Charter-Metro Chess, 59–60, 168
cheerleading, 36, 135–36
chess: bughouse, 230n1; history of competitive, 36–39; increase of, 9; makeup of
  participants, 10; tournament description,
  1–3. *See also* scholastic chess
*Chess Bitch: Women in the Ultimate Intellectual
  Sport*, 138–39
Chess in the Schools, 38
Chess Life for Kids, 38, 52
children, childhood: advice on researching,
  260–63; choices in activities, 226–27;
  dealing with nerves, 194; developing
  coping skills, 212–13; emotional value of,
  47; friendships in competitive activities,
  199–204; fun in competition, 208–13;

children, childhood (continued)
high-achieving, 168–69; hurried lives
of, 7; importance of sampling different
activities, 225–27; importance of
winning, 184–92; interviewing, 180–84,
256–60; judging, evaluation of, 165–70;
middle-class vs. working-class activities,
24, 32; parental rewards for competition,
189–91; understanding of activities,
244n2; understanding of awards, 187–89;
views on colleges, careers, 210–11; as
young professionals, 33. See also
family life
choreography theft, 171
class: and children's activity choices, 141–44;
inequalities of, 12–13; and parents'
expectations for children's careers,
142. See also middle class; upper-middle
class; working class
clocks, chess, 55
coaches, teachers: chess, 56; dance, 42–43,
72, 142, 171; from formerly Communist
countries, 173–74; and high achievers,
169–70; lack of certification for, 156–58,
238n29; licensing for soccer, 114–20; need for
parental caution, 226; paid, 34, 63–64;
vs. parents, 174–76; soccer, 34, 63–64;
winning at any cost, 173
college admissions, 13–16
commensuration processes, 164–65
competitions, tournaments: as check on
coach, teacher skills, 178; and college
admissions, 16; and Competitive Kid
Capital, 91–92; conflicts, scandals,
171–77; crying at, 197, 245n23; dance,
69–80; entrepreneurs profiting from,
153–58; problems at, 107–8; reward
structures for, 162–65; through history,
27–44, 48; time, space limitations for,
159–62. See also prizes, awards
competitive childhood activities: acquiring
skills in, 89–91; addictiveness of, 223;
admissions boost of, 13; appearing to
be recession-proof, 218, 219; backlash
against, 214–15; beginning ages for, 86;
as character development, 14; as child
care, 156, 242n8; common structural
elements, 176–77; data on families
interviewed, 87t–88t; defined, 8–9; and
educational credentials, 10–13, 14–16;
evaluation by judges, 192–99; fee-based
vs. free, 30; as feminine or masculine,
204–8; friendships in, 199–204; as fun
activity, 208–13; getting started with,

85–89; history of, 24–36; as key to
middle-class life, 8; lessons learned
from, 16; long-term effects of, 211–12;
middle-class dominance of, 48; need for
regulation, standards, 177–78; opting out
of, 215–19; organizing, 158–62; parental
rewards for, 189–91; participation vs.
competition, 32; professionalism of,
33; studying, 8–10; as training, 13–14;
unequal distribution of parents' roles
in, 150–51; as way of life, 6–8. See also
dance; history, of competitive childhood activities; scholastic chess;
soccer
competitive/elite category, for dance, 73
Competitive Kid Capital: acquisition of,
16–20; bouncing back, from loss to win,
97–100; as cultural, social, symbolic
capital, 92; five skills of, 17–20, 91–92;
gained in elite sports, 46; generalist path
for, 111–14; internalizing importance of
winning, 92–97; parents' expectations
for, 84–85, 219–23; performing before
others, 108–11; performing under stress,
103–8; specialist path for, 114–20;
unequal distribution of, 25; working
under time pressure, 101–3
competitors, supporting, 132–33,
134–35
concerted cultivation, 7
conflicts, scandals: academic red-shirting,
172; age of competitors, 171–72; among
parents, 176; choreography theft, 171;
coaches, teachers vs. parents, 174–76;
competition fallbacks, 73, 173; conflicts of
interest, 171; poaching, of players, 170–71
cram schools, 14
crying, at competition, 197, 245n23

dance, competitive: about, 69; age levels,
categories for, 73–74; bouncing back,
from loss to win, 99; choreography theft,
171; commensuration in, 165; competition owners, 156; competitions for, 70–74;
complaints about, 209; concessions sold,
76; conflicts of interest, 171; costs of,
76–77; dealing with nerves, 193–94, 195;
defined, 69, 231n12; emphasis on
appearance, 129–30; and fallback ages,
173; fees for, 70; as for-profit organizations, 241n5; and graceful gender script,
131–35; history of competitive, 41–44;
increase of, 9; lack of standardization
in, 71, 77; low dropout rate for, 217, 219;

makeup of participants, 10; mothers' roles in, 240n53; and parents' expectations for children's careers, 142; performing before others, 108–10; performing under stress, 106–8; poaching in, 170–71; prizes, awards, 74–76, 185; rehearsal space for, 160; reward structures for, 163; scoring, 74–75; selection processes for, 166; skill acquisition in, 91, 127t–28t; soloists, 201; specialist path for, 116; as stigma for boys, 147–48; studios evaluated, 77–80; on television, 69; time pressure in, 102
Dance Educators of America, 42
Dance Masters of America (DMA), 42
Dance Moms, 43, 69, 167, 171
DanceSport, 43, 164, 241n1
Dancing with the Stars, 69
December Nationals, chess, 56–57
Dodworth Academy, 41
Double Dutch jump-roping, 30
downward mobility, protecting against, 13
Dweck, Carol, 182, 199

Echo Boomers, 12, 45
educational system, 13, 45–46, 47
educational credentials, and competition, 10–13
entrepreneurs, in childhood activities, 154–58
exercise, children's need for, 129

fallback ages, 73, 173, 221
family life: balancing siblings' needs, 117–18; and competitive activities, 6–8, 44–45; emotional value of children in, 47; influencing activities, 149–51. *See also* children, childhood; parents
Farrey, Tom, 62, 158, 159
Federation of Dance Competitions, 71
field sites, selecting, 249–50
figure skating, 34–35
Fischer, Bobby, 37
flights, in soccer, 63
fun, in competition, 208–13

"geeks," 145–46
gender: in activities, 9; children's views of, 204–8; constrained, transformed by activities, 151–52; and family influence in choosing activities, 149–51; importance to parents, 121. *See also* boys; girls

generalist path, 16–17, 111–14
girls: acquiring Competitive Kid Capital, 126–31; aggressive, 124, 135–37; and class expectations, 141–44; defined in school setting, 122–23; defined in society, 123–24; emphasis on appearance, 129–31; focus of traditional activities for, 129–30; graceful, 131–35; link between sports, business success, 124; and middle-class variations, 125; pink warriors, 137–40; preference for femininity, 205–7; skills acquired in dance, soccer, 127t–28t. *See also* gender; tomboys
graceful gender script, 131–35
Gulick, Luther, 27

habitus, 17
hair, and sports, 130, 136
hegemonic masculinity, 129–30
Heisman, Dan, 38, 53
high achievers, 168–69
history, of competitive childhood activities: from 1980s to present, 32–36; about, 24–26; and American families, 44–45; chess, 36–39; dance, 41–44; early organizations, 232n16; and higher education, 45–46; from postwar to 1970s, 30–32; from Progressive Era to World War II, 26–29; soccer, 39–41
homosexuality, fears of, 146–47, 148
hypercompetitiveness, 32–36

The Incredibles, 8
interview challenges, 254–55
interviews, number and length, 250
Irish step dancing, 42, 243n35

judges, evaluators, 192–99

Karabel, Jerome, 15

lacrosse, 14, 217
Lareau, Annette, 7–8, 24, 121–22
leagues, soccer, 63
Levine, Madeline, 212
Little Girls in Pretty Boxes, 34–35
Little League Baseball, 28, 29, 30, 172

Mad Hot Ballroom, 69
Markovits, Andrei, 47–48
maternal employment, and organized activities, 32–33
May Nationals, chess, 57
medals, 57, 95, 162, 164, 184–86

Metro Chess, 58–61
Metro Soccer Co-op, 67–69, 86, 160–61
Metroville Elite Dance Academy: about, 77–80; age of competitors, 86; high achievers at, 169; lack of jealousy in, 200; rehearsal space for, 160; selection processes for, 166–67; stress, performing under, 106–7; students pleasing teachers, 193; teacher/parent conflict, 175
middle class: activities, vs. working class, 21, 141, 166; busy family schedules of, 7–8, 24–25; data on, 183t; defined, 23; gender divide in, 22; and girls' scripts, 141–43; need for children's credentialing, 11, 13–14; variations in, 125. See also class; working class
mouth organ contests, 28
movies, about winning, 95
music, 35
music memory contests, 28

National Burt Lerner Elementary (K–6) Championship, 57
National Collegiate Athletic Association (NCAA), 47
national level competition, 72, 159
National Scholastic K–12/Collegiate Championship, 56
"nerds," 145–46

opting out, of competitive activities, 215–19
organization, of competition, 158–62
organization, of research, 50–52
outline, of book, 20–23

parents: ambivalence over competitive activities, 222–23; vs. coaches, teachers, 174–76; and college admissions, 13–16; conflict among, 176; cost of children's education, 13; desires for children, 224; helicopter, 12, 215; immigrant outlook of, 115; importance of competitive activities to, 219–22; importance of gender to, 121; and inequality of class, 12–13, 141–44; infighting among, 67–68; influencing children, 209–10; in interview process, 251–55; investigating program, qualifications, 178; meeting and interviewing, 250, 251–53; occupations of, affecting children's activities, 141–42; opting out of competitive activities, 215–19; previous experience with activities, 142; responsibilities in children's activities, 33; rewards given

by, 189–91; socialization among, 230n5; and time pressure for kids, 101–2; view of competitive children's activities, 178–79; winning at any cost, 173. See also family life
participation vs. competition, 32
Pascoe, C. J., 130, 206
patches, badges. See prizes, awards
Pee Wee hockey, 30
performing before others, 108–11
performing under stress, 103–8
piano contests, 28
piano playing, 112
pink warrior gender script, 137–40
poaching, of players, 65–66, 170–71
Polgar, Susan, 138
Pop Warner Football, 28, 29, 30
preprofessional category, for dance, 73
pre-school, 11
Pricing the Priceless Child, 47
prizes, awards: affected by competitive children's activities, 47; in dance competition, 74–76; hierarchy of, 187–88; importance of, to children, 184–92; increased emphasis on, 48; as motivation for winning, 18, 92, 95–96, 95–97, 162–63; for older children, 191; public nature of, 198–99; purchasing, 188; in scholastic chess, 57; as status, 209. See also competitions, tournaments
problem of the high-achieving child, 22, 113, 115, 168–70, 217, 221
prodigy labels, 35–36
products, sold for children's activities, 155, 158
professional category, for dance, 73
Progressive Era, 26–27
Public School Athletic League for Boys (PSAL), 27
Public Schools Athletic Girls League, 123

race/ethnicity, in activities, 10
Race to Nowhere, 212
ratings, chess, 53–54
recreational category, for dance, 73, 79
red-shirting, academic, 172
reward systems, for activities, 162–65
ribbons, 22, 57, 75–76, 162–63, 184–86, 188, 191–93, 209, 223
The Right Move, 38
role confusion, 175–76

safe play space, 31–32
schedules, 19, 67, 102, 117, 160, 162, 209, 262

scholarships, for soccer, 64, 237n23
scholastic chess: age, rating manipulation,
173; aggression in, 138–39; algebraic
notation for, 236n11; "blitz" games,
237n12; bouncing back, from loss to
win, 98; child's view of, 180–82; clubs in,
58–61; coaches, teachers vs. parents,
175; commensuration in, 165; complaints
about, 208–9; dealing with nerves,
194–95; defined, 52; dropout rate for, 217,
219; equipment for, 54–55; evaluation and
rankings, 195–97; FIDE ratings, 236n9;
girls' appearance in, 130–31; high
achievers in, 168–69; lessons, camps for,
55–56; and male hierarchy, 145–46; as
nonprofit organization, 241n5; organization of tournaments, 52–55; performing
before others, 110–11; performing under
stress, 104–6; and pink warrior gender
script, 137–40; poaching in, 170–71;
prizes, awards, 186–87; and ratings,
52–54; selection processes for, 168;
siblings in, 149–50; skills acquired in, 90;
space for, 161; specialist path for, 115–16;
as stigma for boys, 146; Swiss system for,
236n7; team activities in, 57–58; time
pressure in, 101; "touch-move," 236n11;
tournament costs, 54; trophies awarded
for, 57
schoolwork, balancing with sports, 103
Searching for Bobby Fischer, 38
second shifts, 7, 20, 213
selection processes, 165–70
self-esteem movement, 30, 163
Sex Roles, 124
Showstopper National Championships,
42, 71
siblings, affecting activities, 117–18
skittling, 58
soccer: age of competitors, 171–72; and
aggressive gender script, 135–37, 142;
bouncing back, from loss to win, 100;
choosing, for masculinity, 146; clubs
evaluated, 67–69; commensuration in,
165; complaints about, 208; dealing with
nerves, 194; dropout rate for, 217, 219;
evaluation and rankings, 197; fees for,
64–65; girls' appearance in, 130; high
achievers in, 169; history of competitive,
39–41; leagues in, 63; makeup of
participants, 10; as nonprofit organization, 241n5; organization of, 61–66; origin
of name, 234n70; performing before
others, 110; performing under stress,

106; poaching, of players, 65–66, 170;
popularity of, 9; practice space for,
160–61; prizes, awards, 186; selection
processes for, 166, 167–68; skills acquired
in, 90, 127t–28t; state championships for,
66; team aspect of, 201–2; time pressure
in, 101; travel, 61–64
Soccer America, 40, 66
softball, girls', 172
So You Think You Can Dance, 43, 70
space limitations, for competition, 160–62
specialist path, 16–17, 114–20
spelling bees, 27–28
sporting culture, 47–48
sportsmanship, 127t–28t
"stick-to-itiveness," 97–98
stuffed animals. See prizes, awards
suburban, urban differences, in activities,
10

teachers. See coaches, teachers
teamwork, 127t–28t
television, dance competition on, 43–44,
147
time: arranging activity schedules, 159–60;
in chess games, 55; for competitions,
tournaments, 160; as evaluation, 197;
pressure of working under, 101–3
Title IX, 124, 150
tomboys, 123, 124, 205–6
tournaments. See competitions,
tournaments
travel teams, soccer, 61–64
trophies. See prizes, awards

U designation, for soccer, 62
Unequal Childhoods, 8, 121–22
United Cheer Association, 36
United States Chess Federation (USCF):
beginnings of, 37; first elementary
championship of, 38; issuing ratings, 53;
prominence of scholastic chess to, 39;
and tournaments, 52
upper-middle class, 3, 13, 23, 25, 28, 66,
88, 123
Uptown-Metro Chess, 59–60, 161
urban, suburban difference, in activities, 10
U.S. Olympic Committee, 31
USSR, chess in, 37
U.S. Youth Soccer (USYS), 40, 62

Waitzkin, Josh, 38
wall charts, chess, 53
Weber, Max, 11

Westbrook Let's Dance Studio, 77–80, 166, 193, 202
West County chess, 60–61
Westfield Soccer Club, 67–69, 161, 176, 195
winning, in childhood activities, 92–97, 127t–28t, 227
working class: activities, vs. middle class, 141; children's unstructured time, 24; in dance, 125; data on, 183t; defined, 240n23;

emphasis on femininity, 141; lack of knowledge of activities, 166. *See also* class; middle class; upper-middle class

year-round seasons, 34
YMCAs, 28, 32
youth coaches. *See* coaches

Zelizer, Viviana, 47